Leopard, H4-1

Early morning mist, H1-4

KRUGER SELF-DRIVE

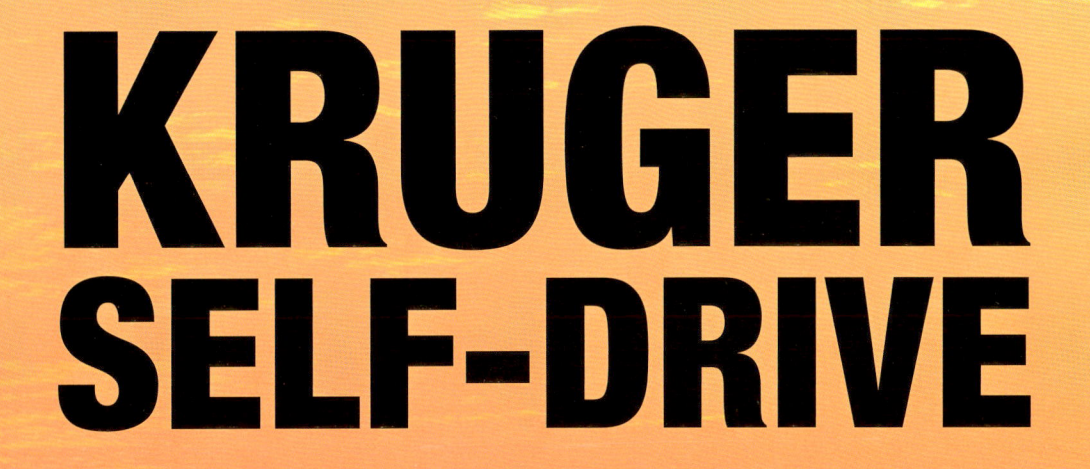

Routes, Roads & Ratings

Text by **Ingrid van den Berg**

Photos by **Philip & Ingrid van den Berg**
Heinrich van den Berg

Published by **HPH Publishing**

African buffalo herd, S55

Contents

INTRODUCTION	**13**
ROUTES	**21**
INTRODUCTION TO ROUTES	22
SKUKUZA ROUTES	28
BERG-EN-DAL ROUTES	30
PRETORIUSKOP ROUTES	32
CROCODILE BRIDGE ROUTES	34
LOWER SABIE ROUTES	36
ORPEN, TAMBOTI AND MAROELA ROUTES	38
SATARA ROUTES	40
OLIFANTS CAMP ROUTES	42
LETABA ROUTES	44
MOPANI ROUTES	46
SHINGWEDZI ROUTES	48
PUNDA MARIA ROUTES	50
ROADS	**53**
INTRODUCTION TO ROADS	54
H-ROADS	56
S-ROADS	110
UNDERSTANDING KRUGER	**237**
DYNAMICS OF THE SAVANNA	239
SUPPORTING FOUNDATIONS	240
ECOZONES OR LANDSCAPES	242
TREES	246
INVERTEBRATES	250
BIRDS	251
REPTILES	266
MAMMALS	268
SELECTED BIBLIOGRAPHY	276
ROUTES AND ROADS INDEX	**277**
MAPS AND ADDITIONAL INFORMATION	**278**

Male lion, H3

White rhino

African elephant herd, S37

Black rhino

INTRODUCTION

The Kruger National Park is not only a national asset for South Africa but is part of a dwindling global treasure and the collective natural heritage of all mankind. It embodies the spirit of wild Africa and offers a glimpse of what this part of the world looked like before human intervention. Although it is primarily a haven for the diverse indigenous fauna and flora and aims to conserve and preserve as much as possible of this pristine natural heritage, it is also there for the benefit and enjoyment of both local and international visitors.

Situated in the South African Lowveld between the northern Drakensberg and Mozambique, the largest national park in South Africa stretches almost 365 km from north to south and 60 km from west to east. Roughly the size of Israel (20 000 square kilometres), it is among the 20 biggest national parks in the world.

It all started in 1899 when the erstwhile president of the Transvaal Republic, Paul Kruger, proclaimed the Sabie Game Reserve. The Shingwedzi Reserve followed. These two reserves were merged in 1926 and land in between was purchased by the state to form the core of the Kruger National Park. Today the park forms part of the Great Limpopo Transfrontier Park (35 000 square kilometres), a cross-border initiative of the Peace Parks Foundation.

The first ranger and warden, James Stevenson-Hamilton, dedicated his life to creating a national park that would be sustained by tourism. Now, a century later, the park caters for more than 1.5 million visitors annually. While the surrounding communities are closely involved with the park and have formed partnerships with the conservation authorities, several private companies also operate in conservancies within the park.

The challenge facing national parks and nature conservation is how to maintain the natural and pristine state of an area such as the Kruger National Park while facilitating tourism and its associated environmental disturbances. To achieve this the park is zoned according to three categories – parts of the park are zoned for development and general tourist activities offering accommodation, an extensive network of tourist roads, picnic sites and educational centres. Then there are sections set aside to remain pristine wilderness areas where any human disturbances are limited. Between the pristine areas and the more developed parts, huge natural zones act as a buffer.

The well-maintained tourist roads make self-driving possible and desirable for the freedom it offers. Spiritual and educational enjoyment derived from one's own observations leads to knowledge, respect and a greater understanding of the natural world.

This book intends to enhance the self-drive experience in the Kruger National Park. Knowledge of animals, birds, rainfall, landscapes and underlying soil and rocks combine to provide a fascinating experience. The more one knows about all these and how they affect each other, the more pleasure will be derived from visiting this world-renowned wildlife destination.

Leopard with cub, H4-2

Interaction between juvenile bateleur and brown snake eagle, H12

Hippos play-fighting, H10

Fever tree forest, S63

INTRODUCTION TO ROUTES

The sections designated for general tourist activities have an exceptional network of roads that access some of the best areas for game viewing in the park.

To the east of the park, the Lebombo Hills form the border with Mozambique. These hills give way to flat plains of weathered basalt. The basaltic soils are rich in minerals and retain water in pans long after the rains have gone. These conditions support the growth of sweet, palatable grasses. Most grazers prefer sweetveld and therefore one may expect to see larger concentrations of plains game such as zebra and wildebeest on the eastern sweet savanna grasslands. Many of the most productive routes are found on the eastern basaltic plains.

On the western side, the granite foothills of the escarpment extend into the park and contribute to an undulating landscape with several dramatic granite outcrops. This area has the highest rainfall in the park. The coarse, older and leached granite soils support more fibrous grass species, which result in sourveld. Mixed veld has both sweet and fibrous grasses.

Routes passing through the western side of the park may not have prolific game numbers, but there is better diversity. These routes are scenically pleasing because of the undulating nature of the terrain and the many drainage systems with riverine vegetation lining the seasonal streams and rivers. Birding is usually good.

The main rivers in the south are the Sabie and the Crocodile, the latter being the southern border of the park. Like the rest of Kruger, the south is dominated by mixed woodland savanna, and habitats range from dense riverine forest to almost treeless plains. Palatable grasses and the wide habitat variety are the main reasons why more animals are found in southern Kruger.

The central part of the park is widely regarded as lion country due to the many reported lion sightings. Most of the roads to the east of Satara traverse sweet grassland savanna where grazers are prolific, and lions and other predators follow their prey. Since visibility is good in savanna grassland, predators are often encountered on game drives.

Towards the west the soil becomes coarser, the grazing

Impala, H4-1

less sweet and broad-leafed mixed woodland dominates large tracts of the park. The prolific bushwillows attract browsers such as elephant, giraffe, kudu, black rhino and impala.

North of Satara the vegetation gradually changes to stunted woodland and eventually to mopane veld. Visibility is not so good in mopane veld and fewer animals are encountered travelling north.

The main rivers in the central part of the park are the seasonal Timbavati and the perennial Olifants and Letaba.

The northern section is characterised by mopane veld, with sandveld in the far north. Established riverine bush is found along the main river courses and on the floodplains of the Shingwedzi River. The Shingwedzi, Olifants, Letaba and Luvuvhu rivers all flow in this section of the Kruger. The Limpopo River forms the far northern border of the park and of South Africa.

The Tropic of Capricorn runs slightly north of Mopani Camp, yet typical tropical vegetation is not evident except in the far northern section. The best game viewing is also in the far north where mopane veld gives way to the diverse woodlands of the sandveld. This area is also the most popular with serious birders who venture there to see the many tropical migratory species and others not found in the south. Apart from being a birding paradise, the far north is heaven for tree enthusiasts. Plains game may be scarce in the mopane veld, but these species are replaced by some of the rarest antelope in the park and vast numbers of elephant. The park's biggest tuskers are found here.

There are 12 main rest camps and several private, bush and concession camps in the Kruger National Park. **The routes given in this book are only the ones that start and end at the main rest camps and the roads that are accessible to all self-driving tourists in the park.**

The listed routes include only suggested prime routes. There are many other possibilities. Routes can be done clockwise or anti-clockwise and can be lengthened or shortened to suit your own interests and available time. Use the road ratings and information to decide on your own routes. Lower-rated routes may be surprisingly good and high-rated routes may also be disappointing at times. Game sightings are mostly unpredictable. **To find and watch is the challenge.**

HOW TO PLAN YOUR ROUTE

- Study the area map.
- Decide on a morning drive (short or long) and/or afternoon drive (usually short) or day drive.
- Look at breakfast and/or lunch options or pack a picnic basket.
- Look at the recommended prime roads for the area. Read more about them to make informed decisions (See the chapter on ROADS.)
- Locate the animal drinking places on the area map.
- Decide on your route by taking all the above into account.
- Make a quick calculation of the distance you plan to travel and divide by 25 km/h to determine the time you should set aside. For example, to cover a distance of 100 km you need to allow about four hours. Decide on your own 'via' roads by consulting the chapter on ROADS.
- Four to five hours for a morning drive is more than enough. An afternoon drive would usually not exceed three hours. A day drive should not be more than 200–250 km. Allow time for relaxing at picnic sites or neighbouring camps. Covering too great a distance will leave you exhausted and inclined to break the speed limit.

The suggested routes show only the main points, with a rough calculation of the time it would take for an unhurried game drive. Calculate approximate time, allowing for picnic breaks and time to spend at excellent sightings.

Isak Pretorius

Lion coalition, S61

European bee-eaters, S1

KRUGER NATIONAL PARK

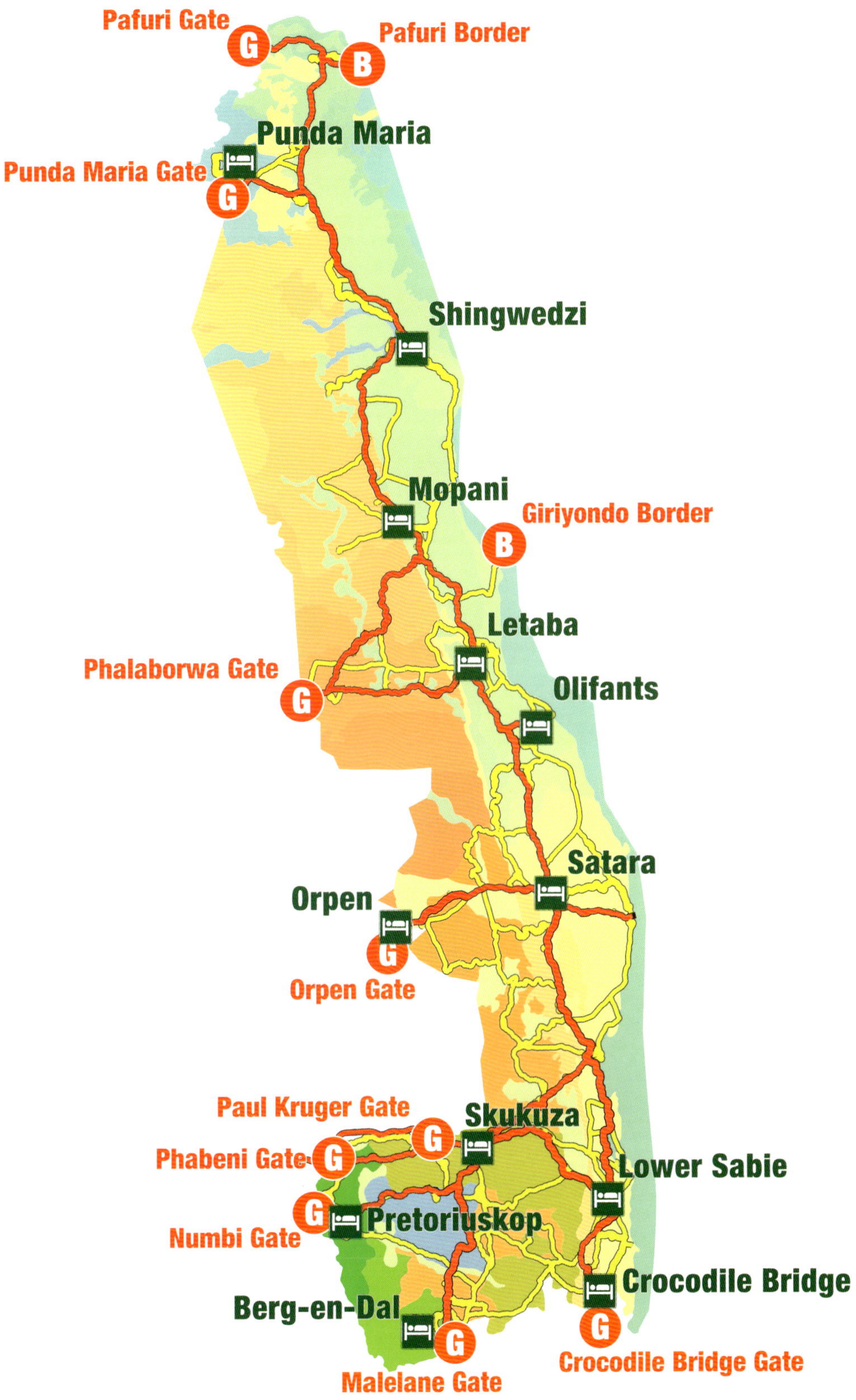

See detailed maps at the back of the book

Liz Hart

SKUKUZA ROUTES

'Sikhukhuza' was the Zulu name given to Colonel James Stevenson-Hamilton who was the warden of the Sabie Game Reserve from 1902. After he was appointed, he imposed new rules in his campaign against poaching, and his name means 'he who sweeps clean or levels the ground'.

The modern-day Skukuza Rest Camp is situated on the southern bank of the Sabie River. The restaurant overlooks the river and a huge sycamore fig tree and other indigenous giants provide shade for visitors and food for a wide variety of birds and monkeys. The camp itself sprawls over a large area with all kinds of accommodation and camping facilities.

There are various trails within the camp, allowing for excellent birding. Even the odd warthog sometimes finds its way into the camp. At night one may expect to see bushbabies (galagos) in the trees or even genets. Always use a flashlight at night.

ROUTES

- Skukuza is situated in the heart of Big Five territory and you can expect to see any of these on any of the roads close by.
- The camp is surrounded by mixed woodland and thorn thickets that occur mostly in the lower contours of the Sabie River catchment areas.
- Predators and scavengers such as lion, leopard, wild dog, cheetah and hyena can be encountered near the camp.
- The Stevenson-Hamilton Memorial Museum houses many interesting artefacts – famous among which is the knife with which ranger Harry Wolhuter single-handedly killed a lion and so saved his own life.

PRIME ROADS

H1-1; H1-2; H3; H11; H4-2; S1; S3; S114; S83; S76; S65.

CLOSEST GET-OUT PLACES

- Lake Panic on the S42 – no ablutions, no picnic facilities
- Nkuhlu Picnic Site on the H4-1 – ablutions, small shop, gas barbeques for hire, take own picnic basket or buy basic food items or meals
- Tshokwane Picnic Site on the H1-2 – ablutions, small shop, gas barbeques for hire, take own picnic basket or buy basic food items or meals
- Orpen memorial koppie – no ablutions, no picnic facilities
- Kruger Tablets – no ablutions, no picnic facilities

PRIME DRINKING PLACES CLOSEST TO THE CAMP

- Lake Panic on the S42 (off the H11): 5.5 km
- Sabie River frontage along the H4-1 and the S3
- Low-water bridge on the H1-1 (5 km from the camp)
- Renosterkoppies Waterhole on the S114 (12 km from the camp)
- Transport Dam on the H1-1 (22 km from the camp)
- N'waswitshaka Waterhole on the S65 (24 km from the camp)

Pretoriuskop Camp
★★★★★
158 km ± 6 hours
H1-1; Transport Dam; Pretoriuskop; H1-1; S3; S1 east; H11

Greater galago, Skukuza Camp

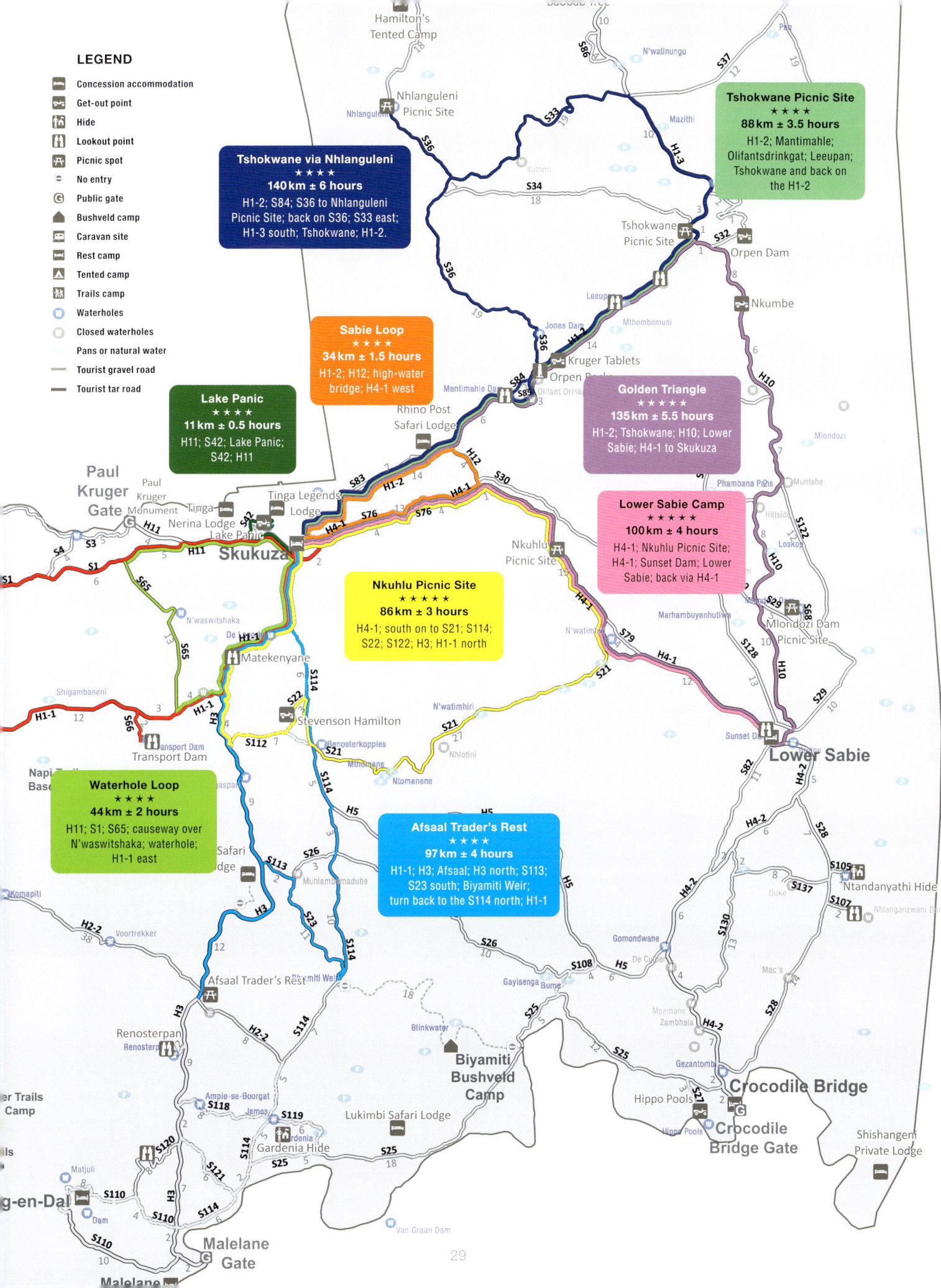

BERG-EN-DAL ROUTES

Berg-en-Dal ('mountain and dale') is a modern, environmentally friendly camp, and is the only one situated in the rugged Malelane mountain landscape. It nestles on the southern bank of the seasonal Matjulu watercourse with a dam built below the main reception area for its water supply. This attracts a variety of animals, especially in the dry season.

When the camp was built, care was taken not to destroy any of the natural vegetation. The result is a paradise for tree-lovers and birders. Tree species not found in any of the other ecozones or landscapes are represented here. Birds are most active from early morning until about 11 a.m. and then again later in the afternoon. Many fruiting trees attract a wide variety of fruit-eating species.

Walks along the inside perimeter of the fence can be rewarding. The vegetation of the stream bed is ideal for leopard and most nocturnal species. Always walk with a flashlight at night.

The **Malelane Private Camp** is not far from the Berg-en-Dal Main Camp.

ROUTES

- In the vicinity of Berg-en-Dal, game densities are relatively low compared to other areas in the park but this does not always affect the variety of game species.
- Grasses on the crests and slopes are not as palatable as in the valleys, where most grazers will congregate.
- Broad-leafed vegetation (e.g. bushwillows) will attract browsers – expect to see kudu, elephant, impala and smaller antelope.
- Giraffe favour knob-thorn and these only occur in the valleys.
- Study the area map and find the places where there should be surface water.
- Leopard and hyena are the prime predators close to the camp. Wild dog is sporadically seen, and lion less often in close proximity to the camp, but further northwards and eastwards.

PRIME ROADS

S110 – the tarred part; H3 – the entire road; S118 and S119 – dirt; S114 – some stretches may be corrugated and unproductive; S25 – dirt road, carries much traffic, sometimes corrugated in places; S23 – dirt road; S120 – most scenic, but rough surface.

CLOSEST GET-OUT PLACES

- Afsaal Trader's Rest – ablutions, gas barbeques for hire, cold drinks for sale, take own picnic basket, small shop, basic foot items or meals
- Gardenia Hide – no ablutions, no picnic facilities

PRIME DRINKING PLACES CLOSEST TO THE CAMP

- Dam in front of reception
- Matjulu Waterhole
- H3 crossing over Matjulu stream
- Bridge over Crocodile River at the Malelane Gate
- Bridge over the Mhlambane seasonal river
- Pools in the Mhlambane seasonal river along the S118 and S119
- Pan at the Gardenia Hide
- Renosterpan
- Biyamiti Weir
- Biyamiti seasonal river with pools (crossing on H3 and S23 up to the weir)
- Animals cross the S114 and S25 on their way to the perennial Crocodile River

White rhino

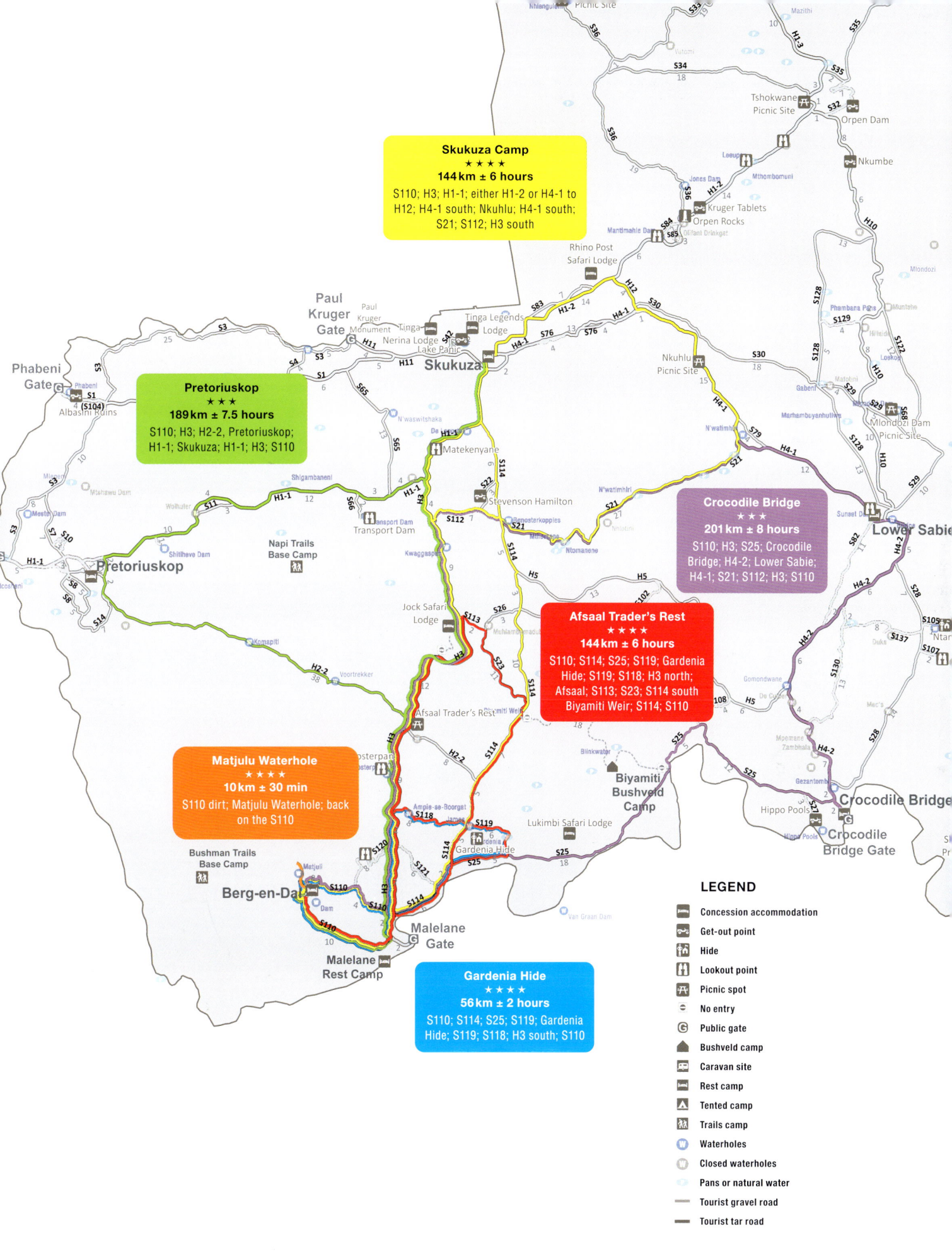

PRETORIUSKOP ROUTES

The camp is situated in the southwestern part of the Kruger National Park and is only nine kilometres from Numbi Gate. Pretoriuskop, the oldest camp in the park, was opened to visitors about a century ago. The pleasant atmosphere, cool climate and abundance of huge trees are a great attraction. It is the only camp where exotic plants such as flamboyants and bougainvillea were planted. Birdlife is prolific and serious birders come here for sightings not easily found elsewhere in the park. The Sable Trail within the park leads past granite boulders and huge marula, fig and Natal mahogany trees.

ROUTES

- The landscape within which the camp is situated is referred to as Pretoriuskop sourveld.
- The rainfall and the altitude here are the highest of all camps in the park. This results in tall grass and thick bush, making game spotting difficult.
- Large bare granite domes are typical, while silver cluster-leaf woodlands dominate the vegetation.
- The underlying geology is granite.
- In summer, grasses grow high and visibility is low.

PRIME ROADS

S14 – Fayi Loop; H1-1 to Skukuza; H2-2 to Afsaal; S7 – Shabeni Loop. There are plenty of white rhino, buffalo, kudu and predators such as lion and leopard. Look out for sable, eland and tsessebe.

CLOSEST GET-OUT PLACES

- S1 at Albasini Ruins – no ablutions, no picnic facilities
- H2-2 at Afsaal – ablutions, gas barbeques for hire, cold drinks for sale, take own picnic basket

PRIME DRINKING PLACES CLOSEST TO THE CAMP

- Shitlhave Dam on H1-1 (8 km); Mestel Dam on S3 south (15 km)
- Nyamundwa on S1 (34 km); Transport Dam on H1-1 (34 km)

Vervet monkey, H1-6

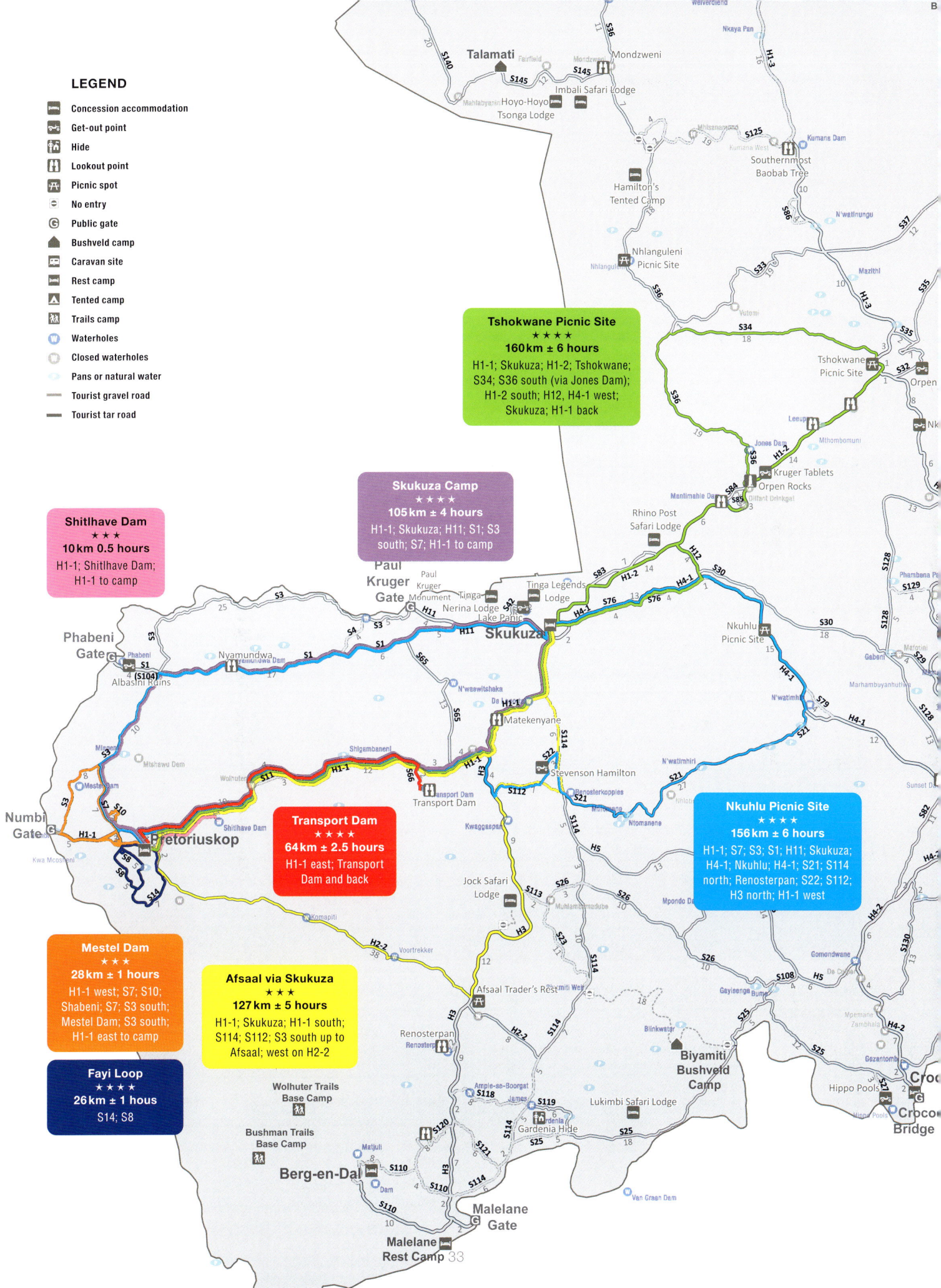

CROCODILE BRIDGE ROUTES

Crocodile Bridge Camp is a delightful little camp in the southeastern corner of the park. It is situated on the northern bank of the Crocodile River, which forms the southern boundary of this world-renowned wildlife destination. On its doorstep is one of the best game-viewing areas of the entire park, called the 'Southern Circle'.

This part of the park is also rich in local history. When one enters the park and crosses the Crocodile River, the remains of a railway bridge for the Selati railway line are still visible. Construction started in 1894. European explorers were lured to the Lowveld by tales of rich gold deposits and there was soon friction between them and the local communities.

The first man to lead an expedition to this area was Francois de Cuiper of the Dutch East India Company in 1725. His party was attacked by local inhabitants in the Gomondwane bush (on the present-day H4-2) and forced to retreat to Delagoa Bay (now Maputo).

Another interesting fact is that when the Sabie Game Reserve (the forerunner of the Kruger National Park) was proclaimed in the late 19th century, Crocodile Bridge was one of the first four ranger posts.

Biyamiti Bush Camp is close to Crocodile Bridge Main Camp.

ROUTES

- Game densities near the camp are probably the highest in the park.
- The camp is surrounded by a typical flat landscape with soils originating from basalt. The grasses are therefore sweet and palatable and huge marula and knob-thorn trees dot the plains.
- Routes from this camp offer some of the best chances of encountering the Big Five on a single drive.

PRIME ROADS

H4-2 – tarred, a lot of traffic, many day visitors use it; S28 – dirt road, excellent visibility.

CLOSEST GET-OUT PLACES

- Ntandanyathi Bird Hide – no ablution facilities

PRIME DRINKING PLACES CLOSEST TO THE CAMP

- The Crocodile River, especially the S27 to the Hippo Pools (8 km)
- Gezantombi pool in the Vurhami stream on the first section of the H4-2
- Gomondwane Waterhole on the H4-2 and H5 crossing the stream
- Several pans in the rainy season on the S130
- Ntandanyathi Hide entrance road from the S28
- Mpondo Dam on the S102

Leopard, H4-2

Dustin van Helsdingen

LEGEND

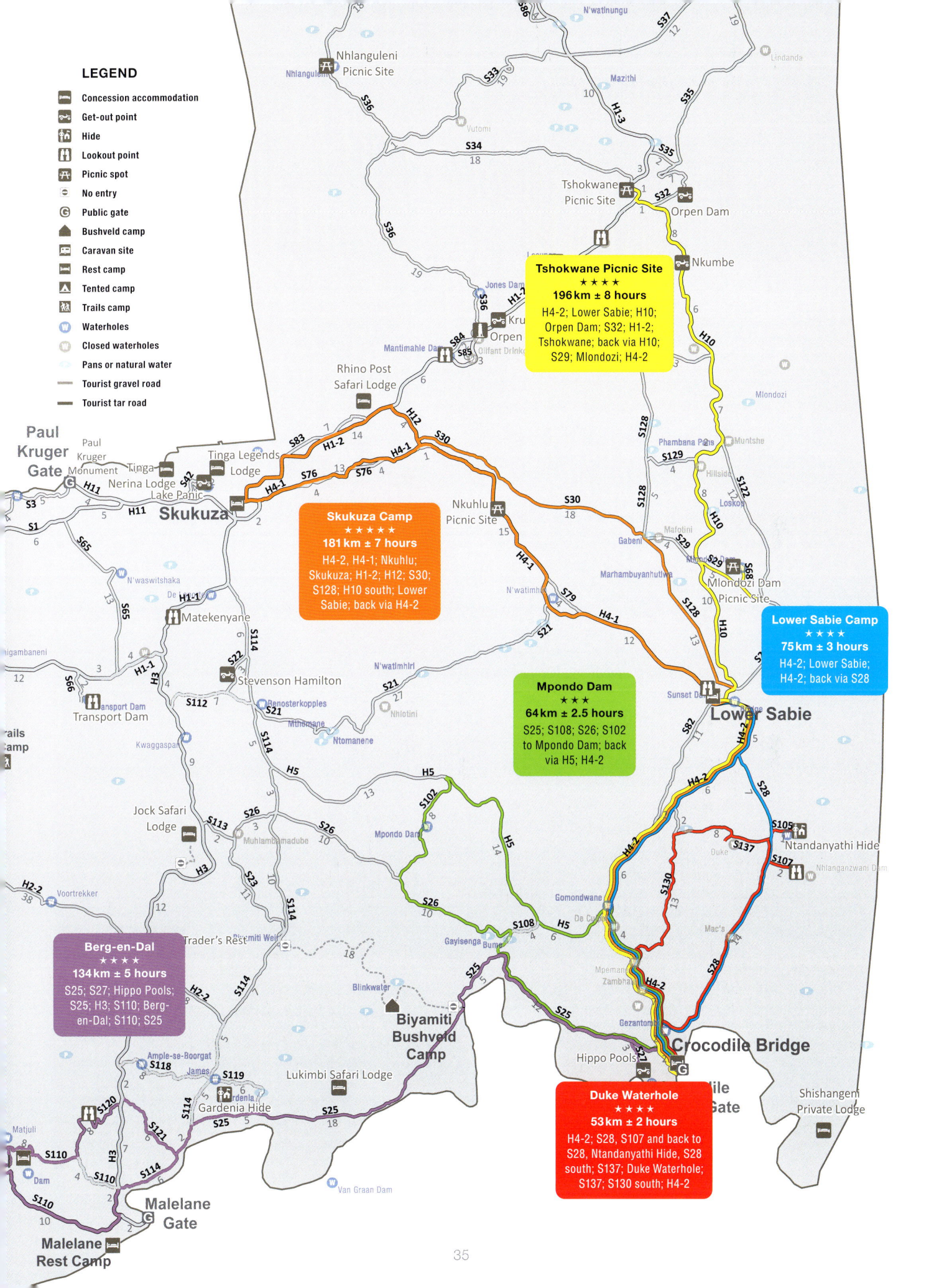

- Concession accommodation
- Get-out point
- Hide
- Lookout point
- Picnic spot
- No entry
- Public gate
- Bushveld camp
- Caravan site
- Rest camp
- Tented camp
- Trails camp
- Waterholes
- Closed waterholes
- Pans or natural water
- Tourist gravel road
- Tourist tar road

Tshokwane Picnic Site
★★★★
196 km ± 8 hours
H4-2; Lower Sabie; H10; Orpen Dam; S32; H1-2; Tshokwane; back via H10; S29; Mlondozi; H4-2

Skukuza Camp
★★★★★
181 km ± 7 hours
H4-2, H4-1; Nkuhlu; Skukuza; H1-2; H12; S30; S128; H10 south; Lower Sabie; back via H4-2

Mpondo Dam
★★★
64 km ± 2.5 hours
S25; S108; S26; S102 to Mpondo Dam; back via H5; H4-2

Lower Sabie Camp
★★★★
75 km ± 3 hours
H4-2; Lower Sabie; H4-2; back via S28

Berg-en-Dal
★★★★
134 km ± 5 hours
S25; S27; Hippo Pools; S25; H3; S110; Berg-en-Dal; S110; S25

Duke Waterhole
★★★★
53 km ± 2 hours
H4-2; S28, S107 and back to S28, Ntandanyathi Hide, S28 south; S137; Duke Waterhole; S137; S130 south; H4-2

LOWER SABIE ROUTES

This camp probably has one of the most exceptional lookouts in the park. Situated on the western bank of the perennial Sabie River, the reception area looks out over a wide expanse of water with hippo grunting in the distance and crocodiles lazing in the sun. On the opposite bank one can see animals coming down to drink. Further to the south lush green lawns are shaded by numerous huge sycamore fig, fever, Natal mahogany and marula trees. This is a real haven in the hot summer months when every bit of shade is inviting.

ROUTES

- The camp is surrounded by mixed woodland with sweet grazing – knob-thorn and marula woodlands are dense in places with pockets of grassland; a good game-viewing habitat.
- Cheetah favour the grassland areas.
- The underlying geology is basalt and yields loam soils.
- Large numbers of animals are attracted to the abundance of water and sweet grass.
- This is Big Five country at its best.
- Excellent birding in the camp and at Sunset Dam.
- The grasslands around the Muntshe Hill are home to some of the largest zebra and wildebeest herds.
- The leaves of the tamboti have a high concentration of tannin, which makes them unpalatable for most wildlife species, but kudu and black rhino seem to have a liking for them. Porcupines feed on their bark and are often seen on guided night drives in this area.

PRIME ROADS

H4-1 north, tarred; H4-2 south, tarred; H10 to Tshokwane, tarred; S28 south, dirt.

CLOSEST GET-OUT PLACES

- Mlondozi Dam – ablutions, cold drinks for sale, gas barbeques for hire, take own picnic basket
- Ntandanyathi Hide – no ablutions, no picnic facilities
- Nkuhlu Picnic Site – ablutions, small shop, gas barbeques for hire, take own picnic basket or buy basic food items or meals

PRIME DRINKING PLACES CLOSEST TO THE CAMP

- Sunset Dam (1 km from camp)
- Sabie River frontage north and south of the camp
- Bridge over the Sabie River south of the camp
- Mlondozi Dam (18 km)
- Ntandanyathi Hide (12 km)
- Duke Waterhole (15 km)

Fighting tree agamas, Lower Sabie Camp

LEGEND

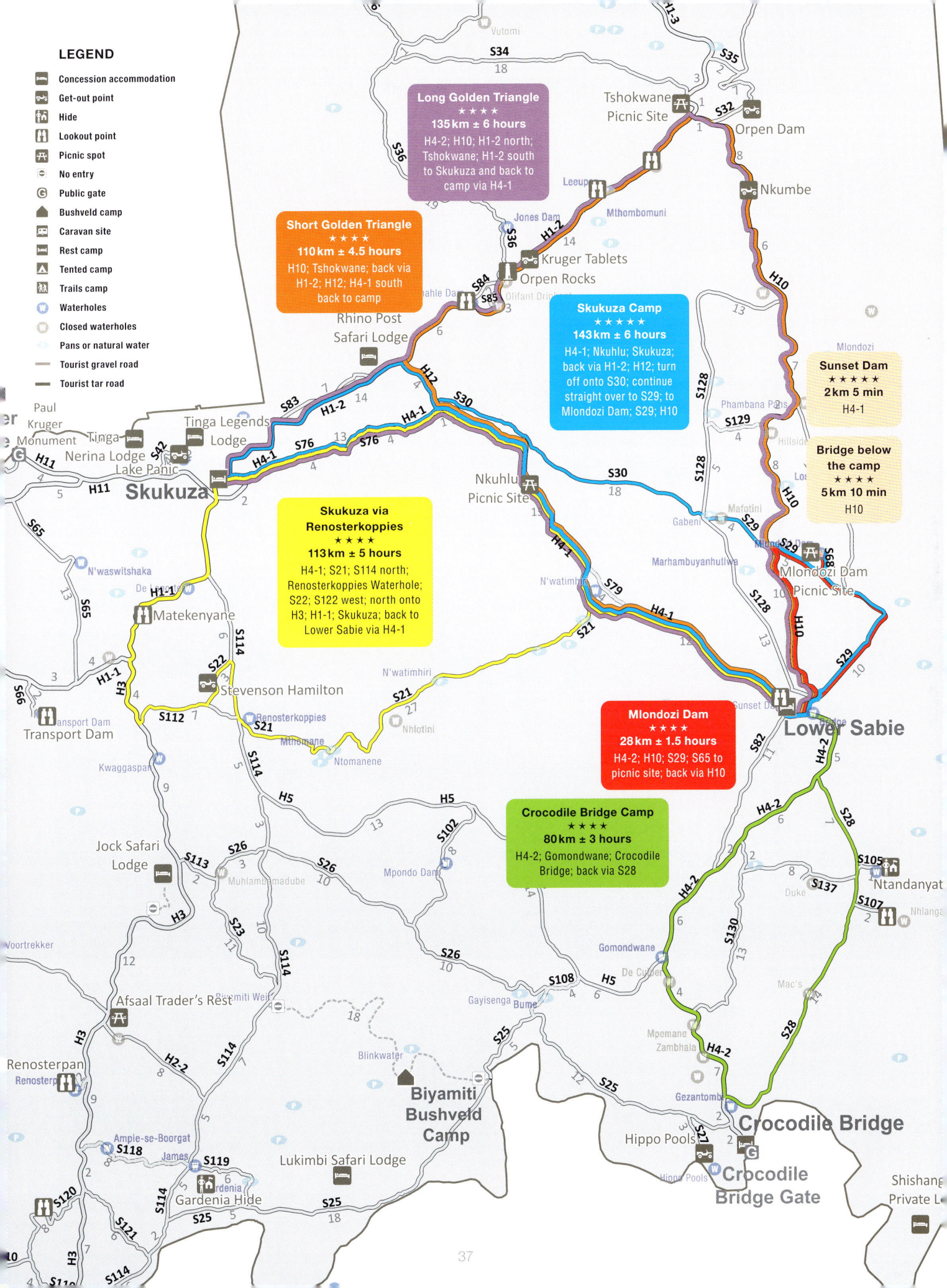

- Concession accommodation
- Get-out point
- Hide
- Lookout point
- Picnic spot
- No entry
- Public gate
- Bushveld camp
- Caravan site
- Rest camp
- Tented camp
- Trails camp
- Waterholes
- Closed waterholes
- Pans or natural water
- Tourist gravel road
- Tourist tar road

Long Golden Triangle
★★★★
135 km ± 6 hours
H4-2; H10; H1-2 north; Tshokwane; H1-2 south to Skukuza and back to camp via H4-1

Short Golden Triangle
★★★★
110 km ± 4.5 hours
H10; Tshokwane; back via H1-2; H12; H4-1 south back to camp

Skukuza Camp
★★★★★
143 km ± 6 hours
H4-1; Nkuhlu; Skukuza; back via H1-2; H12; turn off onto S30; continue straight over to S29; to Mlondozi Dam; S29; H10

Sunset Dam
★★★★★
2 km 5 min
H4-1

Bridge below the camp
★★★★
5 km 10 min
H10

Skukuza via Renosterkoppies
★★★★
113 km ± 5 hours
H4-1; S21; S114 north; Renosterkoppies Waterhole; S22; S122 west; north onto H3; H1-1; Skukuza; back to Lower Sabie via H4-1

Mlondozi Dam
★★★★
28 km ± 1.5 hours
H4-2; H10; S29; S65 to picnic site; back via H10

Crocodile Bridge Camp
★★★★
80 km ± 3 hours
H4-2; Gomondwane; Crocodile Bridge; back via S28

37

ORPEN, TAMBOTI AND MAROELA ROUTES

The Orpen Gate is one of the principal access points to central Kruger and was named in honour of the Orpen family who donated seven farms totalling 24 500 hectares to the park. Consequently the entrance gate that used to be where the Rabelais Hut can still be seen on the S106 and was moved to its present position in 1954. A small main camp with a shop and other amenities was also built here. The accommodation was soon insufficient to meet the popular demand and consequently the Tamboti Tented Camp and the Maroela Caravan Camp were built on the banks of the nearby Timbavati River. Tamboti Camp was named after the grove of tamboti trees on the riverbank and Maroela after one of the most common trees in the park.

Talamati Bushveld Camp and **Marula Camp** are satellite camps to Orpen Main Camp.

ROUTES

- The sweet grass in the vicinity of the camps attracts many browsers.
- This in turn attracts cheetah, lion and leopard.
- Wild dog are also seen from time to time.
- A small waterhole outside the Orpen Camp fence offers game viewing throughout the day.
- The seasonal Timbavati River and the riverine vegetation offers great game viewing from the Tamboti and Maroela Camps.

PRIME ROADS

S41; S39; H7; H1-4; H1-3; S100; H6; S126; southern section of S90; S140.

CLOSEST GET-OUT PLACES

- N'wanetsi Picnic Site on the H6 – shaded lookout platform, ablutions, gas barbeques for hire, cold drinks for sale, take own picnic basket
- Tshokwane Picnic Site on the H1-3 – ablutions, small shop, gas barbeques for hire, take own picnic basket or buy basic food items or meals
- Muzandzeni Picnic Site on the S36 – ablutions, gas barbeques for hire, cold drinks for sale, take own picnic basket
- Timbavati Picnic Site on the S40 – ablutions, gas barbeques for hire, cold drinks for sale, take own picnic basket
- Sweni Bird Hide on the S37 – no ablutions
- Nhlanguleni Picnic Site on the S36 – ablutions, gas barbeques for hire, cold drinks for sale, take own picnic basket
- Ratel Pan Hide on the S39 – no ablutions

PRIME DRINKING PLACES CLOSEST TO THE CAMP

- Nsemani Dam on the H7
- Girivana Dam on the S12

Plains zebra play-fighting, H7

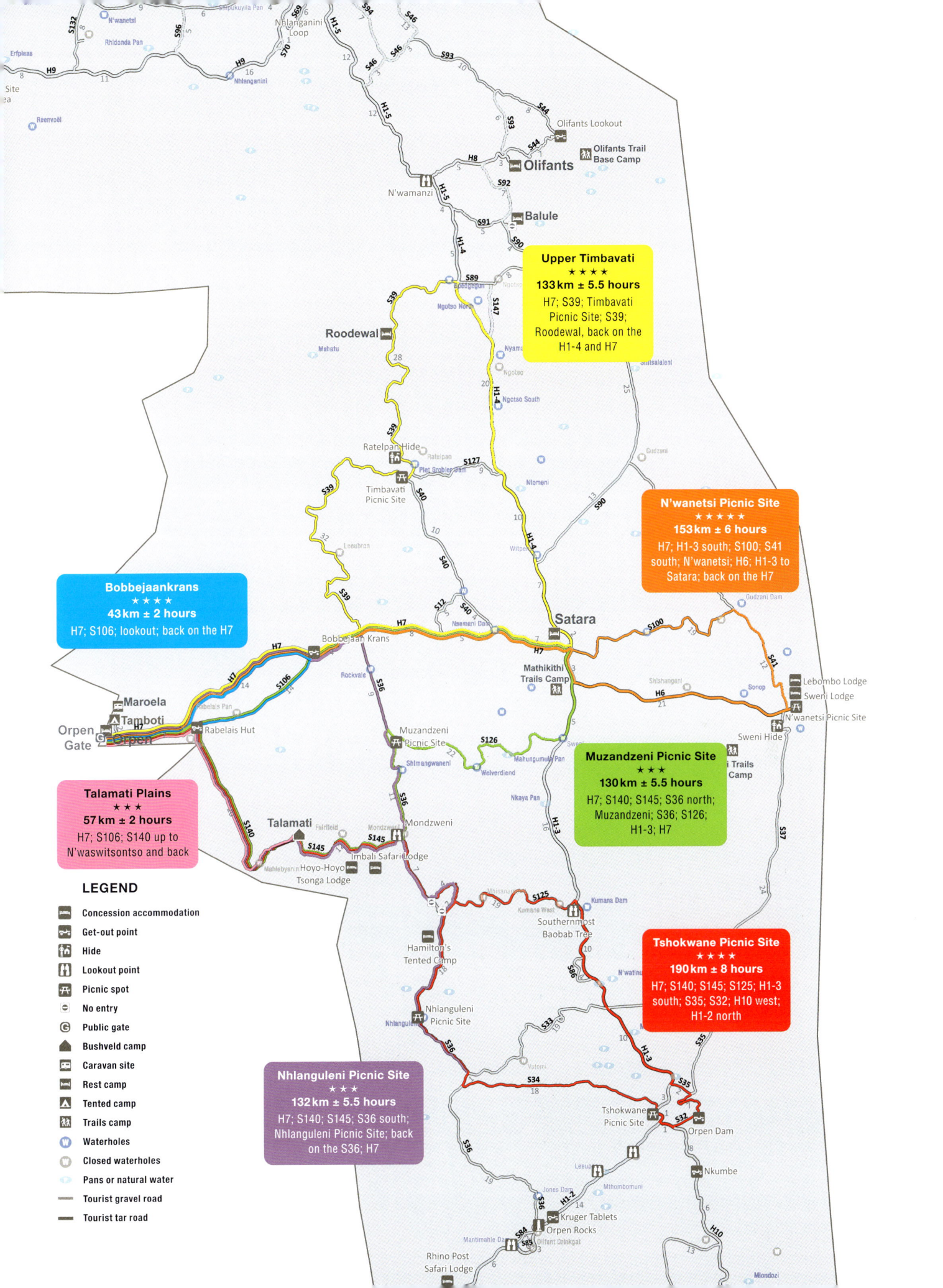

Upper Timbavati
★★★★
133 km ± 5.5 hours
H7; S39; Timbavati Picnic Site; S39; Roodewal, back on the H1-4 and H7

N'wanetsi Picnic Site
★★★★★
153 km ± 6 hours
H7; H1-3 south; S100; S41 south; N'wanetsi; H6; H1-3 to Satara; back on the H7

Bobbejaankrans
★★★★
43 km ± 2 hours
H7; S106; lookout; back on the H7

Muzandzeni Picnic Site
★★★
130 km ± 5.5 hours
H7; S140; S145; S36 north; Muzandzeni; S36; S126; H1-3; H7

Talamati Plains
★★★
57 km ± 2 hours
H7; S106; S140 up to N'waswitsontso and back

Tshokwane Picnic Site
★★★★
190 km ± 8 hours
H7; S140; S145; S125; H1-3 south; S35; S32; H10 west; H1-2 north

Nhlanguleni Picnic Site
★★★
132 km ± 5.5 hours
H7; S140; S145; S36 south; Nhlanguleni Picnic Site; back on the S36; H7

LEGEND
- Concession accommodation
- Get-out point
- Hide
- Lookout point
- Picnic spot
- No entry
- Public gate
- Bushveld camp
- Caravan site
- Rest camp
- Tented camp
- Trails camp
- Waterholes
- Closed waterholes
- Pans or natural water
- Tourist gravel road
- Tourist tar road

SATARA ROUTES

Satara is perfectly located in the best game-viewing areas of the park. The camp is surrounded by fertile plains that attract many grazers. Little wonder that it is regarded as the best place in the world for lion sightings in the wild. Birding is excellent within the camp. A small waterhole just beyond the perimeter of the camp attracts a steady flow of game.

In the late 19th century, before its proclamation as a national park, the area was surveyed in preparation for human settlement. One of the surveyors had a Hindi-speaking Indian assistant who suggested the number 17 (satrah in Hindi) for the farm. A misspelling of this word became the name of the rest camp called Satara, which was established in 1928.

Roodewal Private Camp is close to Satara Main Camp.

ROUTES

- To the west is a strip of Ecca shale with sweet grazing, while the soils in the far west have underlying granite and gabbro, and grasses tend to become unpalatable in winter.
- The frequency of lion sightings is extremely high around Satara.
- Game is prolific on most of the routes radiating from Satara.
- The Central Region of the park stretches from the Sabie River northwards to the Olifants River.
- The grassy plains around Satara are referred to as the central plains.
- To the east of Satara are the basalt plains with sweet grazing fringed by the Lebombo Mountains on the border of Mozambique.

PRIME ROADS

H7; H1-3; S100; S41; H6; S90; S39; S126.

CLOSEST GET-OUT PLACES

- N'wanetsi Picnic Site on the H6 – shaded lookout platform, ablutions, gas barbeques for hire, cold drinks for sale, take own picnic basket
- Tshokwane Picnic Site on the H1-3 – ablutions, small shop, gas barbeques for hire, take own picnic basket or buy basic food items or meals
- Muzandzeni Picnic Site on the S36 – ablutions, gas barbeques for hire, cold drinks for sale, take own picnic basket
- Timbavati Picnic Site on the S40 – ablutions, gas barbeques for hire, cold drinks for sale, take own picnic basket
- Sweni Bird Hide on the S37 – no ablutions
- Nhlanguleni Picnic Site on the S36 – ablutions, gas barbeques for hire, cold drinks for sale, take own picnic basket
- Ratelpan Hide on the S39 – no ablutions

PRIME DRINKING PLACES CLOSEST TO THE CAMP

- N'wanetsi Dam on the H6
- Nsemani Dam on the N7
- Girivana Dam on the S12
- Kumana Dam on the H1-3
- Orpen Dam on the S32
- Gudzani Dam on the S41
- Piet Grobler Dam on the S39

Striped skink pair, H4-2

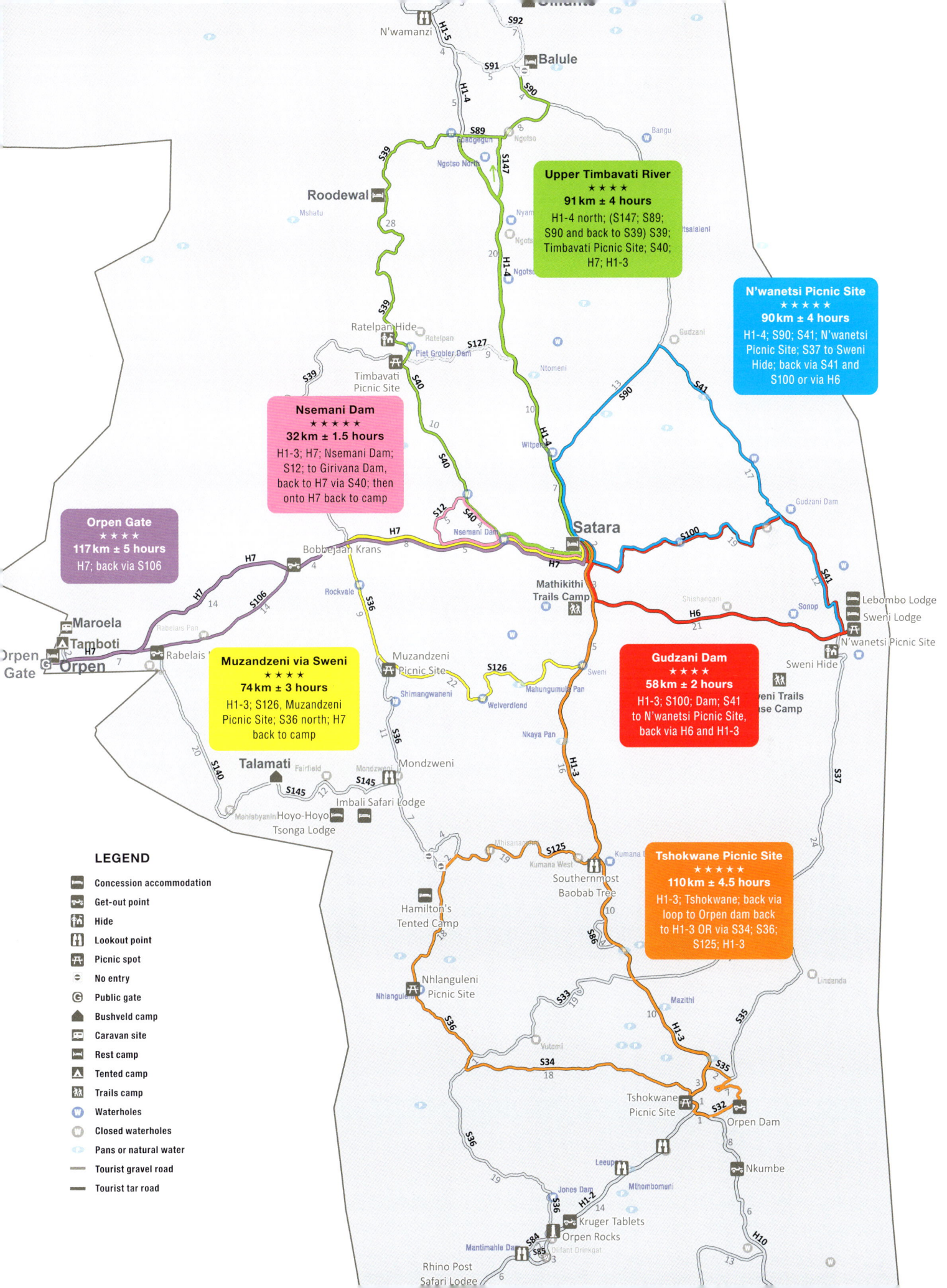

Upper Timbavati River
★★★★
91 km ± 4 hours
H1-4 north; (S147; S89; S90 and back to S39) S39; Timbavati Picnic Site; S40; H7; H1-3

N'wanetsi Picnic Site
★★★★★
90 km ± 4 hours
H1-4; S90; S41; N'wanetsi Picnic Site; S37 to Sweni Hide; back via S41 and S100 or via H6

Nsemani Dam
★★★★★
32 km ± 1.5 hours
H1-3; H7; Nsemani Dam; S12; to Girivana Dam, back to H7 via S40; then onto H7 back to camp

Orpen Gate
★★★★
117 km ± 5 hours
H7; back via S106

Muzandzeni via Sweni
★★★★
74 km ± 3 hours
H1-3; S126, Muzandzeni Picnic Site; S36 north; H7 back to camp

Gudzani Dam
★★★★
58 km ± 2 hours
H1-3; S100; Dam; S41 to N'wanetsi Picnic Site, back via H6 and H1-3

Tshokwane Picnic Site
★★★★★
110 km ± 4.5 hours
H1-3; Tshokwane; back via loop to Orpen dam back to H1-3 OR via S34; S36; S125; H1-3

LEGEND
- Concession accommodation
- Get-out point
- Hide
- Lookout point
- Picnic spot
- No entry
- Public gate
- Bushveld camp
- Caravan site
- Rest camp
- Tented camp
- Trails camp
- Waterholes
- Closed waterholes
- Pans or natural water
- Tourist gravel road
- Tourist tar road

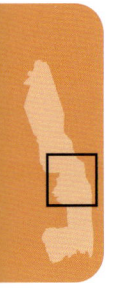

OLIFANTS CAMP ROUTES

This is the camp with the best panoramic views in the park. Towering more than a hundred metres above the Olifants River in the valley far below, the shaded viewing platform offers hours of wildlife entertainment. Elephant and antelope come and go. Leopard and lion are regularly seen. Hippo and crocodile are always there and the abundance and diversity of birds is great. The camp is situated on a hill and many of the bungalows have a river view – visitors can sit on their verandas enjoying the surrounding bushveld.

Balule Camp is situated on the banks of the Olifants River. Many years ago **Reitz's Pontoon** was used to cross the river. Today a low-water bridge connects the S90 with the S91 and S92.

ROUTES

- The Olifants River area is in the transition zone between the southern thornveld and wooded savanna and the northern mopane veld.
- Game density is lower than in the south but diversity is great.
- Mopane bush is dense and visibility generally not good.
- Browsers do better than grazers in this area.
- The best game drive routes are those following river courses.
- It is prime elephant territory.
- The Olifants River is home to the largest crocodile population.

PRIME ROADS

S92; S91; S90 (first section from Balule); S44; S93; S89; S39, S147.

CLOSEST GET-OUT PLACES

- N'wamanzi Lookout – no ablutions, no picnic facilities
- Olifants Lookout – no ablutions, no picnic facilities
- Letaba Rest Camp – full-house amenities
- Timbavati Picnic Site – ablutions, gas barbeques for hire, cold drinks for sale, take own picnic basket

PRIME DRINKING PLACES CLOSEST TO THE CAMP

- After good rains the pan at the S93 and S44 fills up and offers good sunset viewing close to the camp
- The bridge crossing over the Olifants River on the H1-5
- The causeway over the Olifants River to Balule on the S92
- Any of the river-viewing spots
- Ngotso stream along the S147

Red-headed weaver male, Olifants Camp

LEGEND

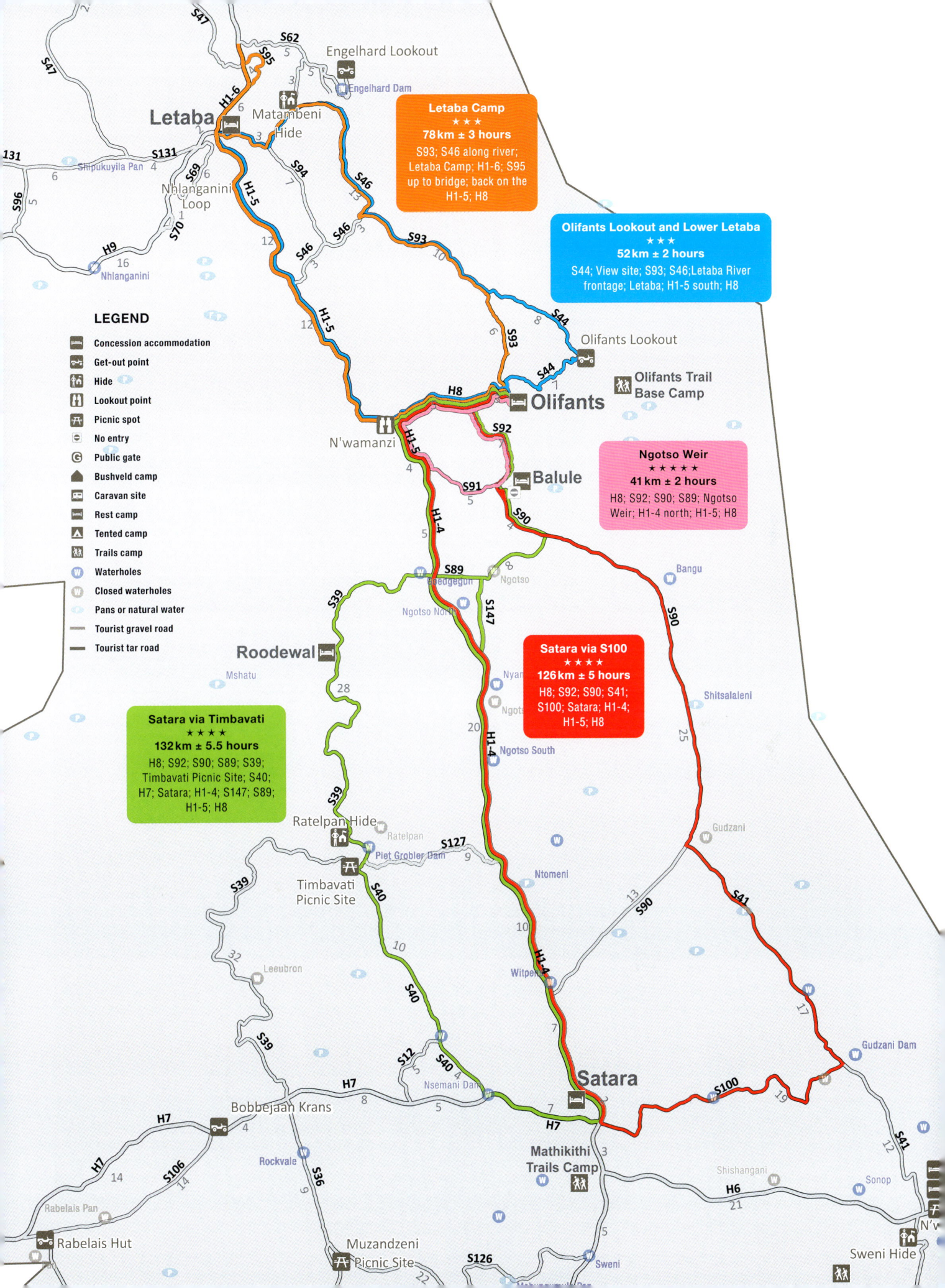

	Concession accommodation
	Get-out point
	Hide
	Lookout point
	Picnic spot
	No entry
	Public gate
	Bushveld camp
	Caravan site
	Rest camp
	Tented camp
	Trails camp
W	Waterholes
W	Closed waterholes
	Pans or natural water
	Tourist gravel road
	Tourist tar road

Letaba Camp ★★★
78 km ± 3 hours
S93; S46 along river; Letaba Camp; H1-6; S95 up to bridge; back on the H1-5; H8

Olifants Lookout and Lower Letaba ★★★
52 km ± 2 hours
S44; View site; S93; S46; Letaba River frontage; Letaba; H1-5 south; H8

Ngotso Weir ★★★★★
41 km ± 2 hours
H8; S92; S90; S89; Ngotso Weir; H1-4 north; H1-5; H8

Satara via S100 ★★★★
126 km ± 5 hours
H8; S92; S90; S41; S100; Satara; H1-4; H1-5; H8

Satara via Timbavati ★★★★
132 km ± 5.5 hours
H8; S92; S90; S89; S39; Timbavati Picnic Site; S40; H7; Satara; H1-4; S147; S89; H1-5; H8

LETABA ROUTES

Midway between the southern and northern boundaries of the park the River of Sand, better known as the Letaba River, wends its way to join the Olifants River to the Indian Ocean. Although the Letaba may become a raging torrent after good rains in summer, it is usually slow-flowing, with many pools among the sandbanks. The river and its tributaries are the main source of water in this, the central part of the park.

The rest camp is known for its beautiful views over the river, its tranquil atmosphere with lots of shade from huge trees, rolling lawns, comparatively tame bushbuck moving among the bungalows, nibbling here and there, relaxed in the sense of safety the camp offers them. Close to Reception, a huge elephant statue intrigues visitors on their way to view the elephant exhibition in the Elephant Hall. This venue also serves as an ecological information centre.

The indigenous gardens with the many aloes and impala lilies attract nectar-feeding birds and tree squirrels. At Letaba it's unnecessary to leave the camp. You have it all there on your doorstep.

LETABA ROUTES

- Letaba and elephants are synonymous. These giants need to drink regularly and are prolific around the river.
- The riverine vegetation in the camp and along the riverbanks offers good birding opportunities.
- Away from the river, the mopane shrubveld on basalt offers mostly sweet grass, although it is sparse.
- Towards Phalaborwa, mopane and bushwillow woodlands are prevalent and game densities are relatively low.
- The area is rich in pre-historical sites. The area was inhabited by successive groups of people and archaeological excavations reveal a fascinating story of Stone Age people who were gradually displaced by other tribes who mined copper and iron and traded with Arabs and others. The Masorini site on the H9 is well worth visiting.

PRIME ROADS

Southern end of H1-6; S95; S62; S46; S69.

CLOSEST GET-OUT PLACES

- Matambeni Bird Hide on S62 – no ablutions, no picnic facilities
- Makhadzi on H15 – ablutions, gas barbeques for hire, cold drinks for sale, take own picnic basket
- Mooiplaas on H1-6 – ablutions, gas barbeques for hire, cold drinks for sale, take own picnic basket
- Masorini on H9 – ablutions, gas barbeques for hire, cold drinks for sale, take own picnic basket
- Nwamanzi Lookout – no ablutions, no picnic facilities

PRIME DRINKING PLACES CLOSEST TO THE CAMP

- The Letaba River north and east of the camp
- Nhlanganini Dam on the H9
- Engelhard Dam on the S62

Woodland kingfisher, H7

Isak Pretorius

LEGEND

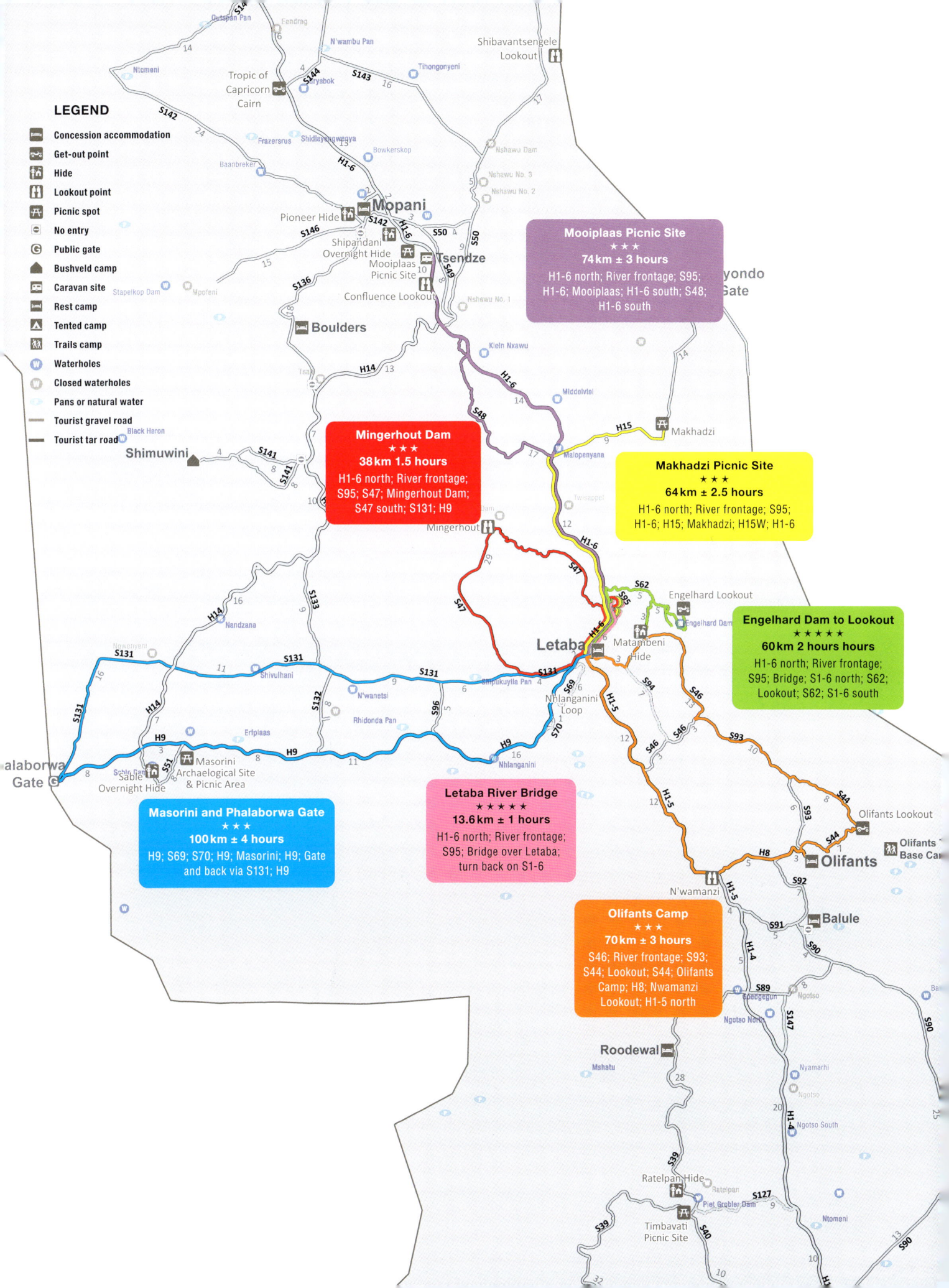

- Concession accommodation
- Get-out point
- Hide
- Lookout point
- Picnic spot
- No entry
- Public gate
- Bushveld camp
- Caravan site
- Rest camp
- Tented camp
- Trails camp
- Waterholes
- Closed waterholes
- Pans or natural water
- Tourist gravel road
- Tourist tar road

Mooiplaas Picnic Site
★★★
74 km ± 3 hours
H1-6 north; River frontage; S95; H1-6; Mooiplaas; H1-6 south; S48; H1-6 south

Mingerhout Dam
★★★
38 km 1.5 hours
H1-6 north; River frontage; S95; S47; Mingerhout Dam; S47 south; S131; H9

Makhadzi Picnic Site
★★★
64 km ± 2.5 hours
H1-6 north; River frontage; S95; H1-6; H15; Makhadzi; H15W; H1-6

Engelhard Dam to Lookout
★★★★★
60 km 2 hours hours
H1-6 north; River frontage; S95; Bridge; S1-6 north; S62; Lookout; S62; S1-6 south

Masorini and Phalaborwa Gate
★★★
100 km ± 4 hours
H9; S69; S70; H9; Masorini; H9; Gate and back via S131; H9

Letaba River Bridge
★★★★★
13.6 km ± 1 hours
H1-6 north; River frontage; S95; Bridge over Letaba; turn back on S1-6

Olifants Camp
★★★
70 km ± 3 hours
S46; River frontage; S93; S44; Lookout; S44; Olifants Camp; H8; Nwamanzi Lookout; H1-5 north

MOPANI ROUTES

Mopani, the newest camp in the park, was completed in 1992. It is situated in a sea of mopane, the dominant vegetation of the north, and was aptly called Mopani Rest Camp. The views over the huge Pioneer Dam are stunning and offer good game viewing from the camp. A striking feature of the camp is the huge baobab towering high above the well-designed grounds. Care was taken not to disturb the natural vegetation when building. All the accommodation units blend in with the natural environment. Birdwatching in the camp is one of the most popular activities. Although they are not autumn months in the southern hemisphere, in September and October the butterfly-shaped mopane leaves take on striking autumn colours.

The Pioneer Dam was built on the Tsendze River. Downstream from the dam the Shipandani game-viewing hide offers sleepover facilities. Visitors love the opportunity to experience a night in the bush in the relative safety and comfort of the rustic hide. Another not so well-placed hide overlooking the dam is not as popular, but occasionally offers waterbird viewing.

Boulders Bushveld Camp, **Shimuwini Bushveld Camp** and the **Tsendze Rustic Camp** are not far from the Mopani Main Camp.

ROUTES

- The camp is situated in mopane shrubveld with underlying basalt rock, but the proximity to the Shipandani and Tsendze seasonal rivers means there is riverine vegetation and therefore a greater diversity of tree species.
- The grass is sweet towards the surrounding eastern plains and attracts more game than the areas to the west (S142 and S146).
- Although game is less abundant on the western roads, the landscape becomes stunning after rains. Pans fill up and water lilies with their delicate-hued flowers appear from nowhere. Silver cluster-leaf is prolific and gives a soft tone to areas where there are seepage lines.
- To the east the Nshawu drainage line with wetland areas and pans is the main attraction, while animals of different kinds are always present at Mooiplaas Waterhole. If you don't see animals it may be because there are predators nearby.
- The Tropic of Capricorn road is a magical sight when huge tuskers approach the waterhole from all directions.

PRIME ROADS

S50; S49; the southern end of S142; S143; H1-6 south up to Middelvlei.

CLOSEST GET-OUT PLACES

- Mooiplaas Picnic Site – shaded lookout platform, ablutions, gas barbeques for hire, cold drinks for sale, take own picnic basket
- Shibavantsengele Lookout – no ablutions, no picnic facilities
- Makhadzi Picnic Site – ablutions, gas barbeques for hire, cold drinks for sale, take own picnic basket
- Shipandani overnight hide – ablutions for overnight guests
- Pioneer Hide – no ablutions, no picnic facilities

PRIME DRINKING PLACES CLOSEST TO THE CAMP

- Pioneer Dam views from the camp
- Mooiplaas Waterhole
- Bowkerskop
- Nshawu Wetlands (seasonal)
- The Tsendze River is seasonal, but pools remain far into the dry season in places

Nile crocodile, S142

Map Legend and Routes

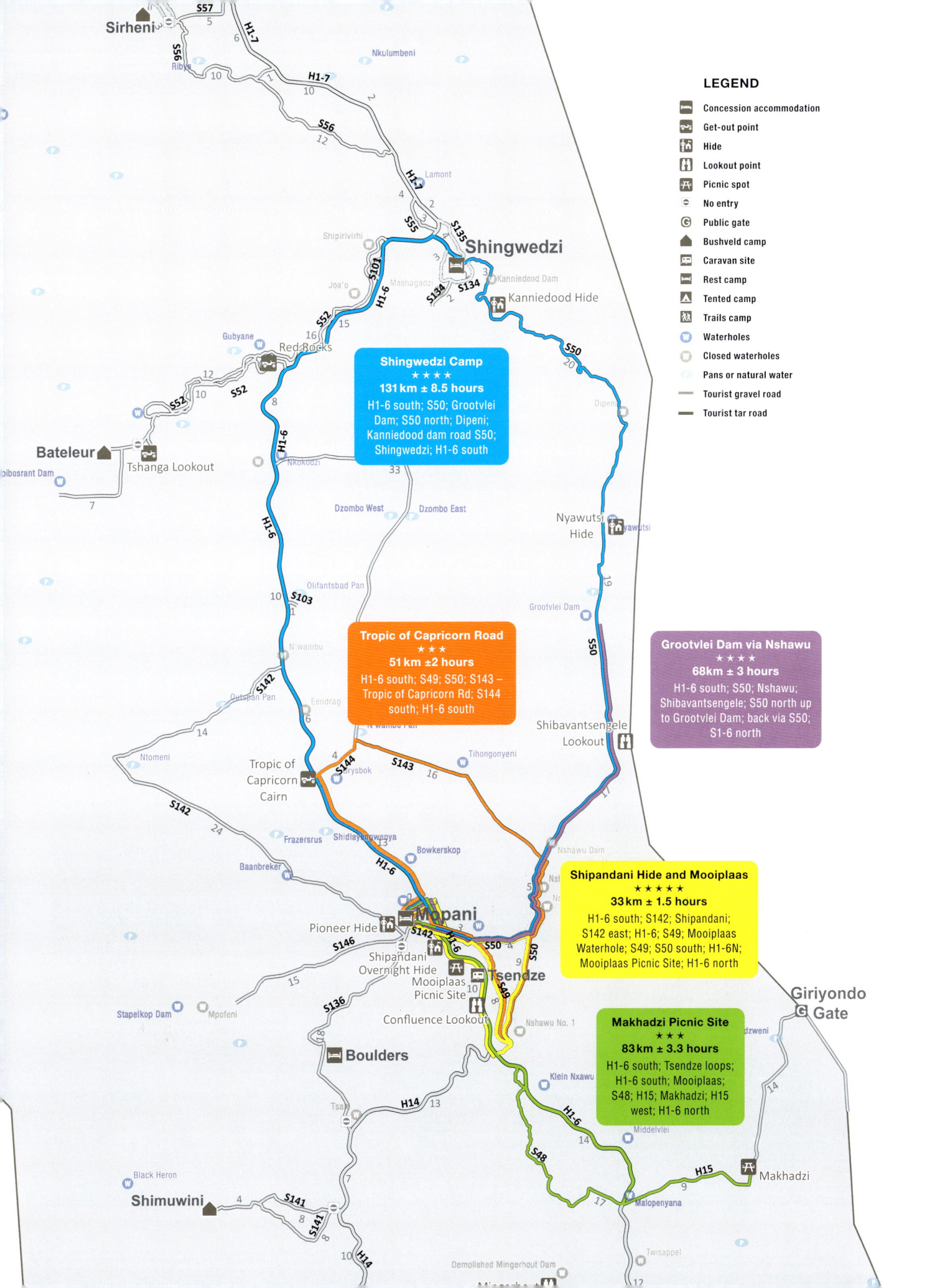

LEGEND
- Concession accommodation
- Get-out point
- Hide
- Lookout point
- Picnic spot
- No entry
- Public gate
- Bushveld camp
- Caravan site
- Rest camp
- Tented camp
- Trails camp
- Waterholes
- Closed waterholes
- Pans or natural water
- Tourist gravel road
- Tourist tar road

Shingwedzi Camp
★★★★
131 km ± 8.5 hours
H1-6 south; S50; Grootvlei Dam; S50 north; Dipeni; Kanniedood dam road S50; Shingwedzi; H1-6 south

Tropic of Capricorn Road
★★★
51 km ± 2 hours
H1-6 south; S49; S50; S143 – Tropic of Capricorn Rd; S144 south; H1-6 south

Grootvlei Dam via Nshawu
★★★★
68 km ± 3 hours
H1-6 south; S50; Nshawu; Shibavantsengele; S50 north up to Grootvlei Dam; back via S50; S1-6 north

Shipandani Hide and Mooiplaas
★★★★★
33 km ± 1.5 hours
H1-6 south; S142; Shipandani; S142 east; H1-6; S49; Mooiplaas Waterhole; S49; S50 south; H1-6N; Mooiplaas Picnic Site; H1-6 north

Makhadzi Picnic Site
★★★
83 km ± 3.3 hours
H1-6 south; Tsendze loops; H1-6 south; Mooiplaas; S48; H15; Makhadzi; H15 west; H1-6 north

SHINGWEDZI ROUTES

The name of this camp was derived from the historic Tsonga name Xingwedzi which comes from the word 'ngwetse' and means 'the sound made by two metal objects rubbed together'. The Shingwedzi Camp is situated on the banks of the Shingwedzi River, a few kilometres downstream from its confluence with the Mphongolo tributary. One of the most distinctive and attractive features of this camp is a clump of lala palms at the entrance to the hutted camp. The single, straight trunks reach high into the sky where they carry their huge hand-shaped compound leaves and fruit that hangs in bunches below them. A collection of huge impala lily shrubs with their lovely pink-red blooms is another typical feature. The river is seasonal but has a huge catchment area. The result is extensive flooding in the rainy season. These floods are a natural occurrence but some of them have been devastating, uprooting huge sycamore figs and other trees in their way. The camp has been flooded several times in the past. Flooding leaves behind widespread floodplains of fertile soils. A unique plant community is typical of such floodplains.

The **Bateleur Bushveld Camp** and the **Sirheni Bushveld Camp** are close to the Shingwedzi Main Camp.

ROUTES

- In mopane veld the best game viewing is along the rivers. The best time for seeing game is in the dry season when the seasonal rivers recede and competition for diminishing water resources is at its peak.
- This is elephant country and huge breeding herds of 50–60 of the largest land mammals in the world congregate at water points.
- The Shingwedzi area was home to the famous Magnificent Seven tuskers. All have now died and their stories and ivory can be viewed at the Letaba Camp.
- Buffalo do well around Shingwedzi and they often come down in their hundreds to drink.
- The Kanniedood Dam was built in 1975 and created a permanent water supply for about 21 km downstream from the camp. In the 2013 floods the dam wall was broken and this changed the entire nature of the previously popular Kanniedood drive. Many pools remain but their positions have changed.
- Gold prospecting at Red Rocks in the early 19th century forms part of the history of the magnificent Shingwedzi River. Fortunately not much of the precious metal was found, and nature was allowed to rest in peace.

PRIME ROADS

H1-7; river drive on northern section of the S50; S56; S52; first southern section of the H1-6.

CLOSEST GET-OUT PLACES

- Babalala Picnic Site – ablutions, gas barbeques for hire, cold drinks for sale, take own picnic basket
- Tshange Lookout – no picnic facilities
- Nyawutsi Hide on the S50 – no ablutions, no picnic facilities
- Shibavantsengele Lookout on the S50 – no ablutions, no picnic facilities

PRIME DRINKING PLACES CLOSEST TO THE CAMP

- Several pools in the Shingwedzi and Mphongolo Rivers
- The Lamont Waterhole on S55
- Causeway across the river below the camp

Impala Lilies, Shingwedzi Camp

LEGEND

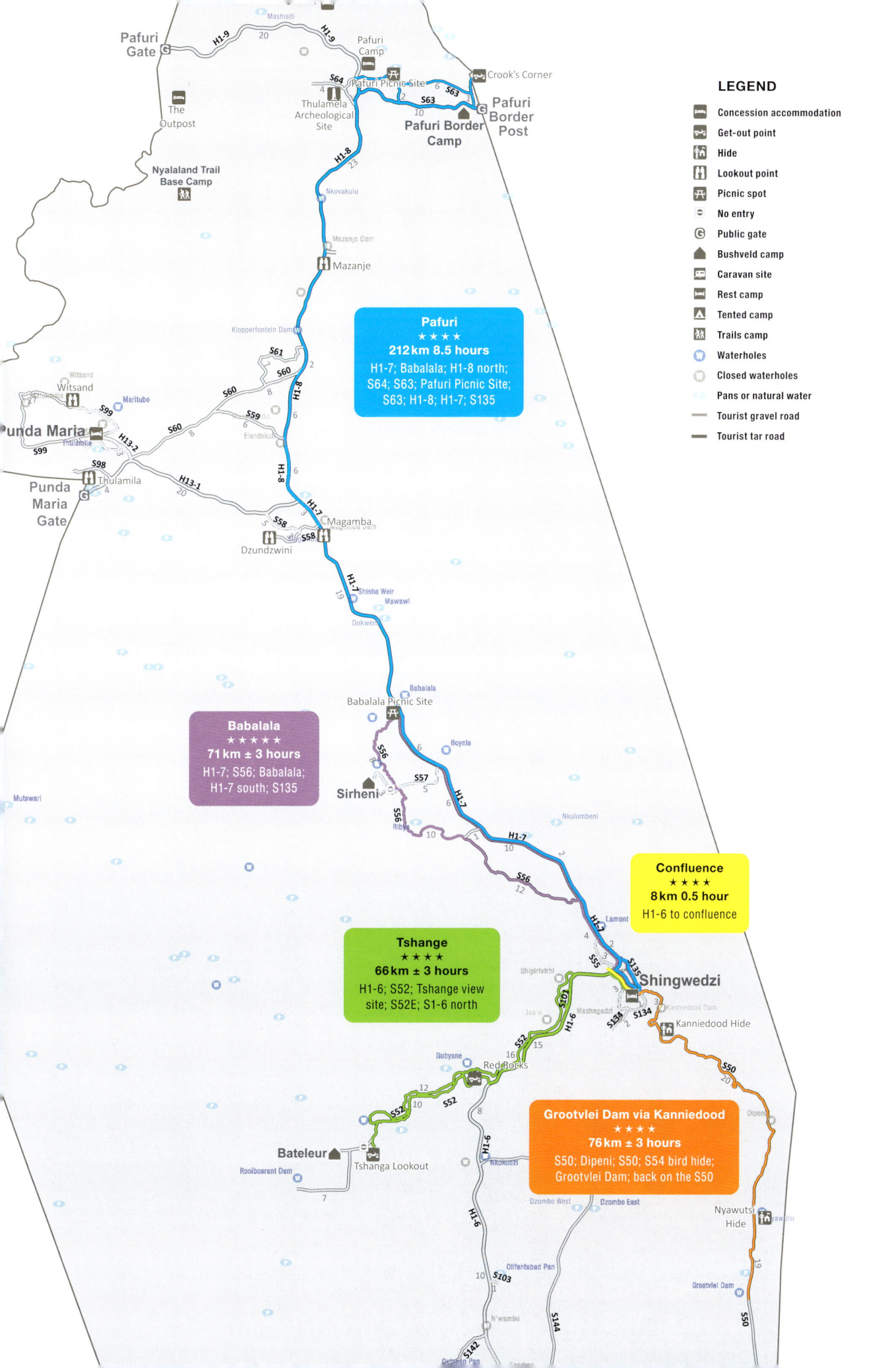

- Concession accommodation
- Get-out point
- Hide
- Lookout point
- Picnic spot
- No entry
- Public gate
- Bushveld camp
- Caravan site
- Rest camp
- Tented camp
- Trails camp
- Waterholes
- Closed waterholes
- Pans or natural water
- Tourist gravel road
- Tourist tar road

Pafuri ★★★★
212 km 8.5 hours
H1-7; Babalala; H1-8 north; S64; S63; Pafuri Picnic Site; S63; H1-8; H1-7; S135

Babalala ★★★★★
71 km ± 3 hours
H1-7; S56; Babalala; H1-7 south; S135

Confluence ★★★★
8 km 0.5 hour
H1-6 to confluence

Tshange ★★★★
66 km ± 3 hours
H1-6; S52; Tshange view site; S52E; S1-6 north

Grootvlei Dam via Kanniedood ★★★★
76 km ± 3 hours
S50; Dipeni; S50; S54 bird hide; Grootvlei Dam; back on the S50

PUNDA MARIA ROUTES

As early as 1919, Captain JJ Coetser was appointed as the first ranger in the far north. His mission was to curb ivory poaching as the north was known as the haunt of smugglers, poachers and hunters. He first established a temporary camp at the natural spring on the S58 before he set up camp near the present Punda Maria. He named the camp after his wife Maria. For many years it was believed that the camp was named after the zebra because in Swahili (the indigenous language spoken there) 'punda' means stripe and 'milia' means donkey. Hence for many years the camp was called Punda Milia. In 1981 this error was corrected and the name Punda Maria was reinstated. It is the only camp where many of the original bungalows are still in use. The lush and diverse vegetation attracts a plethora of bird species, and dendrologists have a feast in identifying the many tree species.

ROUTES

- The Punda Maria area supports fewer big game species than elsewhere but offers a diversity of rare antelope species such as roan, tsessebe, eland, Lichtenstein's hartebeest, Sharpe's grysbok and the tiny suni antelope.
- Big herds of elephant and buffalo are often seen. A game-viewing hide overlooks a waterhole and can be reached direct from the camping area.
- The number of different bird and tree species surpasses that of any other area in the park.
- The entire north is rich in ancient history. Important archaeological sites reveal much about the early inhabitants and settlements.
- The underlying geology is fascinating and very different from the rest of the park.
- The sandveld is known as the flower garden of the park.
- The extreme north is the driest part of the park while the area around the camp is the lushest with huge trees and several springs and creeks.
- The eastern part of this area is the only place where mature mopane woodland occurs.

PRIME ROADS

S99; S61; S58; S63; S64; H1-7; S56.

CLOSEST GET-OUT PLACES

- Babalala Picnic Site on the H1-7 – ablutions, gas barbeques for hire, cold drinks for sale, take own picnic basket
- Pafuri Picnic Site on the S63 overlooking the Luvuvhu River – ablutions, gas barbeques for hire, cold drinks for sale, take own picnic basket.
- Crook's Corner at the confluence of the Luvuvhu and the Limpopo rivers – no ablutions, no picnic facilities.

PRIME DRINKING PLACES CLOSEST TO THE CAMP

- The waterhole just outside the camp (view from the hide in the camping area)
- The natural spring at Thulamila
- The natural spring on the S99
- The natural spring on the S58
- Klopperfontein Waterhole and dam on the S61

Chacma baboon S63

Map Legend and Routes

Pafuri
★★★★★
132 km 5.5 hours
H13-2; S60; H1-8 north; S64; S63; Pafuri Picnic Site; S63; H1-8; H13-1; H13-2

Mahoni Drive
★★★★★
29 km 1 hour +
H13-2; S99 circumnavigating Dumbo Hill; H13-2

Klopperfontein
★★★★
62 km 2 hours +
H13-2; S60; S61; Klopperfontein Waterhole and dam; H1-8 south; H1-7 south; S58; Dzundzwini; H13-1; H13-2

Thulamila Hill
★★★★
19 km ± 1 hour
H13-2; H13-1; S98; Thulamila; H13-1; H13-2

Shingwedzi
★★★★
151 km 6 hours
H13-2; H13-1; H1-7 south; Babalala; S56; H1-7S; Shingwedzi; H1-7 north; H13-1; H13-2

LEGEND
- Concession accommodation
- Get-out point
- Hide
- Lookout point
- Picnic spot
- No entry
- Public gate
- Bushveld camp
- Caravan site
- Rest camp
- Tented camp
- Trails camp
- Waterholes
- Closed waterholes
- Pans or natural water
- Tourist gravel road
- Tourist tar road

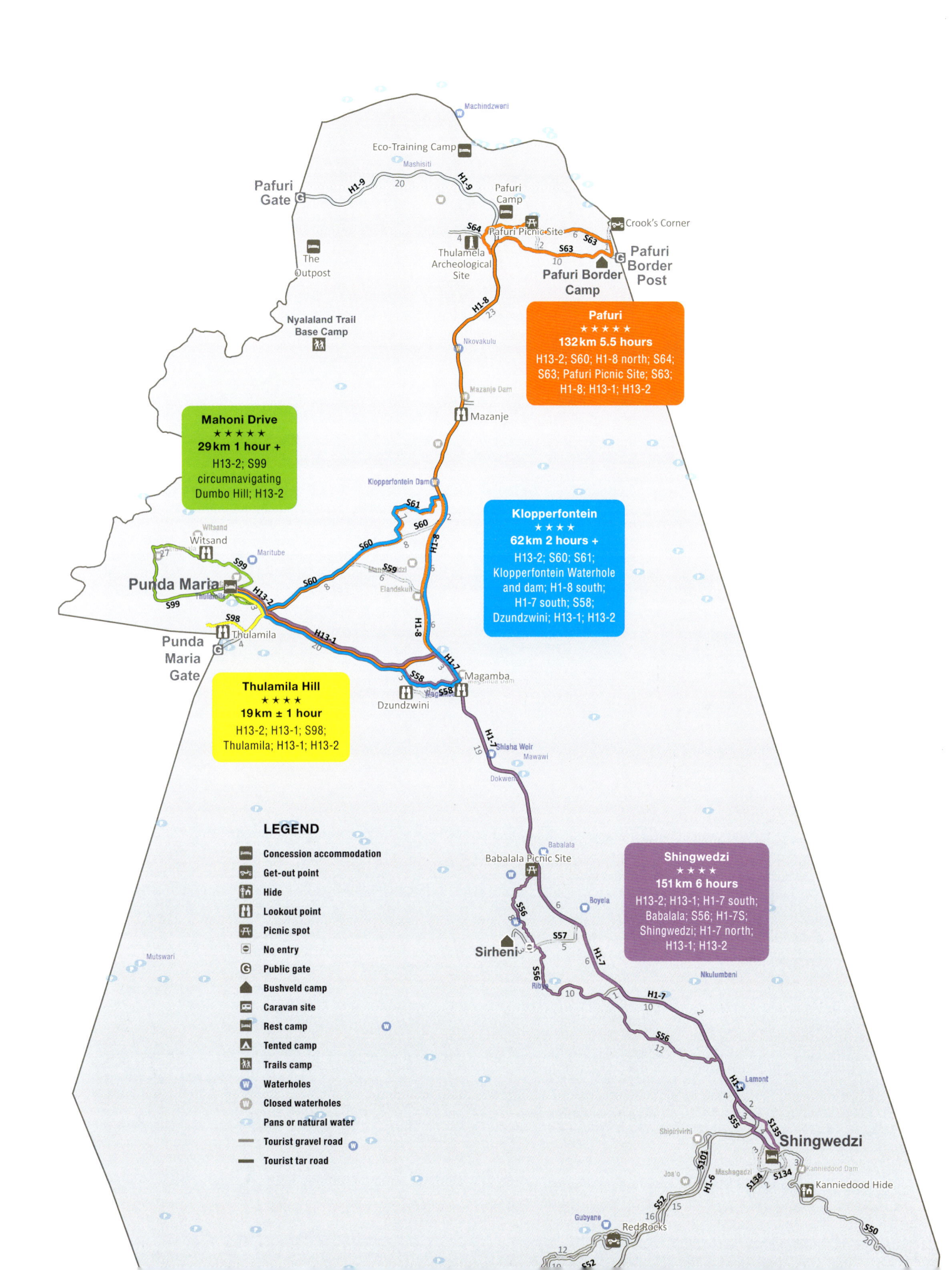

Orpen Road, H7

Roads

INTRODUCTION TO ROADS

Self-driving in the park is a good option – the maps are accurate, many roads are tarred and the gravel roads are well maintained. For optimal game spotting relax and slow down. Simply enjoy the experience of being in the bush.

Plan a steady, relaxed drive for the first 3–4 hours followed by a break at mid-morning at a waterhole or picnic site. The recommended speed for game spotting is 25 km/h on both tarred and gravel/dirt roads. Use this speed to calculate the time you will spend on your chosen route. Most sightings may be missed when you are driving at the maximum speed limit.

There can be no guarantee of sightings of any particular animal in any particular spot, but at the same time it is unpredictability that makes the game-viewing experience so fascinating. Spend time birdwatching and tree spotting. It is amazing how often animals appear 'from nowhere' when you stop to look at birds or trees. Game is not evenly distributed in the park despite the rich diversity of species. Knowledge of the geology, climate and plant distribution will greatly enhance your ability to know what to look for and where.

The availability of surface water greatly influences the movements and concentrations of game. It may happen that a man-made waterhole is temporarily dry or closed. In most cases this is done intentionally as part of the management plan of the park, or to give over-utilised areas a chance to regenerate.

MAKING SENSE OF THE ROAD NUMBERS

You may find the road numbers confusing because there is not necessarily a system in the numerical order.

- **The H roads are the main roads** between the entrance gates and rest camps or between one main camp and the next. They are mostly tarred except for the H5 and the H15, which are gravel roads. The H1 starts at Numbi Gate and continues up to the Pafuri Gate in the north. There are nine sections numbered H1-1, H1-2, H1-3, etc.

- **The S roads are the secondary roads** and they are mostly gravel or dirt roads or tracks. Exceptions are the S1, which is a tarred road between the Phabeni Gate and Skukuza Rest Camp; the southern section of the S110 from the H3 to the Berg-en-Dal Rest Camp; and the section of the S63 between the H1-8 and the Pafuri Border Post.

- **The tarred roads** carry heavier traffic than the backroads but they are wider, and the vegetation lining them is not covered in dust during the peak of the dry season. Game animals near these roads seem to be more relaxed and used to vehicles. **The speed limit is 50 km/h.**

- **The dirt or gravel roads** (backroads) can be dusty and corrugated in places or may even be temporarily closed after heavy rains, but fewer vehicles use them and you may enjoy sightings without getting stuck in traffic jams. **The speed limit is 40 km/h.**

★★★

ROAD NUMBER
ROAD NAME

🦁 ★★   🦌 ★★   🦅 ★★★   🌳 ★★★

🐾 Distance; road conditions; ecozones
🚩 Places of interest on this road

Description of the road

ABOUT THE RATINGS

The ratings given for the different routes and roads have no scientific basis. Various people who have an intimate knowledge of the Kruger roads assisted in the ratings given. These ratings **cannot be anything but subjective** and should merely serve as a general indication of what to expect. **Game sightings are mostly unpredictable and one may expect surprises almost anywhere.** The ratings reflect optimal conditions in the best game-viewing seasons. Give your own ratings and make notes for future visits.

★ A mostly quiet road with little activity

★★ A quiet road, but there may be activity

★★★ Average game and plant diversity, not particularly scenic

★★★★ Usually good game and plant diversity and/or scenically pleasing

★★★★★ Has all the attributes for good sightings and/or is scenically pleasing

🦁 = Probability of encountering predators

🦌 = Density of herbivores

🦅 = Birding potential

🌳 = Scenic beauty and tree diversity

🐾 = Distance, tarred or dirt; number of ecozones traversed

🚩 = Hotspots not to be missed

← S122

← Muntshe Loop   12

← Tshokwane   ⛺   34

Cheetah on the lookout, S29

H1-1

★★★★
H1-1
NAPI ROAD BETWEEN NUMBI AND SKUKUZA

★★★★　★★★　★★★★　★★★

- 54 km; tarred; traverses four ecozones
- Transport Dam; Shitlhave Dam; Matekenyane granite dome; Napi Boulders

The Napi Road, one of the oldest in the park, connects the Numbi Gate to Skukuza. It is also the first part of the main road (H1) that traverses the park from south to north.

Typical of the Napi Road are the **isolated inselbergs** (free-standing hills or koppies) of granite/gneiss boulders that dot the landscape. Not to be missed is the turn-off to the giant granite dome called **Matekenyane**. This provides a wonderful vantage point overlooking the entire Lowveld in all directions. In the far west is the northern Drakensberg escarpment, often shrouded in clouds. The granite foothills below the escarpment extend across the southwestern parts of the park. To the east are the flat plains of weathered basalt and, visible on the far horizon, the low Lebombo Hills.

Predator and Big Five sightings are relatively good along the entire route. Look out for leopard close to rocky outcrops, in trees and at watering points. Lion can be expected anywhere and cheetah sightings are often reported, especially in the vicinity of the Transport Dam. Hyena sightings are common, as they run along the road in the early mornings or at a den. Look out for a den close to the turn-off to the Transport Dam. Occasionally wild dogs are encountered along this road, but a pack has an extensive home range and is constantly on the move.

Good browsing and an assortment of grazing throughout the year offers an ideal habitat for a great variety of game species. There is a high probability of seeing elephant, kudu, impala and giraffe. Buffalo need large spaces and a lot of grazing, as do white rhino. The **Transport Dam** is a good place to see game. All the large herbivores have to drink regularly and, on hot days, may wallow to cool off. White rhino usually drink towards evening but elephant and buffalo may drink at any time of the day. The open savanna around the dam allows good visibility and abundant grazers provide ample prey for lion and cheetah.

Klipspringers are sure to be found at the **Napi Boulders and other granite inselbergs**, especially those near the intersection with the H3. Their habit of standing completely immobile for long periods, staring over the plains, makes them difficult to spot at times. They are usually seen in pairs, often with young. This is one of the most habitat-specific species in the park.

Tall grasses and thick bush make game viewing difficult in the western section but this is ideal summer **habitat for sable antelope** and grazers such as zebra, wildebeest, buffalo and white rhino. Towards winter, game often moves away to sweet and much more palatable grazing along the narrow strip of thornveld in the Shitlhave section.

The **western extremity** of the road passes through **broad-leafed sour bushveld**. Here, altitude and rainfall are the highest in the park. The watersheds are pronounced, with sharply incised drainage lines, while the soil is deep sand or sandy with loam. These soils are poor in nutrients and yield unpalatable grass cover, but support dense and diverse, mainly broad-leafed, tree cover.

About ten kilometres east of the Numbi Gate, as you approach the **Shitlhave Dam**, the geology changes dramatically, and this in turn influences the vegetation. There are fewer broad-leafed trees: **thornveld** (mainly knob-thorn) replaces them. Here, the grass is sweet and extremely palatable. Look out for rare antelope such as roan, sable and tsessebe. At Shithlave Dam the road passes close to the water's edge; a shallow mud pool on one side of the dam is an ideal spot for wallowing animals.

Between the Shitlhave area and S65 the soils are sandy and **short-tree bushwillow woodland** is the dominant vegetation. Look out for silver cluster-leaf growing along seepage lines and the occasional black monkey orange in the sea of bushwillow. The dense, untidy sickle-bush shrubs with their curved pods and the widespread round-leafed teak make up most of the understorey. Marula and the occasional green thorn may be seen on the uplands.

Between the S65 and Skukuza, the road winds through rather dense **thorn thicket**. The soils here are generally shallow, but in places they have a high clay content and are rich in minerals due to the leaching from adjoining watersheds. This makes them suitable for a higher diversity

Mathekenyane, H1-1

of tree species. Knob-thorn is plentiful but other species such as green thorn (torchwood), false marula, tamboti and buffalo-thorn are well represented. Sickle-bush forms much of the understorey. Look for the occasional umbrella thorn with its typical flat crown, monkey apple and wild gardenia. There are a few spectacular specimens of the wild gardenia right next to the road.

Thorn thickets are the preferred habitat of **black rhino** and this would be a very special sighting. They are browsers and favour tamboti and sickle-bush.

Due to the wide variety of habitats, birding is excellent along the entire route. The area around Pretoriuskop is particularly good for a few special bird species.

Spotted hyena, H1-1

Spotted hyena, H1-1

H1-2
MAIN ROAD BETWEEN SKUKUZA AND TSHOKWANE

★★★★

🦁 ★★★ 🦌 ★★★ 🦅 ★★★★ 🌳 ★★★★

- 42 km; tarred; traverses five ecozones
- Sand River; Mantimahle; Olifantsdrinkgat; Leeupan

This is an excellent drive that offers a diversity of landscapes and the possibility of seeing most of the general game found in the park.

In the south, the road starts at the popular low-level bridge over the perennial **Sabie River** near Skukuza. Hippo, water monitor and crocodile are often seen near the bridge and you may want to linger as you cross. Look out for the rare finfoot that only occurs along the Sabie River. Other birds such as herons, kingfishers, weavers and storks often abound. Unfortunately this road carries heavy traffic and one is often forced to move on.

After about six kilometres of rather uninteresting **thorn thicket**, the H1-2 crosses another low-level bridge over the seasonal **Sand River**. Scan the sandbanks for game, as elephant, antelope and also predators are often seen crossing the riverbed. As the road runs along the northern bank of the Sand River, several **short loops** allow a better view of what is happening in the riverbed. Elephant and buffalo can often be seen in the reeds around waterholes. Lush **riverine vegetation** is testimony to plenty of subterranean water, even though the river itself is not perennial. Game on its way to water often crosses the road. Jackalberry, knob-thorn and fig trees fringe the riverbed. Baboon and monkey use these for sleeping and shelter. Look out for lion in the riverbed and leopard in the riverine vegetation.

North of the H1-2 intersection with the H12, the vegetation gradually changes from thorn thickets to more **open bushwillow woodland**. The wide tarred road allows good visibility. Look out for cheetah along this stretch. In this vicinity, giraffe kills by lion occur regularly. Good teamwork is needed for a lion pride to bring down a huge animal such as a giraffe. Apparently a few prides in Kruger have discovered that chasing a giraffe over a tarred road often causes it to slip and fall, giving the hunters the opportunity to overpower it. A giraffe carcass can feed a big pride for many days.

The area around the **Mantimahle Dam** on the western side of the road is good for game viewing. Lions favour the dam wall as a vantage point for watching game come and go across the savanna below. Lately this dam has changed and become a bit overgrown; when there is water, it is far away from the

Inquisitive lion cub H1-2

Lion cub trio H1-2

Plains zebra confronting African wild dogs, H1-2

loop road that leads to the viewing spot. It is nevertheless a pleasant open stretch of savanna with marula and knob-thorn trees. Look out for impala, zebra, kudu, waterbuck and giraffe.

The entire area around the Mantimahle Dam and 4 km north on this road is extremely good game country because of the **thornveld with underlying gabbro rock**, which yields soils rich in minerals. The grasses here are sweet and the vegetation consists mainly of thorn trees such as large knob-thorn and buffalo-thorn, but also marula and round-leafed teak. Drive slowly along the tarred road and be vigilant. Soon you will reach a turn-off to Olifantsdrinkgat (Afrikaans for 'elephants' drinking place' or waterhole). It is a dirt track but worth exploring. At a small dam and a closed watering point further on you may be lucky to encounter buffalo, elephant, white rhino, giraffe, zebra or even predators. Note the vegetation at the end of the track. The prolific evergreen shrubs with the dark-green simple leaves are magic guarri, which are an indication of clay soil, sweet grass and pans in the rainy season. Sweet grasses attract grazers which, in turn, attract predators.

After the next signpost to the S36, the vegetation changes back to bushwillow woodland for a short, featureless stretch before thornveld with underlying gabbro takes over again. From the Kruger Tablets (on the huge boulders) up to Leeupan is an extremely rewarding game area. Grazers such as zebra and blue wildebeest occur in greater numbers, impala in bigger herds and browsers such as giraffe, kudu and duiker are often seen. Predators may be anywhere. Warthog favour the clay depressions. Keep an eye open for magic guarri bushes to indicate where there may be pans in the rainy season.

Don't miss the turn-off to **Leeupan** (Lion Pan). Note the change in vegetation as Delagoa thorn trees and associated many-stemmed albizia become dominant, while magic guarri shrubs grow in profusion in depressions where pans form in the rainy season. This is an indication of a change in the underlying geology. The road now enters the stretch of **Delagoa thorn thickets on Ecca shales**.

There may not be much game activity at Leeupan during the dry season, but when there is water in the pan it is a place where one can spend hours just watching the interactions between animals. Herons, storks, spoonbills, hamerkops and smaller waders find good foraging in the shallow water.

Shilolweni Dam is broken. Northwards and well beyond Tshokwane, **open knob-thorn and marula savanna** becomes the dominant vegetation type. Due to the underlying basalt, the soil is fertile and the grass sweet – therefore, it attracts much game.

H1-3

BETWEEN TSHOKWANE AND SATARA

★★★★★

- 53 km; tarred; traverses two ecozones
- Kumana Dam; Kumana baobab; Mazithi Pan; Nkaya Pan

This is one of the best drives in Kruger. Visibility is excellent (without dust), the road passes reliable water sources and game is plentiful. Too much traffic may be the only problem. The landscape here is characterised by gently undulating plains without high ridges or hills.

The reason for the abundance of game lies in the geology, soil and vegetation of the surrounding plains. Almost the entire road runs through **knob-thorn/marula savanna plains** that are underpinned by basalt, covered by a layer of calcrete. The grasses are sweet and the landscape is mostly park-like and open, with knob-thorn and marula as the dominant tree species. Leadwood, apple-leaf, sycamore fig, river thorn, sausage tree and tamboti also occur, especially along the drainage lines. The soils tend to retain water well into the dry season and therefore game gathers on these plains for nutritious grazing.

The **N'waswitsontso watercourse** and its tributaries are seasonal but because the soils are high in clay content, water is retained in the depressions and forms semi-permanent pools even into the dry season. The same applies to the **Sweni watercourse**, which joins the N'wanetsi River in the east of the park.

Two permanent watering places for game in this area are the **Kumana Dam** and the **Mazithi Pan**. The Kumana Dam is a very rewarding game-viewing area and always has something of interest going on. Spend some time searching on both sides of the road. Look for hippo and crocodile, but grazers such as zebra and blue wildebeest regularly come down to drink during mid-morning. The Tshokwane/Satara south area boasts the highest density of zebra and blue wildebeest in the park. Huge buffalo herds are often seen here, but they come and go within an hour or two and avoid lingering. It is fascinating to watch the interaction within such a herd – the leaders showing the way and others flanking and protecting the cows and calves in the centre. When this is done, they congregate and wait for the leaders to cross the road first. They instinctively know that they are vulnerable at the water's edge. Buffalo are extremely courageous and will fight lions when these attack.

Close to the Kumana Dam there is a signpost and turn-off to a huge baobab, and it is well worth taking this detour. The **Kumana baobab** is probably the southernmost specimen in the park. For those who have never seen a baobab up close, this is a special sighting. This particular tree may be well over a thousand years old since the species is very slow-growing. The trees bear leaves only briefly and their huge white flowers are believed to be pollinated by bats. Apart from the beautiful **riverine vegetation** consisting of jackalberry, weeping boer-bean, sausage tree and others, this is also known as a good leopard-sighting spot.

Giraffe and leopard eye to eye, H1-3

African wild dogs at play, H1-3

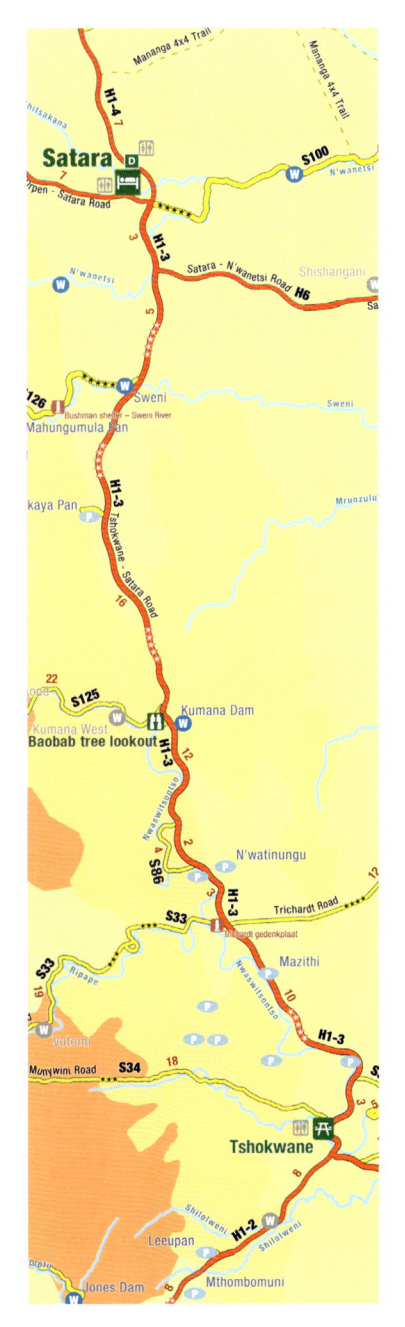

Young lion carrying steenbok lamb, H1-3

Graeme Mitchley

Take the turn-off to **Nkaya Pan** to see if there is water. Note the change in vegetation as you near the pan. Delagoa thorn trees, many-stemmed false-thorns and evergreen magic guarri shrubs represent the typical vegetation found in **Delagoa thorn thicket** landscape. Here, Karoo sediments (Ecca shales) underlie the thorn thicket vegetation. Due to the clay soil the pan retains water for a long period into the dry season after good summer rains. When conditions are favourable one can spend an entire morning here just watching game coming and going. It is a favourite drinking place for big buffalo herds and predators. Resident crocodiles, herons, bustards, Egyptian geese and other water-associated birds find enough food around here. Note the huge leadwood tree close to the pan. Leadwoods grow well where the soil is very dense. Due to the presence of dense thickets and thorn trees (formerly called acacias), one can expect black rhino and a healthy diversity of general game species.

Once you are back on the tarred road, heading north, the thorn thicket landscape soon changes back to **knob-thorn/marula savanna**. Note the huge stand of lala palms before the bridge over the **Sweni River**. These palms grow in low-lying areas where the soil is deep but poor in nutrients. They become more common north of the Olifants River on soils of basaltic origin. This is one of only two palm species in Kruger. The other is the date palm, which usually grows either on riverbanks or in riverbeds. Look out for these palms as you cross the Sweni bridge. Their leaves are fern-like and green as opposed to those of the lala palm, which are fan-shaped and silver-grey.

The area around the Sweni River crossing is usually productive. Look out for leopard here, but also for the elusive serval. Photographic evidence proves that people have seen them around here.

There is a good variety of bird habitats along this road. Birding enthusiasts can expect waterbird sightings at the dams and pans; sightings of plains and grassland birds such as the ostrich, kori bustard, ground hornbill, secretary bird and a plethora of smaller species; raptors ranging from fish eagle to all other eagles, hawks and sparrowhawks; and tree-perching birds, which may include an array of fruit feeders and nectar feeders.

H1-4
BETWEEN SATARA AND THE OLIFANTS RIVER

★★★★

🦁 ★★★★   🦌 ★★★   🦅 ★★★   🌳 ★★★

- 39 km; tarred; traverses three ecozones
- S90 junction; Ntomeni Waterhole

Male steenbok, H1-4

Traversing what are known as the 'fertile plains' of Satara, this road offers excellent visibility for game viewing, particularly in winter when the grass is short.

The **knob-thorn/marula woodland** stretches from Satara up to the H1-4 intersection with the S90. These park-like plains attract grazers such as zebra, blue wildebeest, impala and buffalo. Wildebeest and buffalo are the preferred prey of lion, and good lion sightings are regularly reported along this route. It is estimated that there are about **2 800 lions** in the entire Kruger National Park and that about 25% of these occur between the Olifants and Sabie Rivers. Of these, at least four big prides frequent areas along this road. A big pride consists of an average of 12 individuals. Prides often split up into smaller groups within their home ranges. Since many lions favour blue wildebeest as prey, be particularly vigilant at watering points when wildebeest are around.

Lions are often seen immediately north of the Satara Camp where a waterhole is situated close to the northern fence. In summer the plains beyond are covered with dense stands of waving red grass (*Themeda triandra*). This grass type only occurs in undisturbed grasslands that are not overgrazed. Regular sightings of cheetah are reported in this vicinity. The flat open savanna suits their hunting style, and their prey includes impala and steenbok, which are plentiful in this area.

From the S90 intersection to just south of the **Ngotso South drainage line** the knob-thorns gradually become more and more stunted. The underlying geology is still basalt covered by a layer of calcrete, but the soil layer becomes shallower and the trees do not grow large. This type of landscape is known as **stunted knob-thorn savanna**. The road crosses two tributaries and then the Ntomeni stream itself. In the vicinity of the **Ntomeni stream and drinking place**, white rhino and other grazers are often encountered.

In the vicinity of **Ngotso South** the landscape becomes rockier and the trees become more stunted. This is typical **Olifants rugged veld** where stunted knob-thorn are the dominant trees, thus forming an open shrub savanna. This is a low-density area for gregarious species but a favoured habitat for kudu and even sable. Giraffe and buffalo are also common. Note that most giraffe in the park occur south of the Olifants River. You will probably see many of these in the Ngotso area where there is enough of their preferred browse such as knob-thorn and leadwood.

Travelling northwards you may notice that magic guarri occurs less and less in clay depressions. In its place you will increasingly see **raisin bush** taking over.

Birding along this road is average. The first Burchell's starlings appear towards the northern section. Look out for Dickinson's kestrel.

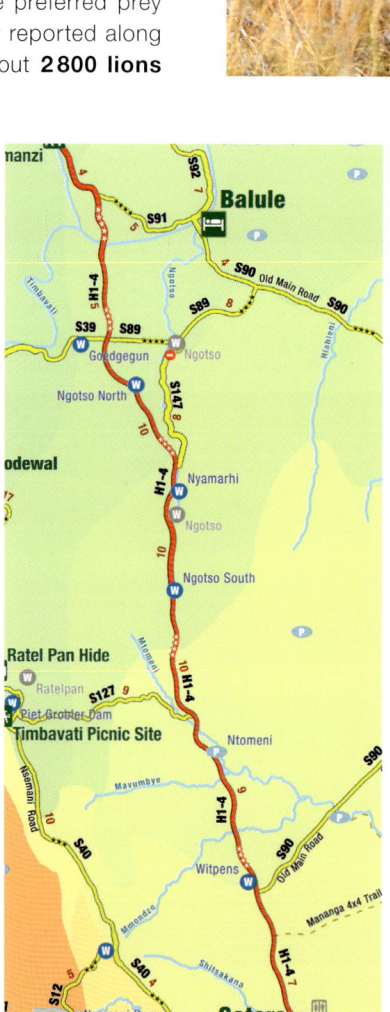

Kori bustard displaying, H1-4

Black-backed jackal pups, H1-4

Southern carmine bee-eaters, H1-4

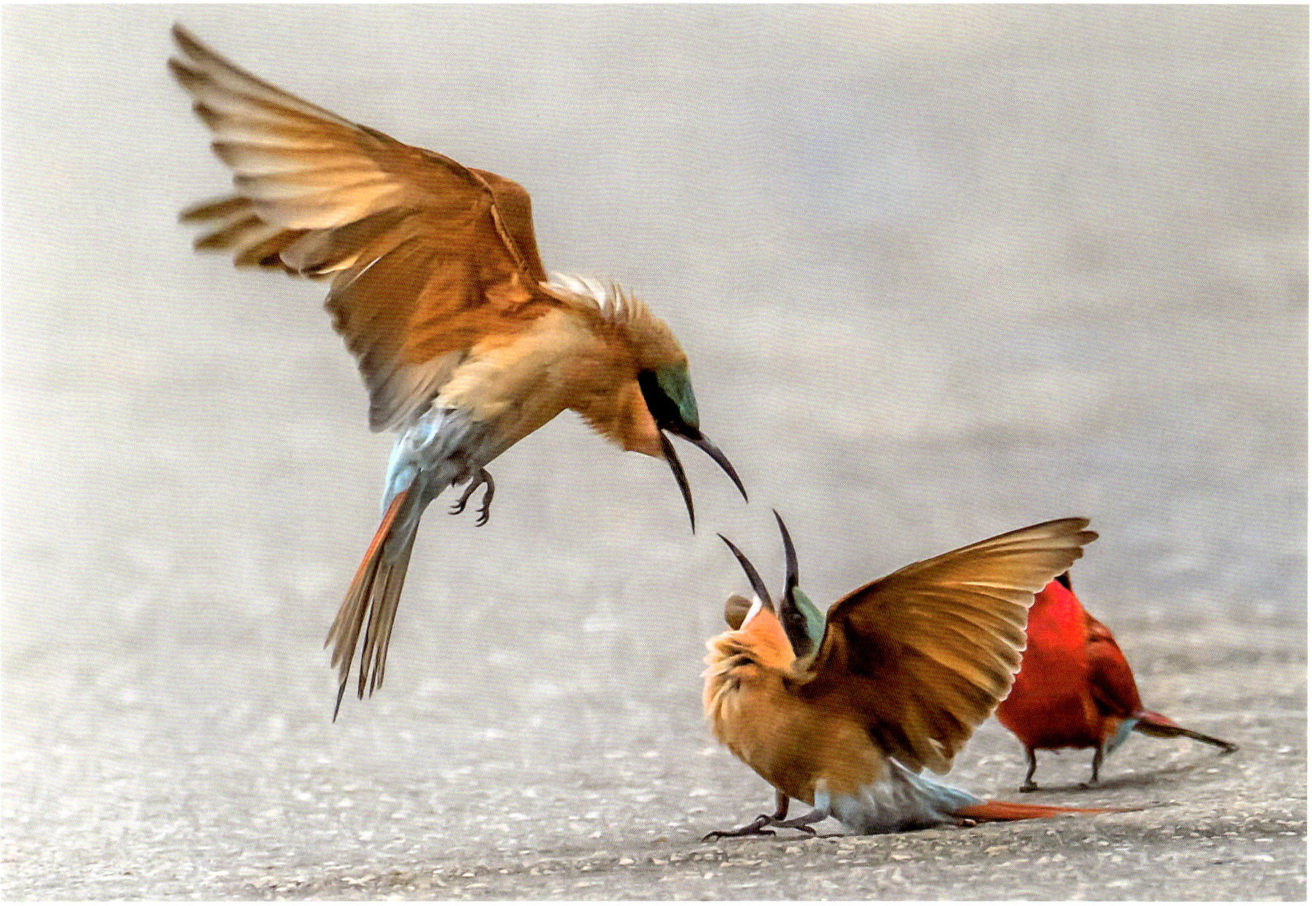

Mohammed and Sarifa Jinnah

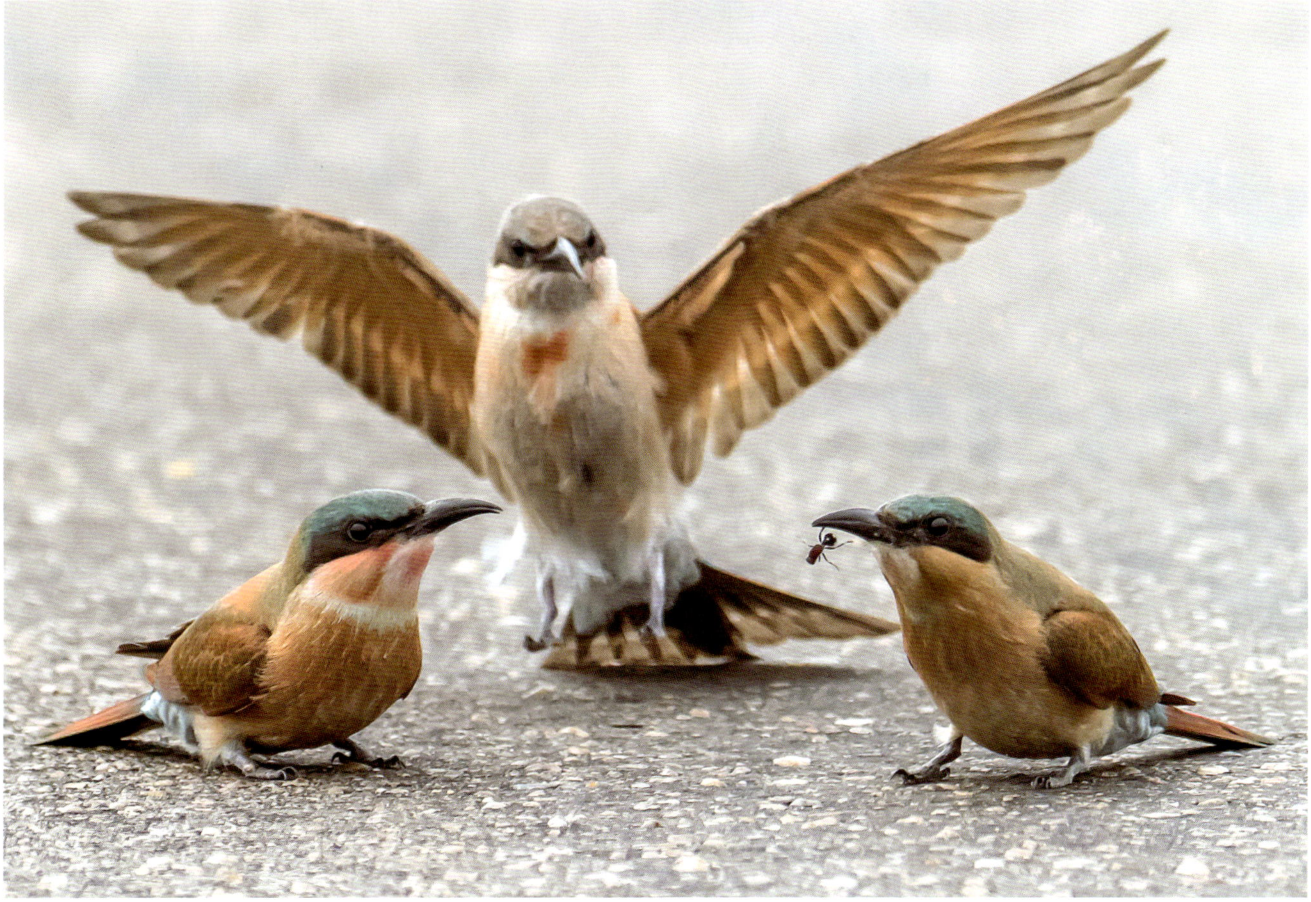

Mohammed and Sarifa Jinnah

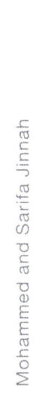

H1-5

★★★
H1-5
BETWEEN THE OLIFANTS RIVER AND LETABA

★★   ★★   ★★★   ★★★

- 28 km; tarred; traverses one ecozone
- Olifants River Bridge and river view; N'wamanzi viewing point

The Olifants River is generally accepted as the division between the southern and northern parts of the park.

The Olifants River is one of the Big Five Rivers in the northern section of Kruger. The others are the Letaba, the Shingwedzi, the Luvuvhu and the Limpopo.

Far less game occurs in the north as the dominant vegetation is **mopane** and many browsers prefer thorn trees (acacias). Less open grassland occurs and the carrying capacity for grazers is much lower than in the south. For the tourist, visibility in mopane savanna may not be as pleasing as the more open bushwillow and thornveld savanna of the south. Nevertheless, the mopane veld has a special attraction of its own. Most animal activity in the north is close to rivers. Roads in the north therefore generally follow river courses.

The bridge over the **Olifants River** offers **impressive views**. On the larger bridges in the park, such as this one, visitors are allowed out of their vehicles to get a better view.

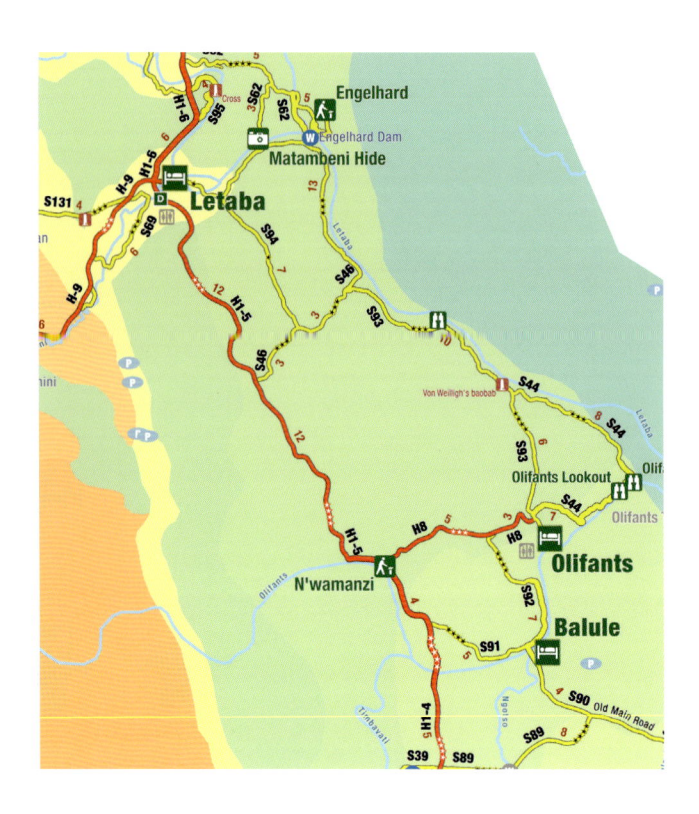

Hippos interacting, H1-5

Red-crested korhaan displaying, H1-5

There are bat colonies under the bridge, which give off a pungent smell. Notice the typical riverine vegetation that fringes the riverbanks. Identify the large knob-thorn, apple-leaf and leadwood specimens.

Immediately after the river crossing the change in vegetation is evident. The underpinning geology is still basalt but the dominant vegetation is now **mopane shrubveld**. This continues up to the intersection with the S91. Thereafter the main road traverses **Olifants rugged veld** again up to the intersection with the H8. Be sure not to miss the turn-off to the **N'wamanzi view site**.

The view over a big stretch of the Olifants River gives a good indication of this important river system. Lately there have been disturbing signs of serious pollution coming from upstream, which is killing the river. Hundreds of crocodiles have already been lost due to this. It is estimated that almost 50% of all crocodiles in the park used to live in this river. The situation to date is being carefully monitored to try and save these ancient creatures from being wiped out here.

After the intersection with the H8 the road closely follows the course of the Olifants River. The stretch that follows is the **most rewarding section** of the H1-5. **Leopard and lion** sightings are very likely; elephant and buffalo are often encountered on the road. Notice the riverine vegetation. Huge **hippo pods** frequent the deeper pools of the river, but floods sometimes change the position of the hippo pools and deposit huge sandbanks and rubble in their place. Many of the age-old sycamore figs and other trees along the river have also been washed away. Hippo used to occur widely in South African rivers, but lately they have been restricted to rivers in game reserves. The Kruger National Park is playing a huge role in this regard. It is estimated that the hippo population in the park stands at about 3 000. The hippo is one of Africa's largest land mammals – third only to the elephant and white rhino.

Hippo are listed as 'vulnerable' on the International Union for Conservation of Nature and Natural Resources' Red List due to poaching for their meat and tusk-like teeth, as well as loss of habitat. They have also historically been killed in areas where they damage crops or pose a threat to human settlement in other ways. According to the Wildlife Conservation Society, there are an estimated 125 000 to 150 000 hippo left in Africa. This represents a decline of as much as 20% during just the last decade. The serious threat of increased pollution of the Kruger's perennial rivers is a matter of great concern.

Despite sweet grazing, **game density in the mopane veld is generally low**. Giraffe numbers are far lower than in the south, but the occasional group may be seen along the major rivers where knob-thorn occurs. Along this road they are a special sighting. You may see impala and the odd zebra and kudu. Waterbuck may be seen in the river valley. Small browsers such as duiker and steenbok are not dependent on regular access to water and may be found anywhere. Despite the low animal density for most parts of this road, lion and leopard sightings are regularly recorded along the river.

The last long stretch to Letaba Camp passes through featureless **mopane shrubveld**. Be careful to keep to the speed limit. Speed traps are set up, and rightly so, next to roads where visitors sometimes lose focus and forget they are in a national park.

Red-crested korhaan calling, H1-5

H1-6
PART 1
BETWEEN LETABA AND MOPANI CAMP

★★★ ★★★ ★★★ ★★

44 km; tarred; traverses one ecozone

Letaba River and bridge section; Malopenyana and Middelvlei Waterholes; Klein Nshawu drinking place; loops onto the Tsendze River; Mooiplaas Picnic Site

The Letaba area is home to some of the biggest tuskers in the park. This pleasant drive northwards towards the Mopani Camp is not only good in the early mornings, but is especially rewarding towards midday when elephant bulls from far and wide gather at watering points.

The entire road from Letaba to Mopani Camp traverses well-developed **mopane shrubveld**, which is based on flat, volcanic basalt. The small soil particles form dense clay soils that tend to crack as they dry out. This breaks the roots of the vegetation and the dominant mopane plants remain stunted shrubs. Regular fires also help to stunt their growth. The scenery is uniform and tends to become monotonous.

There is a fair amount of game but it is widely dispersed. Despite the sweet grazing, game viewing is only average. The exception is the **first few kilometres from the Letaba Camp** where the road runs parallel to the Letaba River and animals may cross it on their way to water. This short stretch of the road is **one of the best around Letaba and in the park**.

From the **high bridge over the Letaba River** you can see the magnitude of this perennial waterway that can carry masses of water to the Olifants River after good rains. In times of drought, stagnant pools remain and are an important life-sustaining source of water along its entire course. Huge amounts of sand are carried down with the water and are deposited as sandbanks along the way. Apart from fish and other water creatures, hippo and crocodiles are abundant. Looking down into the water, you can often see catfish (barbel) and other species swimming around. Towards late afternoon, waterbuck and nyala are often seen moving across the sandbanks and floodplains.

Although the road runs parallel to some minor drainage lines, these watercourses are usually dry and do not necessarily attract game for water. North of the intersection between the H15 and the S48 the **Middelvlei Waterhole is a really worthwhile watering point** on this road. There you may see

Elephant drinking, H1-6

Luca Neto

Southern ground hornbill with snake prey, H1-6

H1-6

ostrich, zebra, impala, perhaps a few blue wildebeest and elephant. Over a period of an hour up to 60 elephant bulls have been reported approaching Middelvlei from different directions. This is also the place to look out for tsessebe.

The **Klein Nshawu** is a seasonal pan close to the road and within the drainage line of the Nshawani tributary of the Nshawu River. This is a popular site to linger when there is water in the pan.

North of the H14 intersection a few **good river loops** may be followed. They look out over the **Tsendze River**, which is mostly dry except for a few stagnant pools. Elephant herds are often spotted down in the river. The riverine vegetation is ideal habitat for leopard. Hyena sightings in the early mornings are regularly reported.

The giant apple-leaf and leadwood trees at **Mooiplaas Picnic Site** are a welcome landmark to the visitor. This spot has full picnic facilities and also offers a **roofed lookout** over the Tsendze River nearby. A semi-permanent pool below the picnic site attracts animals throughout the day, which range from elephants to impala. This site is the source of interesting tales about lions and leopards.

Adjacent to the Mooiplaas site, the new **Tsendze caravan and camping site** offers an extraordinary bush experience of solitude and tranquillity. The camp, without modern facilities of electricity and the internet, is a real gem. The focus here is not on game drives, but rather on a unique bush experience.

Woodland kingfisher, H1-6

White-fronted bee-eater pair, H1-6

Female paradise flycatcher, H1-6

Lilac-breasted roller, H1-6

H1-6
PART 2
BETWEEN MOPANI CAMP AND SHINGWEDZI

★★★ | ★★ | ★★★ | ★★★

- 56 km; tarred; traverses five ecozones
- Bowkerskop Waterhole; Tropic of Capricorn; Shingwedzi River

The northern section of the H1-6 from the Mopani Camp to the Shingwedzi River traverses prime elephant country and often offers unexpected sightings along the way.

The northern section of the park is elephant country and most of the estimated 12 000+ elephants in the park are found here. The chances are therefore very good for **excellent elephant sightings**. Considering that each Kruger elephant pushes over up to four mature trees per day (according to research by Bob Scholes) and that there are about 300 mature trees per hectare, it is not surprising that scientists are getting worried about elephant overpopulation. The estimates are that Kruger loses 1% of its mature trees each year. In the eastern grasslands 60% of large trees have been lost over the past 50 years. Another worrying factor is that there is not enough evidence of regrowth and young trees of certain species.

The first point of interest north of Mopani Camp is the **Bowkerskop Waterhole** situated near the **Shipandani Stream** (a tributary of the Tsendze), which is usually dry. This is a well-used waterhole with many animals coming to drink. To the east the waterhole borders extensive flat plains of basalt with sweet grazing and mopane shrubs. This area is still part of **mopane shrubveld** where trees vary in size according to the richness of the soil.

The **Tsendze watercourse** is the main drainage system from the north. Apple-leaf and leadwood mark the watercourse and its tributaries.

Shidayangwenya is one of a series of pans that forms here after good rains. It is hidden among tall mopane trees and is frequented by elephant. **Grysbok Pan** is another, named after the tiny Sharpe's grysbok that occurs only in the northern parts of the park.

Slightly north of this waypoint, the vegetation changes to **thornveld** due to an intrusion of **gabbro**. Mopane diminishes, and the dominant vegetation becomes a combination of round-leafed teak, apple-leaf, buffalo-thorn, marula and knob thorn. The grass here is sweet and attracts grazers. Elephants are particularly fond of round-leafed teak. This area south and north of the S144 intersection has the potential for **good game viewing** due to the sweet grass that should attract grazers.

At this point you cross the **Tropic of Capricorn** (23° 26' 18") which is clearly demarcated. This is the southernmost point at which the sun passes directly overhead at noon, which it does on the summer solstice, 21 December – the longest day in southern Africa. Although one enters the tropics north of this point, the first real tropical vegetation becomes apparent only in the Luvuvhu River area.

A short loop road leads to the **banks of the Tsendze watercourse** and passes through a grove of mature tamboti trees. The striking feature of this tree is the bark that is dark to black, thick, rough and neatly cracked into regular rectangles. It exudes poisonous latex when a branch is broken, yet kudu, impala and vervet monkey eat the dry fallen leaves. Birds seem to congregate in this area and one can expect to see coucal, spurfowl, dove, barbet, kingfisher and shrike.

Slightly north of the **N'wambu Waterhole** is the turn-off into the Shongololo road. Five kilometres further on, a turn-off to the east leads to **Olifantsbad** (Elephants' bath) S103. This mostly dry and overgrown pan can attract a lot of game when it has water. The rest of the road, up to the intersection with the S52, traverses rather uniform mopane shrub. Game densities are generally low although elephant may be encountered.

North of Olifantsbad, the road traverses a short stretch of **thornveld** before it enters **mopane shrubveld** again. The final 15 km stretch towards the Shingwedzi Camp runs parallel to the **Shingwedzi River** and it provides reasonably good game viewing. Elephant are usually encountered as well as zebra, impala and kudu. Look out for hyena, which often have dens along this stretch of road. The S101 is just one of several shorter loop roads leading out of the H1-6 onto the riverbank and back. Game densities increase noticeably as the road nears the camp.

Yellow-billed oxpecker on buffalo, H1-6

A short loop to the west of the road, and before the bridge over the Shingwedzi River, leads to the **confluence of the Shingwedzi and Mphongolo Rivers**. Look out for the rock python, an unmistakable snake that may grow up to six metres in length. It is often seen curled up in a fork of one of the massive riverine trees.

Lovely riverine vegetation and lala palms fringe the Shingwedzi River on the way to the camp. The good views over the wide sandbanks of the river are a trademark of this popular camp.

The H1-6 ends at the high-water bridge that goes over the Shingwedzi River.

African elephants, H1-6

H1-7
SHINGWEDZI TO H13-1

★★★

★★★ ★★ ★★★ ★★★

- 51 km; tarred; traverses three ecozones
- Babalala Picnic Site; Shisha Wetlands

Mopane veld has a beauty of its own. Although featureless at times, the colours of the vegetation and the wide skies evoke a feeling of endless space and wilderness. Despite the general low density in game numbers, good sightings are reported on this road.

Sightings include predators such as lion and leopard, cheetah and serval. But more special are the sightings of rare antelope such as tsessebe, roan and eland.

From the south up to the **Babalala Picnic Site**, the road traverses open **mopane shrubveld** with an underlying basalt base. The basalt weathers into turf soils (also called vertisols) and the mopane growing on this type of soil are mostly short. The grass growing between them is sweet. This makes the eastern mopane veld completely different from the western parts, where the soils are coarse with underlying granite. It is therefore a good area to expect game, but animal densities are relatively low in the north and watering points are scarce and far apart.

For the first seven kilometres from the south the road runs along the **Mphongolo River** until the turn-off to the S56, which also runs alongside the river. Giraffe often occur on this first stretch due to knobthorn on the banks, as do kudu and other antelope. It is a good stretch for birding. Lions are often reported and, closer to the river, leopard and hyena are often seen.

The **Nkulumbeni stream** is one of the few watercourses draining the eastern catchment areas and spilling into the Mphongolo River that joins the Shingwedzi. A short loop road marked as S53 leads through stunted mopane towards an area that is marshy after good rains, and open grassland.

Tsessebe is the fastest of all antelope; even the young can keep up with their mothers mere hours after birth. They favour basaltic grasslands and mopane plains and are often seen near N'warihlangari, Boyela and Babalala waterholes. They are extremely territorial. The dominant bull may be seen alone keeping watch on one of his territorial markers, which may be a termite mound or even a dung heap. His females and the sub-adults that form the breeding herd move around within his territory. After a year, young males are evicted from the breeding herd to join the bachelor herd of males.

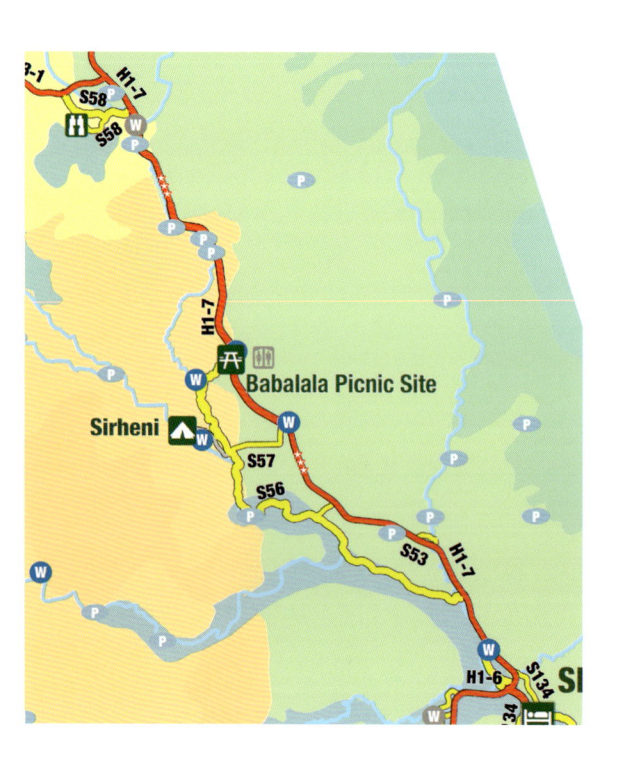

The other rare antelope you may encounter in the north is **eland**, the largest of all antelope species. They form aggregated herds but very large herds are seldom seen in the park. Both males and females have horns and although they form mixed herds, only the dominant males service the cows on heat. The total number of this antelope in the Kruger is estimated at more than 300 individuals. Since they are almost completely independent of surface water, they are seldom seen at waterholes. They eat a wide variety of plants and often roam plains far away from the tourist roads.

Roan antelope populations are declining in the park. The latest estimate of 50–70 individuals has declined from the estimated 328 of the census of 1985. The few that may still be present will most likely be seen in drainage lines of the north where they feed in open grasslands. Although they seem to like areas where the grazing is not very good, their decline may be attributed to the outbreak of anthrax – but

Roan antelope, H1-7 — Gerhard Vosloo

Eland pair, H1-7

also to habitat degradation caused by drought, overgrazing and increased predator pressure.

The Babalala Picnic Site is situated next to a small waterhole. Tables and chairs under an **enormous sycamore fig** are inviting for a picnic. There are braai facilities for hire, cold drinks for sale, and toilets.

The grasslands around the picnic site offer one of the best chances to see cheetah in the northern part of the park. These predators favour open grassland with enough space to run down their prey. Although they are the fastest predator, they can only maintain a high speed for about half a kilometre, after which they have to rest. It is during this time of rest that they are the most vulnerable to other predators robbing them of their prey.

Early summer thunderstorms result in millions of termites emerging from the ground in parts of the north, attracting a feeding frenzy of eagles, hawks, buzzards and falcons that gorge themselves on these high-protein delicacies.

North of Babalala the road continues for a short stretch through **mixed mopane and bushwillow woodland** on **granite** where the grazing is mostly sourveld and game densities are even lower. After a few kilometres the road roughly follows the eastern banks of the seasonal **Shisha stream**. During the wet season several important and protected **tropical wetlands** develop along this drainage line. **Some of South Africa's rarest birds** are summer visitors that migrate down this route and use the **Shisha Wetlands** as key stopovers on their route. Three different crake species are among the migrants. These are the common black crake, the corn crake and the African crake.

The intersection with the H13-1 indicates the end of the H1-7 part of the main route to the north.

Tsessebe, H1-7

H1-8
H13-1 TO LUVUVHU AND PAFURI

★★★

★★★   ★★   ★★★   ★★★

- 38 km; tarred; traverses two ecozones
- Baobab Hill; bridge over the Luvuvhu River

Game densities along this road are fairly low but the anticipation of visiting one of the most beautiful areas in the Kruger National Park makes up for this. Game densities increase dramatically as you reach the floodplains of the Pafuri area.

Natal spurfowl, H1-8

The road to Pafuri initially leads through flat or gently undulating basaltic plains of **shrub mopane**. The rocky ridge at Klopperfontein is the start of the broken landscape of the Luvuvhu catchment area. In the distance the outliers of the **Soutpansberg** become visible. This extensive mountain range tilts downwards to the east with a drop in rainfall and altitude as it enters the park.

When **Baobab Hill** looms up ahead, the heart beats faster. Stop here for a while and see if you can spot a spinetail. These are fast-flying insect feeders that nest in these huge trees and are a star species for birders. Years ago, Baobab Hill was a campsite for migrant labourers from Mozambique who were recruited for the Johannesburg gold mines. Hunters and ivory traders also used this road during the late 19th and early 20th centuries.

From here the road descends steeply into the **Luvuvhu and Limpopo River valleys** that stretch out far beyond. This is the Pafuri area – a magic and almost sacred world of scenic beauty, tropical splendour, age-old baobabs, majestic riverine forest and fever trees fringing the wide silent river.

Mopane vegetation ends abruptly at the alluvial plains. The **floodplain vegetation** consists of thornveld and fever trees, which gives way to riverine vegetation on the banks of the river.

The **Luvuvhu River** rises in the far west outside the park as a fast-flowing stream. As it crosses the Karoo sediments (sandstone ridges) on its way to the Pafuri area, it cuts through the underlying sandstone to form a deep, narrow gorge known as the Lanner Gorge (unfortunately not accessible to the self-driving tourist). The character of the Luvuvhu River changes completely as it emerges from this gorge. The swiftly flowing stream enters a broad floodplain and the silt it carries is deposited as a rich alluvial layer across the plain. This plain joins with the alluvial fringes of the Limpopo River to form a fascinating dry **riparian forest habitat**. In dry years, the channel of the Luvuvhu itself may be waterless, yet there is enough underground water to support the lush riverine forest. It is difficult to believe that the Pafuri area is one of the driest areas in the park with a rainfall of about 400 mm per year.

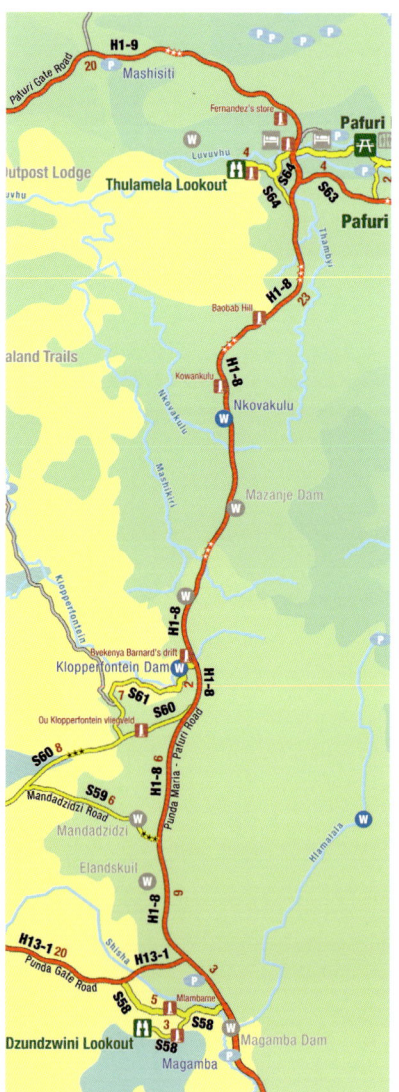

Every now and again heavy floods affect the area and bring about extensive changes. The floods of 2000 were devastating, but those of 2012 and 2013 also brought about far too many changes. Huge trees were washed away and large parts of the riverbank denuded of vegetation.

Crossing the bridge takes you onto the H1-9, the last stretch towards the Pafuri Gate.

Male nyala, H1-8

H1-9
PAFURI GATE ROAD

★★★

★★★ ★★ ★★★ ★★★

- 20 km; tarred; traverses two ecozones
- Baobab trees

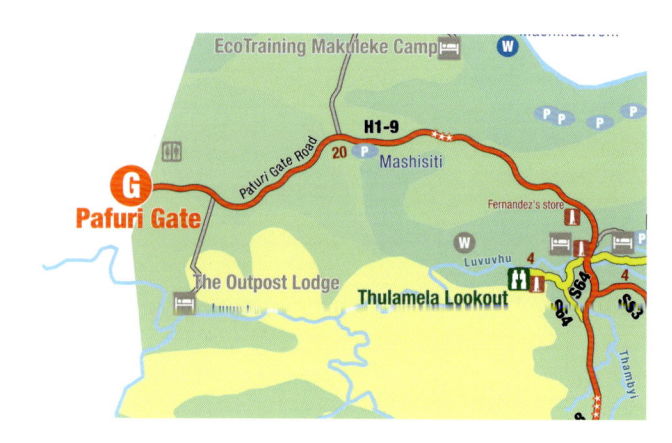

This road traverses the Makuleke area between the Luvuvhu and Limpopo Rivers and stretches from the Luvuvhu bridge to the Pafuri Gate. This section of the park is owned by the neighbouring Makuleke people but is managed by SANParks. It traverses flat and deep sandveld with rugged sandstone hills in the distance.

The major section of the road between the gate and the bridge over the **Luvuvhu River traverses sandveld** with its typical plant communities and types. The soils of the sandveld are derived from sandstone and are deep and sandy, well-drained and relatively infertile. Some of these sediments were deposited millions of years ago by raging windstorms blowing sand in from the Kalahari.

It is surprising to know that the Pafuri area east of this road between the two rivers is the **driest area in the entire park**, with an annual rainfall of a mere 400 mm per year. Only 100 km from here, the Soutpansberg (Entabeni Peak) gets about 1 900 mm per year. Away from the rivers the vegetation reflects this low rainfall. **Corkwood trees** are scattered between the mopane shrub. Corkwood is common to hot, dry places with well-drained sandy soils and rocky outcrops. The Afrikaans name for this tree is 'kanniedood', meaning 'cannot die'. Its most striking features are its robust, fleshy stems and branches with conspicuous, often peeling, papery bark exposing a shiny, greenish undersurface.

Fine old baobabs are dotted all along the road. Some of these are estimated to be as much as 4 000 years old. Look out for spinetails (two species), red-winged starlings and buffalo weavers that are usually associated with baobabs. Note the low **sandstone outcrops**.

The northern sandveld is **one of the most ecologically diverse areas in the park**, incorporating a variety of microclimates and vegetation types. A series of pans along the Limpopo River are of special interest but not accessible to the general tourist. The pans are the home of an extraordinary fish species, the lungfish, and are also feeding grounds for all kinds of waterbirds, especially summer migrants. To do birding along these pans you need to book accommodation at one of the private lodges in the area.

Mottled spinetail, H1-9

Meves's starling, H1-9

Green wood-hoopoe family interacting, H1-9

Dwarf bittern, H1-9

H2-2
VOORTREKKER ROAD
★★★

★★★ ★★ ★★★ ★★★

- 44 km; gravel, corrugated in places; traverses three ecozones
- Historical places; Ship Mountain; Jock of the Bushveld story

The historical H2-2 is a most interesting drive with several hotspots. The diversity of ecozones and habitats provides a basis for good game viewing.

From 1836 to 1860 the Voortrekkers used this route with their ox wagons between Delagoa Bay (present-day Maputo) and the interior. Pretoriuskop Rest Camp was named after one of these men, **Willem Pretorius**, who died on this transport route in 1848. These early travellers suffered many hardships – malaria was rife; the tsetse fly, the carrier of *nagana* or sleeping sickness, was a real threat; lions targeted the oxen; and the bush was dense and unforgiving. The many graves along the route are testimony to these hardships. Yet, despite all the challenges, this remained the preferred route for many transport riders in years to come. **Percy Fitzpatrick** was one of these. He is best known for his book *Jock of the Bushveld*. Many of the incidents he describes in the book can be linked to locations on this road. Look out for the plaques commemorating his brave dog Jock, who was born along this route. The first concrete dam in the park was built on the **Ntomeni Spruit** (creek) close to the road. In this vicinity, a plaque commemorates the outspan of early travellers.

The rolling hills of the southern parts of the park are characterised by a landscape built on **granite**. Granite weathers into coarse quartz sand and fine clay. The latter washes down into the valleys and the clayey soil supports fine-compound-leaved thorn trees (most people know these as acacias) and more palatable sweet grasses. Note that the knob-thorns grow mostly in the depressions where the clay has accumulated. On the higher ground of the ridges the soil remains sandy and is less fertile, supporting large-leafed thornless trees such as the bushwillows and cluster-leaves, and sour, unpalatable grasses.

The eastern section of the road winds through **mixed bushwillow woodlands** with weeping bushwillow, large-fruited bushwillow and silver cluster-leaf as the dominant trees. Sickle-bush, round-leafed teak and monkey apple form the dominant undergrowth. The far western section of the road traverses typical **Lowveld sour bushveld** with the woody plants dominated by knob-thorn, russet bushwillow, large-fruit bushwillow and silver cluster-leaf.

More or less between Thomas Hart's grave (see the plaque next to the road) and Ship Mountain, the vegetation noticeably changes from broad-leafed plants to **thornveld**. This is an indication that the underlying geology also differs. This happened over time when the granite layer cracked in places. The granite floor underwent changes due to heat and pressure to produce gneiss and scattered intrusions of **gabbro** (an intrusive igneous rock), which penetrated the granite layers in places to form **dykes**. Gabbro rock is similar to basalt but is generally older and harder. Such a dyke stretches from slightly west of Biyamiti in the Lukimbi Concession area, crosses the H3 more or less at Afsaal, runs parallel to, and south, along the H2-2 before it crosses the road, and extends in a narrow strip almost to the Phabeni Gate area. The soils derived from gabbro are finer than those from granite: thick black-cotton-type soils that become waterlogged and sticky when wet but support nutritious grasses with knob-thorn and marula trees.

Ship Mountain is particularly striking and was an important navigational landmark for early travellers. At first glance it resembles the upturned hull of a capsized ship. There is however more to the mountain than simply its resemblance to a ship. It consists of a massive pile of loose, lichen-covered boulders. What makes it remarkable is that no other hills in the area are geologically similar – the mountain was literally dumped onto the landscape when the gabbro penetrated the granite floor of the Lowveld aeons ago.

The fertile soil along the strip of underlying gabbro yields good grazing and attracts large herds of grazers. Look out for zebra, blue wildebeest and warthog at the foot of Ship Mountain. Grazers are usually followed by predators. Look out for lion, leopard and cheetah. This road is also good for kudu, giraffe, duiker and the odd elephant. Look out for rare antelope species such as sable, tsessebe, roan and eland.

The diverse mix of bushveld and the moderate vegetation density creates an ideal habitat for **white rhino**. Sadly, white rhino had been shot out by 1896. The first ones to be reintroduced into the park were released in this area during the 1960s. More than fifty years later, this is still the best area to look for white rhino. Yet now the white rhino is in peril once again. The decimation caused by 19th-century big-game hunters is being repeated by 21st-century poachers.

Birding is particularly good all round. Because many visitors avoid gravel roads, traffic is not so heavy on the H2-2 and it is possible to do a leisurely birding drive.

Young impala male, H2-2

H3
BETWEEN MALELANE GATE AND THE H1-1

★★★★

★★★★ ★★★ ★★★ ★★★

- 56 km; tarred; traverses five ecozones
- Mhlambane bridge; Afsaal Picnic Site; Biyamiti river basin

The H3 is a superb drive through a historic area, whether taken from the south, i.e. the Malelane Gate, or from the north. Game viewing is good over the entire route.

The area from the Crocodile River roughly up to the north of Skukuza comprises the original **Sabie Game Reserve** that was proclaimed by President Paul Kruger in 1896. During the 1800s this area was the popular hunting ground of both professional and sports hunters. This soon resulted in the depletion of game. Kruger, the president of the Transvaal Republic (ZAR) at that time, proclaimed the game reserve in an attempt to curb the slaughter of antelope. Lions and other predators however were declared vermin and were exterminated.

Today this entire area is once again teeming with all types of game, including predators that are now one of the main attractions of the Kruger National Park. Lion sightings are a good possibility while white rhino sightings are almost a certainty. The chances of seeing elephant, giraffe and kudu are excellent since they are all browsers and favour bushwillow, the dominant vegetation along most of the road. Impala have a wide tolerance for all kinds of habitat and are both grazers and browsers – you are sure to have several good sightings. Look for zebra and blue wildebeest in the **Afsaal** region. **Leopard** may surprise you anywhere along this road, but be extra vigilant in the **Biyamiti basin**.

Wild dog packs are often spotted along this road, usually running and playing, sometimes hunting. Hyena often make dens in culverts next to tarred roads. Look out for adults or pups in the early mornings.

The road traverses several ecozones and therefore offers a variety of vegetation types, with an associated variety of game and birds. The southern stretch passes through **Malelane mountain bushveld** and skirts the eastern side of the **Tlhalabye Hill** (630 m) where the soils are generally coarse and shallow and originate from granite. Grasses here are generally sour and not very palatable, but towards the foothills and drainage lines (near the Matjulu

Male lion, H3

African wild dogs feeding, H3

bridge) the grass tends to be sweeter. This attracts a wide variety of grazers and browsers. The big trees are mainly knob-thorn, but both russet and red bushwillow occur, as do purple-pod cluster-leaf and silver cluster-leaf. The shrub layer consists mainly of sickle-bush.

The vegetation gradually changes to typical **mixed bushwillow woodlands**. The bridge over the seasonal **Mhlambane River** offers excellent views onto the riverbed and elephant are often seen digging for underground water in the dry season. In this vicinity, wild dogs are often encountered.

'Renoster' may be the Afrikaans word for rhino, but the name **Renosterpan** does not necessarily mean that you will see rhino here. It is however a **good drinking place for many animals** of the area. Park your vehicle in the shade of a tall jackalberry and wait for animals while enjoying the sounds of the bush. On the way there, the road passes through healthy silver cluster-leaf stands – an indication of a seepage area.

As you approach Afsaal, the vegetation changes abruptly to open thornveld with stunted knob-thorn shrubs and sweet grassland where the road traverses a dyke of underlying gabbro. This narrow strip attracts plenty of grazers and predators – an excellent area for lion and leopard sightings.

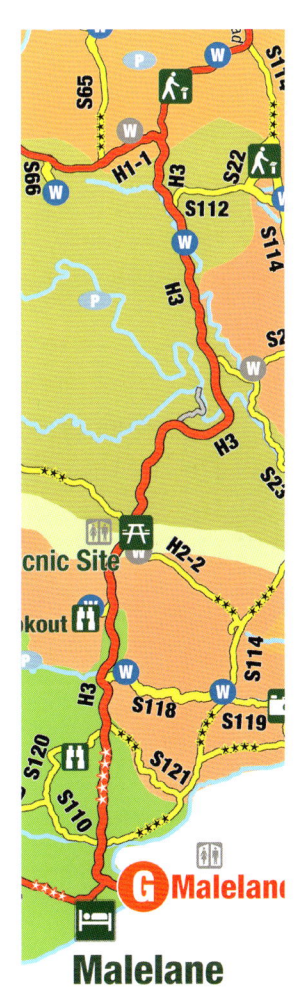

Afsaal is one of the most popular picnic sites in the park. It has a lovely setting amongst thick clusters of red ivory trees. There is a fast-food outlet and shop for something to drink and munch, and gas braai (barbeque) equipment is for hire for those who want to picnic. Look out for mongoose foraging in the grass. A huge jackalberry and a weeping boer-bean straddle a large termite mound close to the entrance of the braai area. Bushbuck are often seen close to the picnic site. The birdlife here is delightful. Look out for woodpeckers, francolins and starlings.

North of Afsaal, the first **granite koppies** (small hills or inselbergs) appear. Look out for klipspringer and large-leafed rock fig when passing the **Makhutlwanini inselberg**. Elephant are often found browsing along this section of the road. Be vigilant as the road winds through the Biyamiti basin where the woodland becomes denser and **game is more concentrated along the watercourse** during the dry season.

Northwards the road passes **Kwaggaspan**. The pan forms a bit of a wetland in the rainy season where waterbuck and even reedbuck may be seen. Other grazers also favour this area with its palatable grass. Soon thereafter the road to the Renosterkoppies S112 turns off to the east and the H3 merges with the H1-1.

H4-1
SKUKUZA TO LOWER SABIE ROAD

★★★★★

🦁 ★★★★★ 🦌 ★★★★ 🦅 ★★★★ 🌳 ★★★★

- 43 km; tarred; traverses three ecozones
- Sunset Dam near Lower Sabie; Nkuhlu Picnic Site and Nwatimhiri Dam

This is one of the most popular roads in southern Kruger. The main attraction is that the road hugs the perennial Sabie River, is extremely scenic and offers ideal habitat for most kinds of predator.

The probability of good sightings and witnessing action is high on this road. The downside is that everyone knows this, and traffic congestion does occur around good sightings. Courtesy and lots of patience is the name of the game.

Along the river it is the **riverine vegetation** that enchants. Many trees on this road are named and numbered. Wonderful specimens of sycamore fig, jackalberry, knob-thorn and river thorn occur. On the opposite side of the river typical **Sabie thorn thicket** is the dominant vegetation. Different kinds of thorn-bearing trees (formerly known as acacias) make up the dominant vegetation. One of these is the horned thorn that is typical and particularly common along this road. Before coming into leaf, the trees are easily recognised by their huge white thorns that resemble the wide horns of African cattle. This tree is number 168.1. in the South African National List of Indigenous Trees.

The **Nkuhlu Picnic Site** is a welcome stopping place halfway between Skukuza and Lower Sabie. Stretch your legs, have your picnic, mind the baboons (they are very clever at snatching food) and take your binoculars to do some birding. There is a small shop, fast-food outlet, gas barbeques for hire, hot water and restrooms.

Most animals are dependent on regular access to water. This is what the **Sabie River** offers. Grazers and browsers from the interior cross the H4-1 to get to the water. Predators

Lion pride on Lubyelubye Rocks, H4-1

Male lion scent-marking, H4-1

therefore often linger close to the river for their meals. Drive slowly and pay attention to the bush. Animals appear unannounced and may surprise you.

The riverine vegetation attracts **primates** such as vervet monkey and baboon. Impala herds loiter along the road, often nibbling here and there, hoping to avoid the hungry eyes of predators. Bushbuck and nyala keep close to the river in the deeper shade, feeding on fallen leaves or fresh shoots off the forest floor. Giraffe and kudu browse the higher shoots and leaves and often cross the road.

Huge **elephant** bulls enjoy the riverine vegetation and are often encountered feeding close to the road or in the reed beds down at the river. Breeding herds with babies do not dawdle when on their way to the water. When you encounter such a herd it is best to keep your distance as they tend to be unfriendly towards interfering motorists. **Buffalo** bachelor groups also keep close to the river but big herds are seldom encountered on this road.

Leopards are masters of camouflage and stealth and are often passed unnoticed. They are mostly active at dusk and dawn but it is surprising how many leopard sightings are also reported in the middle of the day.

Two or more resident **lion prides** may be frequenting the area between Skukuza and Lower Sabie. Scan the river banks and look deep into the bush. Be on the alert for shape combined with sandy coat colour for lions at rest. Lions often specialise in killing certain types of prey. Old buffalo bulls are often taken by lion along this road.

H4-1

Grey heron on hippo's back, Sunset Dam

Early risers are bound to come across **hyena** trotting back to their den. These predator-scavengers often den in road culverts along this tarred road. Look out for the telltale white droppings in the vicinity of a culvert next to the road.

The **N'watimhiri Dam** is another favourite in the wet season. Sweet grass around the dam attracts grazers such as impala, waterbuck and others. Hippo make use of the garden on their doorstep and whenever there is water in the dam, hippo soon make themselves at home. When conditions deteriorate, they simply move back to one of the many deeper pools in the Sabie River.

Look out for klipspringer on the rocky terrain next to the bridge crossing the seasonal **Lubyelubye River**.

This busy road is also a **birding hotspot** in the Kruger. Expect to see raptors, waterbirds, perching birds such as bee-eaters, shrikes and others, terrestrial birds and vultures when there is a kill. Storks, hamerkop and hadeda ibis are often seen foraging in the pools.

Sunset Dam is situated close to **Lower Sabie Rest Camp**. It is an extremely popular place for tourists and particularly photographers. There is ample parking close to the water's edge, and excellent photographs can be taken here. Several hippo pods have made this dam their home. Unfortunately, this has led to the enrichment of the water by their dung, resulting in a green, mossy colour and sometimes unwanted invader plants. In spite of this many animals come to drink, including impala, warthog, zebra, waterbuck and kudu. Look out for white and **black rhino** drinking in the late afternoon on the far edges of the dam. Several huge crocodiles like to bask in the sun at the water's edge.

Egyptian goose with young, Sunset Dam

African harrier hawk foraging, H4-1

Lilac-breasted roller pair, H4-1

H4-2
GOMONDWANE ROAD

★★★★

🦁 ★★★★ 🦌 ★★★ 🦅 ★★★★ 🌳 ★★★★

- 35 km; tarred; traverses three ecozones
- Sabie River and the Vurhami and Gezantombi waterholes

The H4-2 is yet another access road into Kruger. This is one of the more productive roads in the south of the park and is rated as one of the best game-viewing drives in Kruger with the probability of excellent sightings of predators and most other game.

In the early 1920s **CR de Laporte**, who was a ranger in the then Sabie Game Reserve, chose this route to build the **first road between Crocodile Bridge and Lower Sabie**. It was not originally established as a tourist route but today it is considered to be one of the most productive tourist roads.

Both the northern and southern sections of the H4-2 pass through **knob-thorn and marula savanna** while the central part passes through **Delagoa thorn thicket**. Since the soils in this entire area originate from basalt, the grass is sweet to ultra-sweet and thus favoured by most grazers. On the clay soils of the central part of the route, magic guarri is common around pans and in low-lying areas, while extensive stands of many-stemmed albizia and Delagoa thorn line the road between the two S130 intersections.

Delagoa thorn, river thorn, jackalberry, buffalo-thorn, umbrella thorn and wild date palm grow along the **Gomondwane/Vurhami drainage line** to the west of the road in the vicinity of the H5 turn-off. The huge solitary trees in the open savanna are marula, knob-thorn or leadwood.

The northern section of the H4-2 runs close along the **Sabie River** and is **extremely rewarding**, since many animals cross the road on their way to the river. The **riverine vegetation** along the Sabie River (close to Lower Sabie), and the **Vurhami**, **Gezantombi** (closer to Crocodile Bridge) and other drainage lines, is **ideal habitat for leopard**.

Look for herds of wildebeest, zebra and buffalo. Waterbuck may linger close to the water. Expect to see giraffe and kudu where there is browse. Impala herds are a common sighting and white rhino do well in this area. Elephant favour the stunted round-leafed teak but may be found browsing or grazing anywhere along this road.

Since **black rhino** keep to dense stands of vegetation with good browse, you may be lucky to see one along the central part of the route. With the abundance of suitable prey, lion and hyena are often encountered. Look out for the white droppings of hyena close to culverts. They often use these as dens.

Male southern masked weaver displaying, H4-2

Scan the branches of the huge weeping boer-beans, knob-thorns and marula trees for leopard. The openness of the woodland in many places makes this route one of the prime areas for spotting cheetah. The movements of wild dog are unpredictable, but they have been known to den in this area.

Birding is good along the entire route. Look for terrestrial birds such as francolin and guineafowl in the more open savanna. Also plentiful and highly visible are insect feeders hunting from perches. Magpie shrike and roller are usually around in the open savanna. Fish eagles are often seen along the Sabie River and at Gezantombi pool.

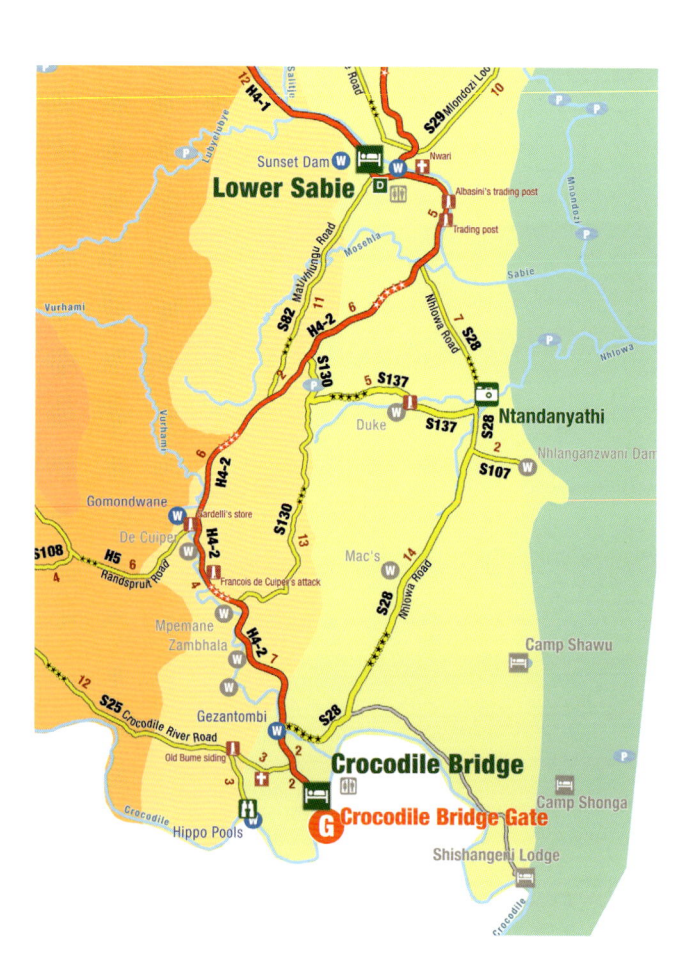

Cheetah pair, H4-2

Newborn lion cubs, H4-2

H5
RANDSPRUIT ROAD

★★★

★★★ ★★ ★★★ ★★★

- 33 km; dirt; average condition; low traffic volumes; traverses three ecozones
- The derelict railway track

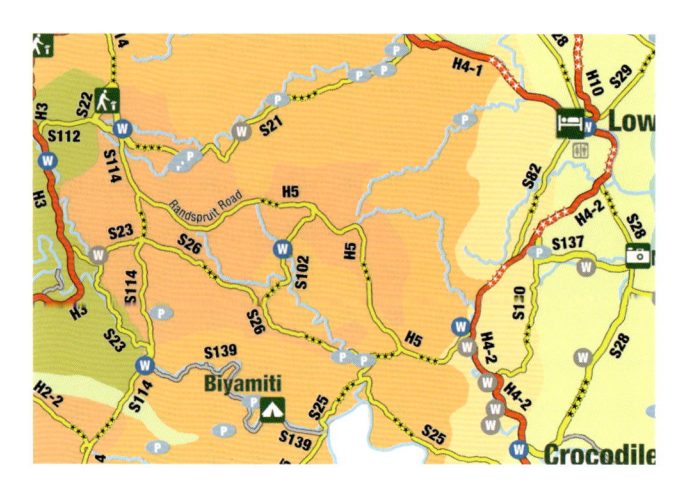

The Randspruit Road is not one of the best game-viewing roads in the park but it offers a lot in terms of historical interest. Although scenic, it can be a tedious road when in a bad condition. On the other hand, there will not be much traffic and you'll have the bush almost to yourself.

Of interest is that the **first recorded battle between Europeans and Africans** took place along this road in 1725. Later, it became a regular **stopover for traders** from Mozambique into the interior. In the early days of the park, the **Selati Railway Line** linked Komatipoort with the interior via Skukuza. Today, the evidence of this line can still be seen along this road.

From the eastern intersection with the H4-2, the Randspruit Road passes through the seasonal **Vurhami watercourse**, which is seamed by **riverine vegetation** such as sycamore fig, weeping boer-bean, leadwood and others. The **Gomondwane watering point** is situated next to the Vurhami.

As the **Delagoa thorn thickets** give way to **mixed bushwillow woodlands**, the countryside opens up a bit. The bushwillow woodlands are indicative of relatively infertile soils. The topography is undulating with low hills, rocky outcrops and drainage lines that feed into seasonal streams and rivers. On the hills the soil is sandy and coarse, supporting a mixture of sweet and sour grazing. On the lower slopes towards the drainage lines, the grass is sweeter.

This area is not really good for grazers, but impala, which are both grazers and browsers, do well. The **habitat suits browsers** such as kudu, giraffe, elephant and the endangered **black rhino**. Look out for them in dense bush. Klipspringer may be seen on the rocky outcrops. Even the rarely seen sable antelope has been recorded on this road. Since the road is narrow, it is possible to get up close to animals browsing alongside it. Approach slowly to avoid scaring them away.

Burchell's coucal, H5

Tree squirrels sunning themselves, H5

H6
N'WANETSI ROAD

★★★★

★★★★ ★★★ ★★★ ★★★

- 19 km; tarred; traverses two ecozones
- N'wanetsi Picnic Site

This lovely tarred road is a pleasure to drive. However, despite the sweet grazing and good visibility, game viewing is not consistently good.

The central **knob-thorn/marula savanna** between the H1-3 and the Lebombo Mountains is rather flat, with shallow drainage lines. The H6 road partly follows the seasonal and usually dry Shishengendzini watercourse. The **Shishengendzini Waterhole** is closed but the **Sonop Waterhole** attracts game in the area. Look for vultures' and owls' nests in the canopy of the high knob-thorn at the Sonop dry waterhole.

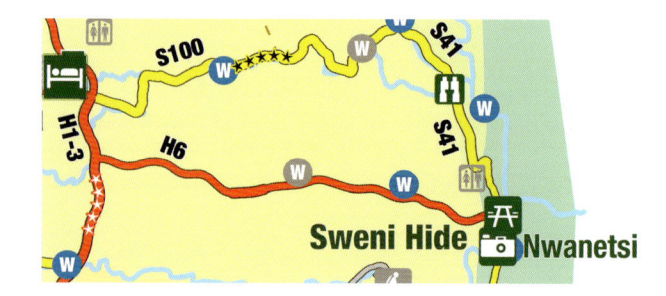

Look out for secretary birds and snake eagles in the flat and open grassy plains with knob-thorn and marula trees.

Look out for **telltale white hyena droppings** next to the road. Culverts along the tarred road are often used as dens. Expect to see hyena in the early mornings on their way back to their dens after a night's hunting. Pups often play outside the den until the adults arrive. These predator-scavengers are mainly nocturnal and will turn in for sleep an hour or two after sunrise. Towards sunset they become active again.

Zebra and blue wildebeest are often seen on the grassy plains where knob-thorn and other shrubs are stunted. Giraffe have a preference for feeding on thorn trees. Expect to find them browsing along the **Shishengendzini watercourse** and towards the eastern parts where the trees are bigger. The central grassland savanna is **buffalo country** and it is possible to find a buffalo herd on its way to water. **Lion** often follow such buffalo herds.

Look out for leadwood dotted over the plains and for round-leafed teak – a shrub that elephants prefer to browse on. Impala and kudu are often seen towards the east. Impala is a favourite prey of **cheetah**, which is often seen along this road. Steenbok, another favourite prey, is also plentiful along this road.

For magnificent scenic views combined with a wholesome picnic meal, plan to prepare a breakfast at the **N'wanetsi Picnic Site**. There are excellent barbeque facilities in a shaded rest area with tables and chairs. **Birding is particularly good** at the picnic site. Look out for euphorbia trees, since these are a typical feature as you approach the picnic site. They grow where the substrate becomes stony and the terrain hilly, where the **Lebombo Mountain bushveld** commences.

Steps up the hill lead to a **breathtakingly beautiful lookout point with shaded seating**. Panoramic views take you from the craggy hills of the Lebombo range to the central plain and down below over euphorbia-clad cliffs to a deep pool in the N'wanetsi River below. In the far distance, the pool at the Sweni Hide is visible. Don't miss the Sweni Hide on the S37 (Trichardt Road).

Lioness with cub, H6 — Isak Pretorius

Spotted hyena carrying pup, H6

H7
ORPEN–SATARA ROAD
★★★★★

★★★★★ ★★★★ ★★★★ ★★★★

- 48 km; tarred; traverses four ecozones
- Nsemani Dam; Bobbejaankrans

The Orpen–Satara road takes you through excellent game country and is one of the better roads for encountering predators such as lion, leopard and cheetah.

From the east, the first section of the road passes through beautiful and open park-like **marula/knob-thorn savanna** with underlying basalt. This is **ideal habitat for cheetah**. These fast and lithe predators hunt by first stalking their prey to within a short distance, then accelerating rapidly before tripping and killing it. Their preferred prey is impala but they will also take immature kudu, waterbuck and steenbok. Despite their speed, they are timid and will easily be chased off their kill by hyena, lion or jackal. After the hunt they have a short rest, then they gulp down their food before a scavenger arrives. There are only 120 to 150 cheetahs in the park. A sighting is therefore special indeed. The cheetah may be on its own, or a male may be accompanied by its brother, or a female by two to four of her cubs.

The marula/knob-thorn vegetation changes to Delagoa thorn thickets just east of the intersection with the S40. Karoo sediments (Ecca shales) underlie this area, and yield clayey soils and sweet grazing. Delagoa thorn, many-stemmed false thorn and magic guarri dominate here. The popular Nsemani Dam lies within this area. Since it is only about 10 km from the camp, it is a favourite afternoon game-viewing hotspot. Elephants come down to drink, white rhino wallow in the mud, impala and waterbuck graze the short sweet grass and, if luck is on your side, you may find buffalo. This peaceful setting and abundance of game with the call of Africa in the background lures everyone here. Don't miss it.

About 4 km west of Nsemani, the road leaves the thorn thickets and enters typical mixed thornveld on gabbro. Large knob-thorn, buffalo-thorn, marula and round-leafed teak are dominant here. The mixed woodland persists until the Bobbejaankrans turn-off.

It is worthwhile getting out at the **Bobbejaankrans** ('baboon cliff') view site to enjoy the scenery and coffee from a flask. The **Timbavati River** is mostly dry, but the underground water is not very deep below the surface. Elephants are often seen on the sandbanks, as are other animals such as buffalo and antelope.

The road follows the Timbavati River for a while. The **riverine vegetation** is cool and inviting on a hot summer's day. Take this section slowly – leopard or bushbuck may surprise you. Even lion have often been encountered here. Baboon and vervet monkey may be foraging next to the road. Baboons feed on virtually anything from swollen grass rhizomes to scorpions and insects, which they find by overturning stones and rotting logs.

Soon after you leave the riverine bush, typical **mixed bushwillow woodland** takes over, but soon the vegetation composition once again changes to **mixed thornveld**.

Gabar goshawk pair mating, H7

Rare white lion, H7

H8
OLIFANTS CAMP ROAD
★★★

★★★ ★★★ ★★★ ★★

- 8 km; tarred; traverses two ecozones
- The views over the Olifants River Valley

This short access road to the Olifants Camp is a popular afternoon drive and predators are regularly encountered.

The arid landscape towards the Olifants Camp has distinct undulations. On the upper and middle slopes of the **hilly terrain**, knob-thorn, bushwillow and cluster-leaf are interspersed with mopane. The aridity is reflected by the low growth of the woody vegetation – many shrubs and small trees. Tall trees are sparsely distributed. The widely spaced trees and shrubs give rise to an open savanna.

The knob-thorns are heavily browsed by elephant, kudu and giraffe, while the open savanna and short grass attract impala, zebra, wildebeest, warthog and waterbuck. **Predators** are often encountered along this road.

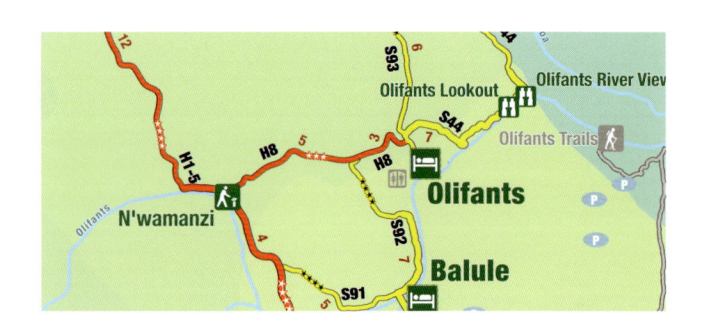

Southern ground hornbill with prey, H8

View from Olifants Camp

★★★
H9
PHALABORWA–LETABA ROAD

★★★ ★★★ ★★★ ★★

- 51 km; tarred; traverses three ecozones
- Nhlaganini Stream and Dam; Shilawuri Hill; Masorini Hill and historical village

Resting African wild dogs, H9

The H9 is the main access road from Limpopo province. Almost the entire route from west to east runs through mixed mopane and bushwillow woodland. The road follows the watershed between the Letaba River to the north and the Olifants River to the south. Game densities are low but game viewing can be surprisingly exciting.

From the west, the first granite hills become visible in the distance even before the intersection with the S51 and H14. Soon the **Vudogwa Hill** (439 m) looms to the south of the road. North of it and next to the road is the smaller **Masorini Hill**. This is where the **archaeological Masorini Village** has been reconstructed. It is worthwhile stopping at this picnic site and taking a guided tour to explore the utilisation of this natural environment and its resources by humans.

Stone Age people occupied this land and probably lived in the numerous caves and shelters on these hilly outcrops. Stone Age artefacts tell us that they were **hunter-gatherers**, collecting edible plants and hunting game. **Iron Age inhabitants** succeeded the Stone Age people and started utilising ore-bearing rocks in the area. The last in a long line of inhabitants of this site were the **Majola tribe**. The men became iron smelters and forgers, while the women grew and processed sorghum. The men supplemented their diet by hunting. The reconstructed village has two terraces with displays depicting the Majola people's lifestyle. During the week, guides are on hand to interpret and show visitors around. Ponder the origin of the glass beads, the clay pots, the metal artefacts and their role in the local economy. It is clear that they must have been traders. With whom did they trade? What did they trade? Was it a peaceful society? Were there any skirmishes? When did they move away from here? Why?

Look out for **klipspringer** ('rock jumper') on the hill. These small antelope are associated with such rocky habitats and move with amazing agility as they jump from rock to rock and bound up the sides of steep rock faces. Sometimes they are hard to find because of their habit of standing dead still for long periods. Once you locate one, you will probably find its mate.

The **mopane and bushwillow savanna** tends to be featureless and game densities are low. Due to the underlying granite, the grasses are less palatable than grasses in the east of the park. Closer to the **Shilawuri Hill** (414 m) and the **Nhlanganini Dam**, game becomes more plentiful. It is usually worth spending some time at the dam. The hippo can be quite entertaining. Elephant regularly drink here, as do buffalo herds. In their wake, lion may follow.

In the vicinity of the shorter Nhlanganini Loop the road traverses a narrow strip of sandveld. The presence of this sandveld strip is extraordinary since the only other place where sandveld occurs is in the Punda Maria area. See if you notice a change in vegetation that indicates the different soil type.

Closer to Letaba, bushwillow becomes less prominent and **mopane shrubs** predominate. The underlying geology changes from sand to shallow clay on basalt, while the grass is sweet and attracts grazers. In the **Nhlanganini drainage line** there are a few large knob-thorns, leadwoods and apple-leaf trees. The conditions here are ideal for elephant, buffalo, wildebeest and zebra. Look out for lion and leopard. Jackal and hyena may be skulking around.

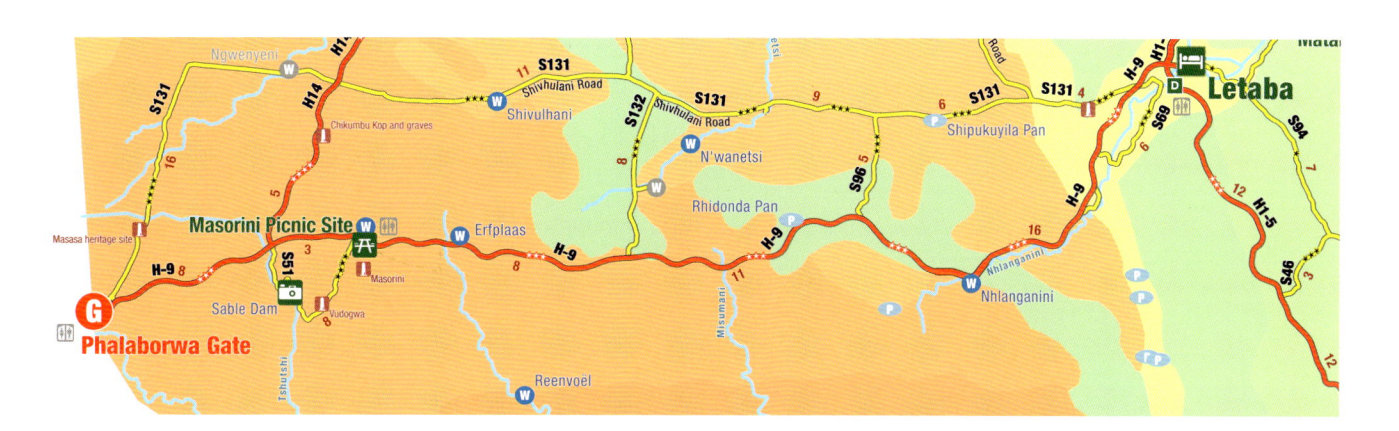

H10
LOWER SABIE TO TSHOKWANE ROAD

★★★★★

★★★★★   ★★★★   ★★★★   ★★★★★

🌀 39 km; tarred; traverses two ecozones

🚩 Muntshe Hill; Nkumbe Hill

The H10 is one of the finest game-viewing roads in the park. Visibility is good and game densities are high. The possibility of sighting all of the Big Five in one game drive is high.

The southern end of this road crosses the **Sabie River**, which is famous for its magnificent sunset views and game sightings in the riverbed. This must surely be one of the most popular bridges in the park.

More often than not elephant or buffalo may be seen among the reeds while hippo yawn for photographers. Giant, malachite and pied kingfishers are usually around to entertain and show off their fishing skills. Herons of different kinds use the fast-running overflow area to fish, darters and cormorants rest on rock perches between diving sessions, and wagtails and plovers pick at the tiniest of insects at the water's edge. Egrets, spoonbills, storks, hamerkops and even marabou storks occasionally make a stop-over. Jacana and different species of duck are often seen. At least three different species of swallow nest under the bridge. They usually perch on the bridge railing between foraging flights.

The full H10 route leads through **knob-thorn and marula savanna** with its short, sweet grasslands and open plains. This is excellent game country and large herds of grazers, with predators in their wake, frequent the area. The southern section initially seems uninteresting with low shrub cover. Soon the shrub opens up and single large leadwood, marula and knob-thorn dot the plains. As the road approaches the **Muntshe Hill**, larger trees become more prominent and the **riverine vegetation** in the drainage line becomes evident. Look out for the huge fever trees (light green), sycamore figs (yellowish stems), leadwoods (tall and upright) and jackalberries (huge, dark-green, rounded canopies, yellowish in early spring) that line the streambed.

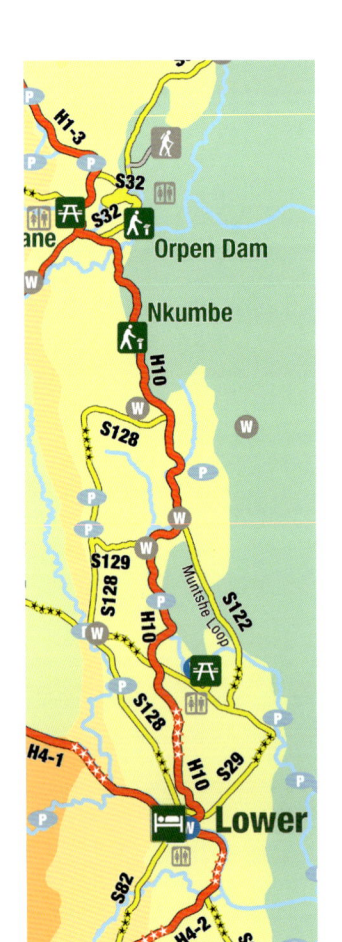

Green-backed heron, H10

Elephant stand out in the open landscape. Each elephant needs between 70 and 300 kg of fodder per day, so they spend up to 19 day hours feeding. Take time to watch elephants and their ways. Be careful of breeding herds. Avoid getting too close. Watch out for bulls in musth – the condition is indicated by a watery discharge from a gland between the ear and the eye and dribbling urine.

The open savanna is ideal habitat for grazers such as buffalo, white rhino, zebra and blue wildebeest. Impala, kudu and giraffe have enough to browse. In the vicinity of the drainage line, where there is water and riverine vegetation, baboons and monkeys occur. Expect to find predators since they tend to take advantage of the high concentration of prey species.

Look out for **reedbuck** between the crossings of S29 and S128. Here, the road runs along the **Mlondozi drainage line** and a vlei area provides the ideal habitat for them. Reedbuck are only active in the early morning and late afternoon. During the rest of the day they lie down in grass tall enough to conceal them. Often, only the horns of the males give away their presence. Dense

Hippo, H10

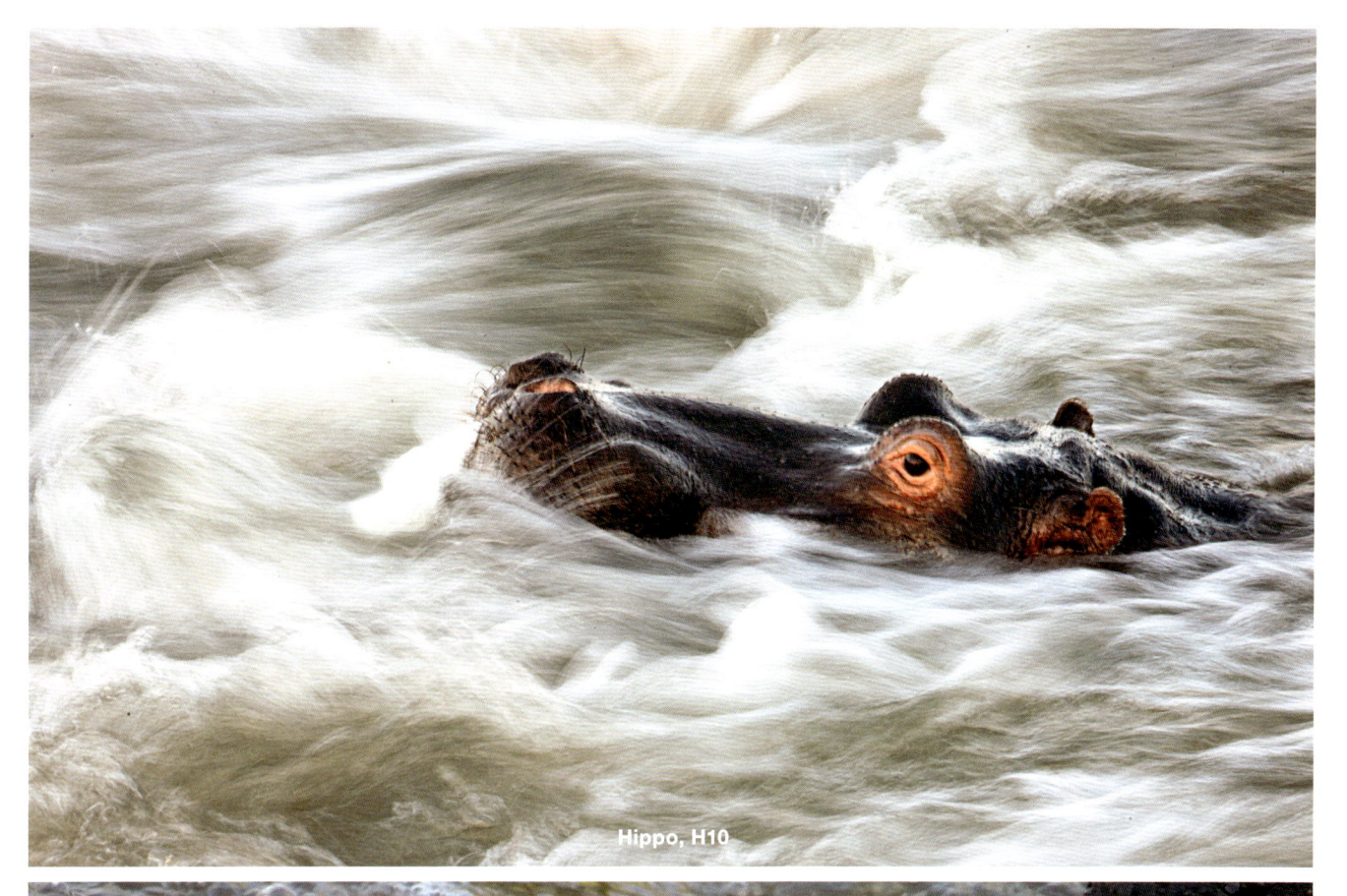

Nile crocodile, H10

Serval, H10 — Mohammed Jinnah

stands of magic guarri indicate brackish sites. The vegetation around these sites is rich in minerals and is favoured by warthog and grazers.

Southern ground hornbill are often seen along this route. They nest in the high trees along the watercourse between the intersection with S129 and northern S128. Terrestrial birds such as ostrich, bustard and francolin are usually seen on the open grassy streches.

Past the northern intersection with the S128, the **Nkumbe Hill** rises sharply above the plains. The grasslands dotted with low shrubs on both sides of the road attract plenty of game. Look out for **klipspringer** on the rocky ridges of the hill.

The high vantage point of the **Nkumbe Lookout** offers one of the grandest vistas of the seemingly endless bushveld. Spend some time there and let the bushveld ambience infuse and rejuvenate your soul. The majestic and **rare Lebombo euphorbias** (*Euphorbia confinalis*) are succulents found only on the **Lebombo mountain range**. This is one of the few places in the park where they can be seen. The resident rock skinks may welcome you where they lie basking on the rocks below the lookout.

North of Nkumbe Hill the road winds down into the **fertile N'waswitsontso valley**. Impala are particularly abundant here. Large herds are often seen grazing and browsing close to the road. Look out for the well-established hyena den next to the road. Their white droppings are distinctive. This is evidence of the rich pickings scavengers can find here.

Even though it is a gravel road and quite corrugated, it is worthwhile to take the detour to the lookout over the Orpen Dam.

Sable antelope herd, H10 — Graeme Mitchley

Klipspringer, H10

H11
KRUGER GATE TO SKUKUZA

★★★

🦁 ★★★★ 🦌 ★★★ 🦅 ★★★★ 🌳 ★★★★

14 km; tarred; traverses one ecozone

Kruger Gate

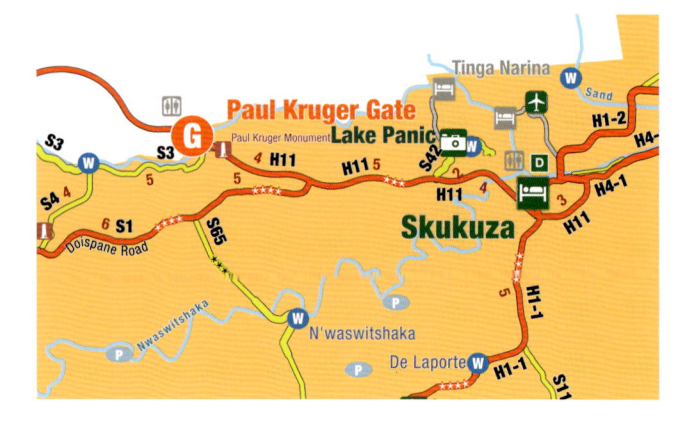

The H11 is quite a busy road, but despite the traffic, good sightings are regularly reported. The animals seem to ignore the presence of vehicles, making it possible to get up close.

The **Kruger Gate** is situated on the banks of the **Sabie River** and is the closest entrance to Skukuza. It is well worth a visit if it was not your place of entry. Apart from the impressive **Paul Kruger bust** hewn in sandstone by the famous sculpture Coert Steynberg, the area at the gate offers good birding and a **craft market** where local crafters sell their wares.

Animals on their way to and from the Sabie River cross the road. The banks of the Sabie provide a perfect habitat for predators such as leopard and lion – the availability of prey, coupled with enough shelter, is an ideal situation. Elephant can be expected, but also rhino, giraffe, impala, zebra and other antelope. Hyena are usually more abundant closer to camps, and these are often encountered in the early morning when these scavenger-predators use the tarred road as a convenient route back to their dens.

The entire road offers **good birding**. The common scavenger of the bird world, the large marabou stork, is often seen close to the **Skukuza Camp**. They are carrion feeders but also forage in the rubbish dumps of human settlements. They often roost in dead trees. Towards evening the members of a flock gather here and greet one another profusely with a beak clapping and clicking ceremony, while desperately balancing so as not to lose their grip on their perch.

Chacma baboon pair, H11

Inquisitive chacma baboon juvenile, H11

★★★★

H12
HIGH BRIDGE AND LINK ROAD BETWEEN H4-1 AND H1-2

★★★ ★★★ ★★★★ ★★★★

5 km; tarred; traverses one ecozone

The high-level bridge and immediate surroundings

The highlight of this road is the bridge. The scenic views up and down the river always delight.

Look out for the **majestic sycamore fig trees** on the southern bank with their distinctive yellowish bark. On the same bank, right next to the bridge, there is a small grove of matumi trees. This tree only occurs along perennial rivers of the Lowveld and is easy to recognise. The leaves are thin and lancet-shaped, and grow upwards like the leaves of a pineapple.

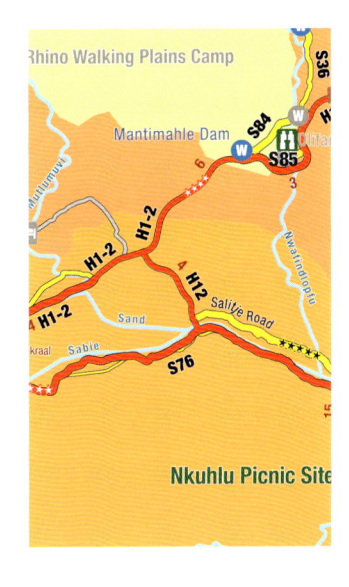

A **resident baboon troop** is usually around to provide entertainment. Never feed any of these primates. Look for elephants feeding amongst the reeds in the riverbed. Older elephants with worn teeth often prefer softer vegetation. The same applies to older buffalo bulls. Reeds provide shelter and food.

You will be sure to spot the occasional **crocodile** or **water monitor** basking on a sandbank or boulder in the riverbed. Hippo might lurk in the deeper pools. Look out for bushbuck in the dense riverine vegetation on the riverbank.

Scan the area with your binoculars – you may see storks, egrets and herons, swifts and swallows, kingfishers, darters and cormorants. A giant kingfisher is usually around, using the bridge railing as a perch from where it swoops onto fish in the swift-flowing Sabie River.

Juvenile chacma baboon, H11

★★★
H13-1
PUNDA MARIA GATE TO H1-7

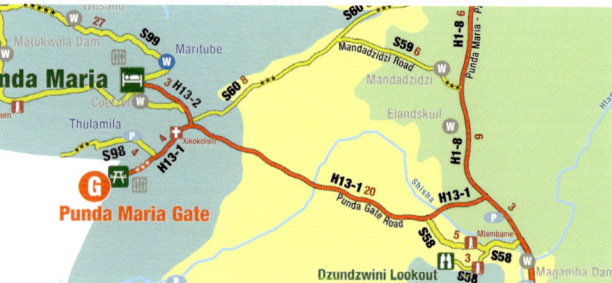

★★★ ★★★ ★★★ ★★★★

- 20 km; tarred; traverses three ecozones
- Several rainwater pans next to the road in the wet season

The Punda Maria Gate gives access to the far northern parts of the park and the H13-1 links the entrance gate to the main H1 road. It is a pleasant drive but overall visibility is poor and game is not easily spotted, even though it is relatively abundant.

The western section of the road passes through typical **sandveld vegetation** before **tree mopane woodland** takes over. The grass is sweet and palatable and attracts grazing animals in both the sandveld and the tree mopane. Expect to see browsers such as elephant, kudu, nyala and impala. The sandveld may also yield the occasional giraffe, zebra and buffalo. Predators are around but neither abundant nor frequently seen.

Sightings may include small antelope such as Sharpe's grysbok, suni, steenbok and duiker; browsers such as nyala, elephant, kudu and impala; and bulk grazers such as buffalo and small groups of zebra. Predators may include hyena, leopard and lion.

The sandveld with its many species of flowering plants is known as the **flower garden of the park**. In summer the huge patches of peach-coloured Pride-of-de-Kaap (Bauhinia galpinii) lighten the spirits with their beauty. Several other flowering shrubs occur, but it's the **diversity in tree species** that attracts tree-lovers from far and wide. The baobab is possibly the most impressive, but others such as the pod mahogany are equally admired. Several species of bushwillow occur but the large-fruited bushwillow is possibly the easiest to recognise. Trees such as the Natal mahogany, leadwood, jackalberry, marula, sausage tree and sycamore fig grow extra large and tall. The white kirkia, with its fairy-tale appearance in autumn before it sheds its leaves, cannot be missed. The sandy soils of the sandveld are deep but cannot retain water adequately, so the vegetation that grows in it needs to be drought resistant. Typical drought-resistant trees are the corkwoods (Commiphora sp.).

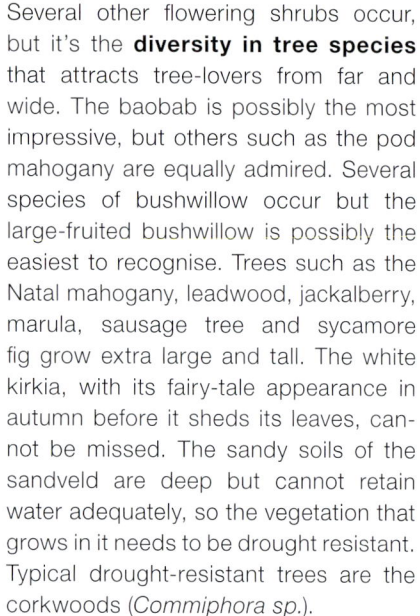

The sandveld ecozone gradually changes into a zone underpinned by Ecca shales. In this zone, the soils are also very deep and the dense clays are rich in minerals. These conditions are favourable for the common mopane to grow into fairly tall trees and form dense woodland. The mopane woodland makes a **spectacular display in August-September** when the leaves change colour before falling. The woodland is fairly uniform, with only tamboti growing in association with the mopane at some places.

European roller, H13-1

Purple roller, H13-1

Lilac-breasted roller, H13-1

H13-2
ROAD TO PUNDA MARIA CAMP

★★★ ★★★ ★★★★ ★★★★★

- 4 km; tarred; traverses one ecozone
- Lovely big trees line the road and create a park-like atmosphere

The H13-2 turns off from the H13-1 and gives access to the Punda Maria Camp. The road is lined with magnificent trees ranging from marula, knob-thorn and apple-leaf to various others.

The access road to Punda Maria Camp and all the other roads leading into this road pass through a **sandveld ecosystem**. The vegetation here is very different from the vegetation of the eastern basaltic plains or the western granite hills and valleys. The main reason for this is that the underlying geology differs so much. The soils are derived from sandstone and are deep, sandy, well-drained and relatively infertile. Some of these sediments were deposited millions of years ago by raging windstorms blowing sand in from the Kalahari. Today, the sandveld is home to a **complex diversity of plants** in which no plant or tree is particularly dominant.

Due to the infertility of the soils, the density of game is generally low. However this is **a mecca for tree-lovers and birders**. On your way to the camp you will probably come across elephant, especially in the late summer when the marula fruit ripens. Several huge jackalberry and marula trees fringe the road and elephant are particularly fond of these. Many specimens of the sjambok pod are scattered among the marula and mopane.

Birding is excellent and diverse, especially in summer once the migratory species have arrived. Common sightings are hornbill, francolin and rollers. Look out for greenbul, robin-chat and scrub robin. Soaring raptors are a common sight.

African elephant, H13-2

H14
PHALABORWA–MOOIPLAAS ROAD

★★★★

★★★★ ★★★ ★★★ ★★★

- 53 km; tarred; traverses two ecozones
- Ngwenyeni drainage line; Letaba River crossing
- Mopani bushwillow woodlands; undulated with streams and rivers, sand on crests, clay in drainage lines. Look for sable, large breeding herds of elephants, giraffe along streams, leopard, lion

This is the shortest access route between Phalaborwa and Mopani as well as the entire northern section of the park. It is also the main access road to Shimuwini and Boulders Camps. When this road was built, care was taken to traverse the most scenic sections of the area between Phalaborwa and the road intersection with the H1-6.

Most of the road traverses **mopane and bushwillow woodlands**. The first landmark when driving from the south is **Shikumbu Hill** (494 m). Similar to the Masorini Hill, this inselberg was also inhabited by 19th-century ironworking communities. Evidence has been found of the homesteads and cattle shelters they built on the top of this hill. The road skirts the lower slopes of the hill on the western side. The rocks and boulders are granite or gneiss, which are **some of the oldest rocks on Earth**. Note the different vegetation along the rocky slopes – large-leafed rock figs and mountain syringa (kirkia) trees do well in this kind of habitat. Giraffe are often seen on the lower slopes. Look out for klipspringer and steenbok.

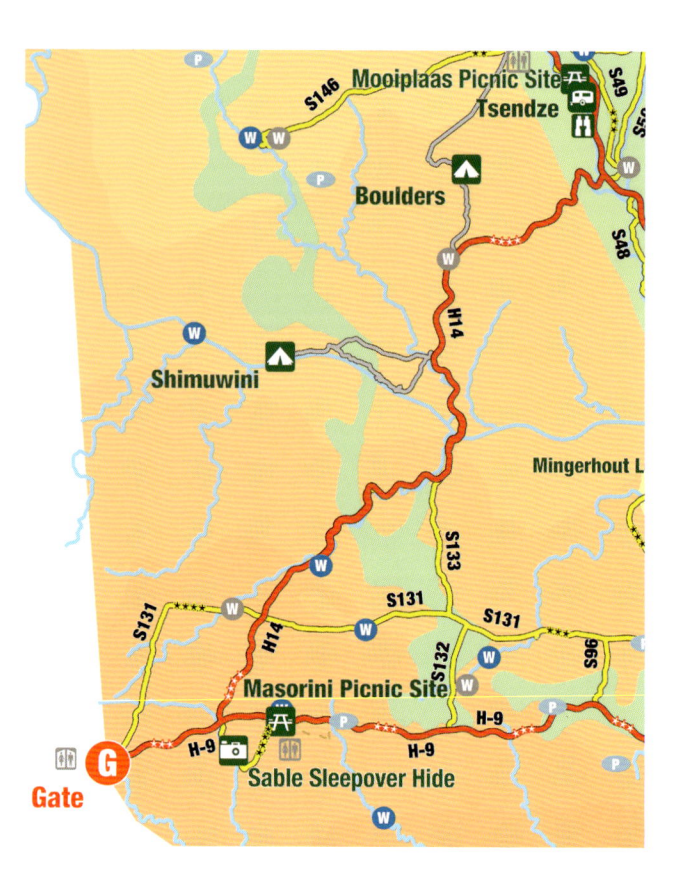

Leopard watching potential prey, H14

Cardinal woodpecker male feeding young, H14

Before the bridge-crossing over the **Ngwenyeni stream**, there is a turn-off to a waterhole where the **Ngwenyeni and Shicindzwaneni watercourses converge**. Thereafter, the road follows the course of the Ngwenyeni drainage line for several kilometres. This is the most scenic section of the road. There are two loops along this watercourse to follow. It is worthwhile investigating these as semi-permanent water pools offer drinking water to game and may just reveal some predators as well. A lookout point at the top of the cliff offers good views of the meandering stream and over the entire area. **Riverine vegetation** includes leadwood, knob-thorn, sycamore fig and beautiful big apple-leaf trees. Large impala herds and waterbuck are usually abundant here.

Soon the seasonal Ngwenyeni stream converges with the **Shivulani stream** and offers **several semi-permanent pools** along its way down to the Letaba River. It is worth taking this last stretch slowly before the Letaba crossing. Where there is water there are usually animals, including predators.

Another landmark is the broad, sandy and perennial Letaba River, which eventually flows into the Olifants River. To the northwest of the bridge the watercourses of the Shivulani (including the Ngwenyeni from the south) and Shipikana (from the north) join the Letaba River. **Birding** in the riverine vegetation around the Letaba River is usually good. Spend some time on the bridge studying the surrounding areas.

The northern section may be rated as the less scenic part of the H14. It is deeply undulating with prominent watersheds and deeply incised watercourses. The vegetation can still be described as **mopane and bushwillow woodlands** with high trees and a well-developed shrub layer, but with a low and poorly developed grass cover. Prominent inselbergs are visible from the road. Game densities are low until the sweeter grasslands beyond the **Kaleka Hill** (southeast of the road) are reached. The road follows parts of the major drainage lines that collect water from the north. Initially it follows the Shipikana, which carries water from beyond the Stapelkop Dam catchment area and then along its tributary, the **Tsale Stream**.

Once the crossing of the Tsendze River is reached, you are already in the **basalt-based mopane shrubveld**, which is less undulating, with sweet grasslands.

Caracal with kitten, H14

H15
GIRIYONDO ROAD
★★★

★★ ★★ ★★★ ★★★

- 28 km; gravel; traverses two ecozones
- Malopenyana Waterhole; Makhadzi Stream, Waterhole and Picnic Site

The road to the Giriyondo Border Gate is a relatively new addition to the public road network in the park. Game viewing is not highly rated, but there may be a few pleasant surprises for the traveller.

Formerly this road was used to transport Shangaan mineworkers from Mozambique to Johannesburg. It was resurfaced when the border was reopened at the time of the Peace Parks initiative. It is a surprisingly busy road, with vehicles travelling this route for **quick access to Massingir** in Mozambique and back into South Africa. No commercial vehicles are allowed through this border post and although only four-wheel drive vehicles are recommended, many heavily laden pick-ups and sedans are regular users.

Despite the traffic, it is well worth investigating this road. For most of the way it runs through fairly monotonous **mopane shrubveld** with sweet grass on basalt soils before it reaches the **Lebombo mountain landscape**.

The **Malopenyana Waterhole** at the turn-off from the H1-6 is a good one. On the northern side of the road a wetland forms in summer. This is a particularly good place to look for **tsessebe**. They are grazers and often seen in association with zebra and wildebeest. Tsessebe are known to be the fastest antelope, capable of galloping at speeds of over 90 km per hour.

In summer, **several pans form along the road** and grazers frequent the area. **Elephants** often gather in the region of the **Makhadzi Stream** crossing. Near the Makhadzi Waterhole is a turn-off to the **Makhadzi Picnic Site**. This site is a big and unexpected surprise and quite different from any other picnic site in the park. The best specimens of **huge, mature, apple-leaf trees** are found here, and one could easily spend a lunch break in their shade. There are **extensive kitchen facilities and ablutions**, while the picnic area has many tables with ample seating. Firewood, charcoal and cold drinks are on sale.

Another surprise is the **Steinaecker's Interpretation Centre**, built in 2003. During a field survey in 1996 the remains of a camp were discovered here. Apparently this was the northern outpost of the fighting unit known as Steinaecker's Horse during the Anglo-Boer War. Archaeologists excavating the site found artefacts to confirm this. Von Steinaecker was quite a character and the exhibition tells his story.

The road beyond the picnic site eventually leads through a gap in the **Lebombo Mountains** where the **Giriyondo Gate** gives access to the **Limpopo National Park** in Mozambique.

Average mopane veld birding applies for most of the way. Special sightings can be expected along the outliers of the Lebombo range near Giriyondo Gate.

Secretarybird, H15

Plains zebra interacting, H15

S1
DOISPANE ROAD
★★★★

- 26km; tarred; in good condition; traverses two ecozones
- Nyamundwa Dam

Many visitors enter the Phabeni Gate into the Kruger National Park and enjoy a rewarding game drive on the S1. The scenery alone is engaging and offers great diversity. A variety of habitats makes for good birding.

The western end of the Doispane road initially passes through **open savanna**. With relatively good annual rainfall of 650–700mm at this end of the road, grass cover is good and pans fill up quickly in summer. From the Phabeni Gate and more or less up to the **Nyamundwa stream** on the S1, the road traverses a geological strip of gabbro set among the granite soils. The soils here are dark with a high clay content and the grasses are sweet and palatable. This attracts a wide range of grazers and also browsers.

The landscape is **slightly undulating** and the road passes through a park-like open area scattered with knob-thorn, marula and bushwillow. Giraffe, kudu and duiker all browse at different levels and are often seen around the intersection between the S3 and S1. This is also an excellent white rhino area. The road descends into the **Sabie catchment area** and soon passes the Nyamundwa stream.

The **Nyamundwa Dam** is in the overlap between two ecozones. This is a most rewarding game-viewing spot and a couple of hours can be spent parked in the shade of a huge knob-thorn tree. It is the favourite drinking place for kudu, giraffe, zebra, impala, buffalo and white rhino. Grazers usually drink during mid-morning. White rhino wallow during hot days but otherwise drink mainly towards evening. Open savanna is a particularly suitable habitat for cheetah, and sightings are often reported in the vicinity of the dam.

African civet, S1

Lion snarling, S1

The dam is deep enough for hippo and crocodile. Waterfowl to be seen include the ever-present Egyptian goose. Spend some time and be rewarded by the beautiful and haunting call of the resident fish eagle.

Soon after the crossing of the Nyamundwa Stream, the landscape changes. The soils become shallower on the crests and slopes. Towards the lower slopes and drainage lines, the clay content increases and these soils are rich in minerals due to the leaching from adjoining watersheds. The soils are suitable for a **higher diversity of tree species** and although the knob-thorn is dominant, trees such as the green thorn or torchwood, marula, false marula and buffalo-thorn are well represented. Sickle-bush forms much of the understorey. Look for the occasional umbrella thorn with its typical flat crown. Next to the road there are a few spectacular specimens of the African or weeping wattle, with its yellow flowers borne in long drooping clusters in November and December.

Near the turn-off to the S4 a series of **granite inselbergs** appears. This is where the famous ranger **Harry Wolhuter** used to camp in the early days of the park. These koppies or granite hills also mark a change of landscape. Eastwards, the climate is drier, the savanna opens up and leadwood and magic guarri become common.

Due to better visibility, game viewing on this scenically pleasing road improves as you approach the H11. A well-used hyena den under a culvert next to the road should not be missed. The young ones often linger outside the den early in the morning, waiting for the adults to return from their hunting and scavenging. It is also an area frequented by the scarce and endangered wild dog. Their numbers in the park are estimated at only 150.

Look out for the widespread and common bushveld bird species but also keep an eye open for raptors closer to the dam or in habitats with good trees for perching.

★★★★

S3
NUMBI TO KRUGER GATE ALONG THE SABIE RIVER

★★★ ★★★ ★★★★ ★★★★★

- 46 km; dirt road (Albasini section 17 km; along the upper Sabie River 29 km); narrow in places; avoid after heavy rains; traverses three ecozones
- Mestel Dam; Sabie River views

The S3 is one of the special jewels of the south. The narrow and winding dirt road offers many surprises and has a special ambience. This is a good road for a morning drive.

From the H1-1 close to the Numbi Gate up to a few kilometres before crossing the Doispane intersection, the S3 passes through **Lowveld sour bushveld**. The high altitude and rainfall (highest in the park) as well as the soils derived from granite are deep and sandy but poor in nutrients. The grasses

African wild dog pair, S3

Pat Scott

Sleeping leopard, S1

growing here are mostly perennial and become unpalatable in winter. This area is well known for its **tall grass** (good for thatching) that can grow up to two metres. Knob-thorn is the dominant tree species but bushwillow and teak are also well represented. Silver cluster-leaf is found in huge stands along seepage lines. Fine specimens of jackalberry and marula occur. The result is a **densely wooded savanna** with sour grassveld growing very tall in late summer. Grazers will eat young sprouts of sour grasses but in winter they move away to mixed veld with better grazing. Despite high game populations, tall grasses and thick bush make game viewing difficult.

Look out for sable antelope since they favour this area. They have a patchy distribution in South Africa but the largest natural population is presently in the Kruger National Park. Their distribution is dependent on cover and availability of water. They prefer open woodland, with adjacent wetlands or grassland with medium to high stands of grass. They avoid areas where tree density is high and grass is short and overgrazed.

The S3 is known to be an excellent white rhino route. In the taller grass areas, white rhino are known to favour grasses growing on termite mounds. The reason is probably that these grasses are richer in nutrients, especially sodium. The availability of good browse throughout the year makes this area particularly suitable for duiker, kudu and giraffe. The dense broadleaf savanna with rocky outcrops is good habitat for leopard and regular lion sightings are reported. Hyena and wild dog, as well as black-backed jackal, may be encountered in the early mornings.

Mestel Dam in the **Phabeni River** attracts general game including white rhino and elephant. It is a small but deep dam. Check for reedbuck in the low-lying areas with high grasses close to the dam edges. Since this is sable country, look out for approaching animals. Predators also need water and may be found on their way to and from water. The road stops well away from the water's edge.

After the intersection with the Doispane road, the S3 soon meanders along the **Sabie River**. **Prime riverine vegetation** delights the eye on the northern verge of the road. On the southern verge, typical thorn thickets fringe the road. Normally this is a quiet dust road with little traffic, where game viewing is usually good. Elephant are almost a certainty and leopard and lion sightings a high probability. Good wild dog encounters have also often been reported. Herds of buffalo on their way to water may cross the road. Plenty of white rhino middens provide evidence of their presence. Impala are the most abundant antelope while kudu, giraffe, zebra, nyala and warthog can also be expected.

Look out for sycamore fig, weeping boer-bean, matumi and jackalberry on the riverbanks. Bushbuck may be browsing the undergrowth of these huge trees while vervet monkeys and baboons also find this an agreeable habitat with plenty of food and shelter. Many hippo tracks lead out of the river to the surrounding thickets – a sure sign of the abundance of hippo in parts of the river with deep pools. Look for basking crocodile on the sandbanks and otter frolicking in the water.

The **Sabie River thickets** are characterised by the presence of knob-thorn, abundant bushwillow, the occasional green thorn and large marula trees. The grass is sparse and mixed. Apple-leaf and silver cluster-leaf appear on the seepage lines while leadwood, thorny cluster-leaf, magic guarri and sickle-bush feature along the footslopes and drainage lines where the grass is sweeter.

Spot the widespread and common bushveld bird species and keep an eye open for raptors closer to the river or where there are good trees for perching.

⭐⭐⭐
S4
LINK ROAD BETWEEN S1 AND S3

🦁 🦌 🦅 🌳
★★★ ★★★ ★★★ ★★★

4 km; dirt road; traverses one ecozone

This is a useful link road to escape the S3 or the S1 to make a round trip back to Skukuza Rest Camp. The ecology of this area is similar to that of S3 and S1.

⭐⭐⭐
S7
SHABENI LINK ROAD BETWEEN H1-1 AND S3

🦁 🦌 🦅 🌳
★★★ ★★★ ★★★ ★★★

7 km; dirt road; traverses one ecozone

The Shabeni road is an alternative to the first section of the Albasini Road (S3), and its vegetation is similar. It also leads out of the H1-1, but closer to Pretoriuskop, and meets up with the S3 after 7 km.

The **sour grassveld** does not attract large herds of the common grazers, but is home to some of the scarcer antelope in the park. Look out for eland, sable and roan antelope. While predators are not abundant here, lion are often reported, as are leopard, occasionally.

Running impala, S7

★★★★

S8
CIRCULAR DRIVE CLOSE TO PRETORIUSKOP

★★★　★★★　★★★　★★★

- 14.5 km; gravel road; confusing signage; traverses one ecozone
- Granite outcrops or inselbergs

This circular road is the best choice for a short game drive close to the camp, but the numbering of this and other roads in the vicinity may be confusing. Maps differ. This road might as well be called the granite outcrop or inselberg road because you will encounter three mini loops around rocky outcrops. Enjoy the scenic splendour.

Leaving camp, the S8 starts at the turn-off to the left just after the day-visitors' picnic site. Soon after the turn-off, there is a track to the right which is the first short loop that circumnavigates a **granite outcrop**. Look out for leopard here.

The **wild teak or kiaat** *(Pterocarpus angolensis)* is one of the special trees limited mostly to the Pretoriuskop area where it is quite dominant. Recognise the tree by its distinctive roundish pods. Its small golden-yellow flowers emerge in spring. Kudu and other browsers love its leaves while monkey and baboon go for the pods.

At the following intersection, turn left and keep left at the fork as you continue along the S8. Soon there is another turn-off to the second short loop leading around another **granite outcrop**. Marvel at the huge boulders. Pretoriuskop is better known for its scenic drives and diversity of beautiful trees and other vegetation, than the number of animals one is likely to encounter, but there is always a chance that something special may surprise you.

The Fayi Loop turns off more or less at the halfway point, but S8 loops back northwards to meet up with the fork in the road. Driving back towards the H1-1 or to the camp, another short road S19 takes you to yet another and more impressive inselberg.

★★★

S10
SHABENI LOOP

★★★　★★★　★★★　★★★

- 7 km; dirt road (Shabeni Loop 3.4 km); traverses one ecozone

The S10 is a loop road out of the S7 that circumnavigates the amazing Shabeni Hill (758 m).

Huge boulders seem to be haphazardly piled next to, and atop, one of the biggest undisturbed rock faces in the park. Look out for **large-leafed rock figs** with their yellow-white twisted trunks and white roots hugging rock faces. There are sure to be **klipspringers** around and it will be a feather in your cap to find a pair of these. They tend to be on the sunny side of the hill in the morning but prefer the shady side in the afternoons. These agile, small, sure-footed antelope form lifelong pair bonds. If you see one, look for its mate, as it should be somewhere nearby. Their hooves are adapted to landing on all fours on a small space. Caracal and leopard both prey on klipspringer and are often found on or close to rocky outcrops. Baboons often make these huge granite hills their home since they provide lookouts and safe sleeping places. The surrounding woodlands offer enough food in the form of insects and fruiting trees.

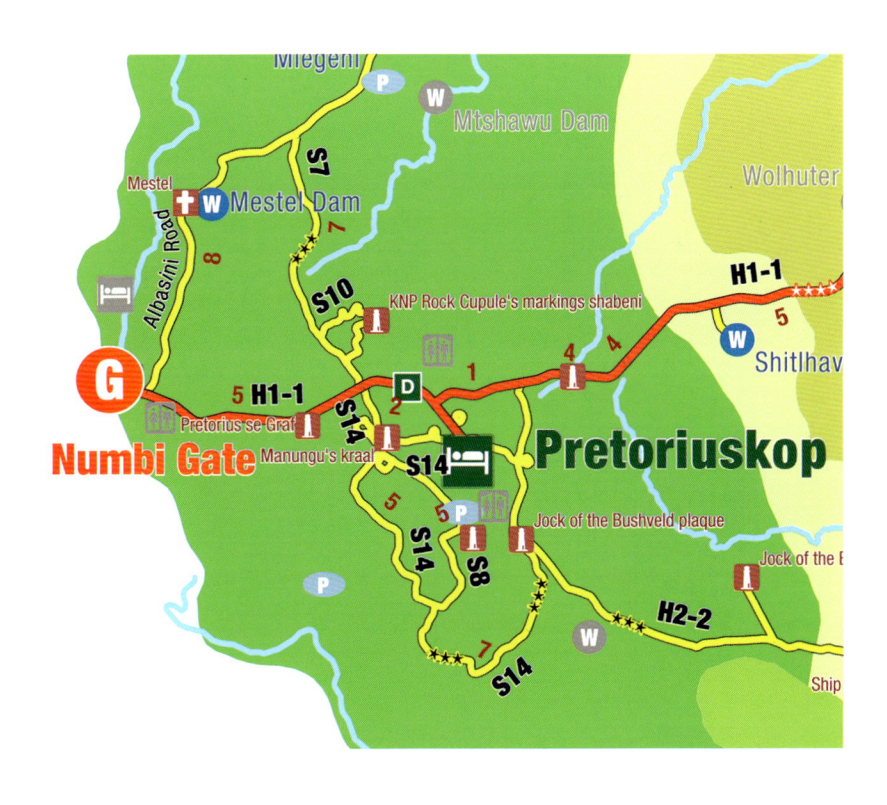

S12
GIRIVANA LOOP

★★★

🦁 ★★★   🦌 ★★★   🦅 ★★   🌳 ★★★

- 5 km; dirt road; narrow and intimate; traverses two ecozones
- Girivana Dam and waterhole

The narrow dirt road passes through thorn thickets, and then red bushwillow woodland, before it joins the H7.

Although the western part is not very rewarding for game, it offers close-up views of birds next to the road.

The highlight of this loop road is the **Girivana Waterhole**. This is a particularly nice dam since it can be approached from three sides. **Lions** are often found drinking here early in the morning. When bigger game is absent, there are often baboons or birds around to attract one's attention. Spending a peaceful hour or so simply watching is a great experience.

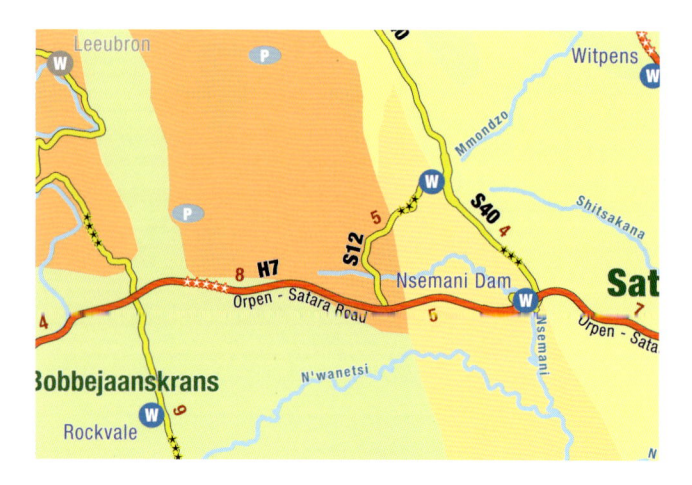

At the side of the road behind the waterhole, on the bank of the watercourse, is a beautiful specimen of a huge **sycamore fig**. Note the distinctive smooth pinkish-yellow bark of the trunk and exposed roots. Note the fluted, relatively short but massive trunk, which is buttressed and gnarled. When it bears figs, all kinds of birds and animals visit the tree. Some feed on fallen fruits, such as warthog, baboon and impala. Others, such as elephant and giraffe, browse if they can reach the new leaves on the high branches.

Birds you can expect at the waterhole and sycamore fig tree are pigeons, parrots, hornbills, barbets, starlings and rollers.

Chacma baboon feeding, S12

⭐⭐⭐
S14
THE FAYI LOOP AT PRETORIUSKOP

🦁 ⭐⭐⭐   🦌 ⭐⭐⭐   🦅 ⭐⭐⭐   🌳 ⭐⭐⭐⭐⭐

- 5 km; dirt road; narrow and intimate
- Fayi Creek; wet grassland; granite boulders

Known for its scenic qualities, this is a road on which to get lost – literally and figuratively. It turns out of the S8, crosses a wetland area and the Fayi Creek, leads through silver cluster-leaf woodland before it meets up with the H2-2.

You are unlikely to find the park's cutest mammal that is only found in the foothills around Pretoriuskop – the tiny **South African hedgehog**. It is small, about the size of a rat, and covered with spines. Changing its sheltering place daily, it can be found curled up in thick dry bush or in rock crevices. It only emerges in the evenings, but may appear sometimes **after rain** to take advantage of emerging insects and surfacing earthworms. If you happen to visit in summer, and it happens to rain and you happen to park for a while, look around and watch out for a **tiny spiky ball on the move**. It might just be the best and rarest of all your sightings in the park.

Whether you prefer silver cluster-leaf forest, granite hills, creeks, wet grassland or marshes, you will find it all on the Fayi Loop. Added to all of this splendour is the possibility of bumping into lion or leopard. This loop is one of the better places around Pretoriuskop to find predators. The vegetation is not as dense as in other places and although grass can be long the visibility is better than in many other places close by. There is also the possibility of seeing common reedbuck in the marshy grassland in the vicinity of the **Fayi creek**. Reedbuck favour long grasses where they can hide during the day. They are active in the early mornings and late afternoons when they graze on the grasses close to the stream.

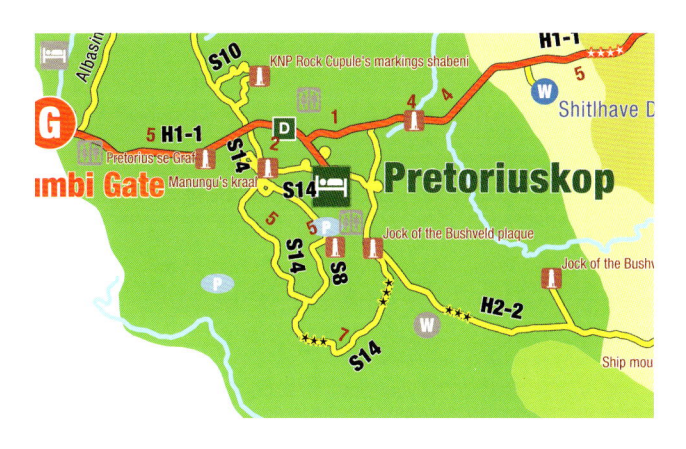

The other specials of this area are eland, sable antelope and roan antelope. Oribi used to be found here, but their numbers have diminished and it is uncertain whether they are still around.

The Pretoriuskop area is home to several special birds not common elsewhere in the park. Check the list of species that specifically occur in the **Lowveld sour bushveld**. Look out for mocking cliff chat, red-winged starling and cinnamon-breasted bunting, species that keep to granite outcrops and will only be found in these locations.

Marsh terrapin, S14

S21
N'WATIMHIRI ROAD

★★★★

★★★★ (lion) ★★★ (antelope) ★★★★ (bird) ★★★★ (tree)

- 27 km; dirt road; narrow and intimate, usually in a fair condition; traverses two major ecozones
- Granite outcrops

This link between the H4-1 and S114 is an appealing choice for its ambience. Despite (or perhaps because of) the gravel road, the intimacy of the nature experience along this route is overwhelming.

On the **eastern end** the landscape is initially **flat to slightly undulating** but it gradually changes towards the **west** where **granite outcrops** create a magic feeling as the road meanders between them, also crossing several drainage lines and dry watercourses. The eastern part of the road winds through dense **thorn thickets**, but the vegetation gradually changes to **mixed bushwillow woodlands**. The mixed grasses attract grazers; with them come the predators. The relatively narrow road means that when you come across animals, they tend to be very close to your vehicle.

A good place to stop and spend some time during the rainy season is a biggish **pan** on the south side of the road a few kilometres from the intersection with the H4-1. This is where rhino like to wallow when the summer heat and flies make life uncomfortable. Several dung middens along the road confirm their presence. Warthog are frequently around and provide good entertainment. Buffalo may also be taking their mud baths here.

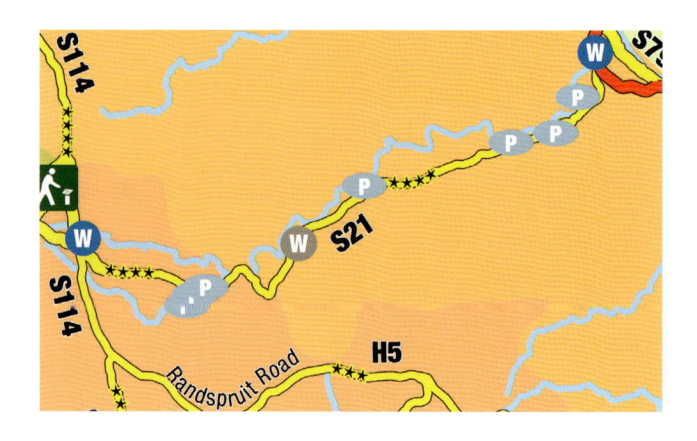

Giraffe and kudu are abundant, as are impala. Wildebeest and zebra can be seen on the more open savanna. There is plenty of browse for elephant and black rhino. Lion sightings are common and leopard and hyena occur. Be extra vigilant at the **granite outcrops**.

The trees along much of this road are magnificent. Look out for knob-thorn and green thorn (torchwood) on the high ground; silver cluster-leaf on the seepage lines; leadwood and apple-leaf lower down on the footslopes; magic guarri around the pans; and sickle-bush cluttering the undergrowth. Towards the granite outcrops there are lovely specimens of the weeping wattle that are particularly striking when in flower from November to February. Their bright yellow flowers hang in long, drooping clusters.

Birding along this road is excellent. When you come across a 'bird party', take time to stop for a while and listen to the magnificent birdsong – especially in spring. Look out for the widespread and common bushveld species, and also for raptors where there are tall trees for perching.

Cheetah, S21

Cheetah pair, S21

S22
STEVENSON-HAMILTON MEMORIAL ROAD

★★★★

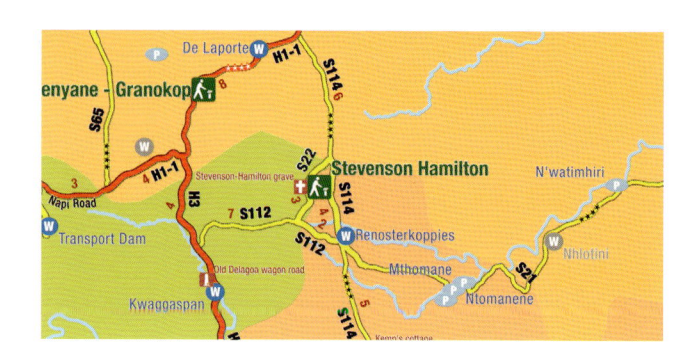

★★★★ ★★★★ ★★★★ ★★★★

- 3.2 km; narrow dirt road; traverses one major ecozone
- Shirimantanga Hill

The S22 is a link road between the S114 and the S112 and skirts the Shirimantanga Hill, where James Stevenson-Hamilton and his wife Hilda requested their ashes to be scattered.

James Stevenson-Hamilton was appointed head ranger of the **Sabie** and the **Shingwedzi Reserves** in **1902**, which formed the core of today's Kruger National Park. A man with vision, his greatest concern was to secure the park for the animals and create a national park that would be sustained by tourism. He vigorously fought mining entrepreneurs and sheep farmers, as well as poachers and hunters, to achieve his goal. In **1926** privately owned farms between the two reserves were purchased and merged to form the **Kruger National Park**. He retired in 1946 and died in 1957 at the age of 90. The huge granite boulders form an apt memorial in his honour.

Game viewing on this road is usually rewarding. Predator and other game sightings are regularly reported. Birding is good since the vegetation offers a variety of habitats.

Red-billed oxpecker on impala, S22

Red-billed oxpecker gathering impala hair for nest, S22

Red-billed oxpeckers gathering impala hair, S22

S23
BIYAMITI LOOP
★★★★

🦁 ★★★★ 🦌 ★★★★ 🦅 ★★★★ 🌳 ★★★★

- 14 km; dirt road; narrow and meandering along the river; usually in a fair condition; traverses two major ecozones
- Views over the Biyamiti River; loop overlooking the Biyamiti Weir; granite outcrops

The S23 follows the meandering course of the river east of the tarred H3 road (the link road is S113) and makes a loop out of the S114. Drive slowly and be vigilant when doing this fairy-tale drive. Unexpected sightings may surprise you.

The **Biyamiti catchment area** stretches from the **Shitlhave Dam** close to Pretoriuskop and eventually spills its contents into the **Crocodile River** in the south. Like many other seasonal rivers, the Biyamiti only **flows in the rainy season**, but several permanent pools along its course supply game with much-needed water.

While the surrounding landscape is typical **mixed bush-willow** and **thorn tree woodland**, the vegetation along the river is typically **riverine**. Leadwood, marula, weeping boer-bean on termite mounds and knob-thorn fringe the river course. A granite outcrop next to the river, almost on the road, offers the ideal habitat for klipspringer. A large rock fig twists its light-yellowish roots around big boulders and one gets a good view of this extraordinary tree close up. Down in the riverbed, buffalo and elephant are often sighted. Big impala herds are an indication of good grazing and browsing. Lions and leopards frequent this area.

Before the southern intersection with the S114, the loop towards a lookout on to the **Biyamiti Weir** is not to be missed.

Keep an eye open for the widespread and common bushveld bird species but also try to spot raptors closer to the river or in habitats with trees where they perch. A wide selection of birds associated with water can be expected at the Biyamiti Weir.

Side-striped jackal, S23

Liz Hart

Klipspringer, S23

S25
CROCODILE RIVER ROAD
★★★★

★★★★ ★★★★ ★★★★ ★★★★

- 43 km; dirt road; carrying high traffic volumes; often corrugated; traverses four major ecozones
- Crocodile River

This route runs to the north of the perennial Crocodile River, which forms the southern boundary of the park. It passes through four different landscape types or ecozones and thus offers great variety in vegetation and animal life.

From east to west it briefly meanders through **knob-thorn and marula savanna** rich in grazing species, then through a **thicket** section with clay soils dominated by Delagoa thorn where the short grass is sweet and seasonal pans are surrounded by magic guarri. The next landscape is rather dull and flat with dense **thorn thickets** of low sickle-bush. Before the S119 turn-off, the sickle-bush gives way to **mixed bushwillow woodlands** until it merges with the S114 on its western extremity.

Game viewing is usually good all along this road. Animals from the interior cross it to drink from the Crocodile River, especially during the dry season. Elephants, giraffe and buffalo sightings are to be expected. Lion often follow buffalo herds. Look out for leopard in the huge riverine trees where the road runs close to the river. White rhino sightings are to be expected where grazing, water and shelter are available in both the eastern and western sections of the route. Browsers such as giraffe, kudu and impala can be found throughout. Look out for the tiny and entertaining **dwarf mongoose** in the vicinity of termite mounds, which they often use as their castles.

The variety of ecozones contributes to a good birding experience. Look out for the widespread and common bushveld species, but also keep an eye open for raptors closer to the river or in habitats with good trees for perching.

Impalas and flowering knob-thorn trees, S25

Leopard in tree, S25

★★★
S26
BUME ROAD

★★ ★★★ ★★★ ★★

🛣 23 km; dirt road; often corrugated; traverses two major ecozones

The Bume Road is one of the quiet backroads that offers peaceful bird- and game-watching away from the crowds.

From the south the Bume Road initially follows the seasonal **Bume River** fringed by **riverine vegetation**. The surrounding landscape away from the river is typical **thorn thicket** that gradually changes to **bushwillow vegetation** as the road winds westwards towards the S114. The terrain becomes **slightly undulating** with higher ground and lower areas. Notice that the trees on higher ground tend to be broadleafed and deciduous. The bigger trees are mostly marula, with red bushwillow amongst them. Notice that thorn trees (e.g. knob-thorn) mainly occur in the low-lying areas. Look out for stands of magic guarri, apple-leaf trees and torchwoods.

The abundant medium-sized multi-stemmed shrubs (or small trees) are mostly **red bushwillow** of the *Combretum* family. They are easily recognisable when they bear fruit. The **four-winged pods** are brilliant reddish-brown with a slight satin sheen when they ripen in late summer and autumn.

Bushwillow woodland offers ideal food for browsers and small antelope such as duiker that feed on the young and fallen leaves. Kudu, giraffe and elephant browse the mature green leaves. Grazing is limited but feeders with a mixed diet such as impala do well. Predators are around, but not easily seen.

Look out for **parrots feeding on bushwillow seeds**. The Bume River weir offers good birding in the wet season.

Unfortunately the road is often corrugated in the dry season when road grading is not possible. On the other hand, since it is one of the less travelled backroads, it offers peaceful game viewing and birding away from the crowds.

★★★★
S27
HIPPO POOLS ROAD

★★★★ ★★★★ ★★★ ★★★★

🛣 3 km; dirt road; often corrugated; traverses two major ecozones

The road off the eastern section of the S25 leads to the banks of the Crocodile River. Like all Lowveld rivers, the Crocodile River is also prone to flooding after exceptional rain in its catchment area. One such flood washed away most of the rocks on the hill above the pools that contained remnants of San paintings. Recently the original deep hippo pool was also washed away, and sandbanks formed in its place, but hippo can still be seen from a distance.

Hippos spend their days with their families either partly submerged in deep permanent pools in perennial rivers or basking in the sun on adjacent sandbanks. Towards evening they leave the pod to find grazing on land. **Hippos kill more people in Africa than any other animal.** They may appear slow, but don't be fooled, they can move with surprising agility. Most deaths occur when an intruder surprises the giant on its way back to the water.

A pod consists of a dominant male with a harem of females and young. Other males may be around but are usually killed or ousted by the dominant bull. The hippo is one of the largest land mammals (weighing 2 000–3 000 kg), third only to the elephant and white rhino – the skin alone can weigh up to half a ton. With its thick and almost hairless skin, it has a problem getting rid of heat. To cool off, it spends about 16 hours a day underwater or covered in mud. It secretes an oily red substance from its skin – not to be mistaken for blood. The red substance moistens the skin, acts as a natural sunblock, and may also provide protection against germs or act as a healing agent. An adult hippo can hold its breath underwater for up to six minutes and typically walks along the bottom of a river rather than swims. A baby hippo holds its breath for only about 30 seconds – but it can suckle underwater by closing its ears and nostrils.

African elephants, S27

Southern ground hornbills, S27

S28
NHLOWA ROAD
★★★★

★★★★ ★★★★★ ★★★★★ ★★★

- 24 km; narrow dirt road; good after grading; corrugated in the dry season; traverses one major ecozone
- Ntandanyathi Bird Hide

The S28 is an extremely popular route as an alternative to the central section of the H4-2. Game viewing and birding are excellent.

The entire route passes through a landscape of **open plains of knob-thorn and marula savanna** with sweet grazing. In the distance, to the east, the **Lebombo Mountains** are visible. Interspersed in the open grassland are low shrubs. Magnificent **leadwood** trees are dotted about and indicate good grazing. Radiocarbon dating has shown that a leadwood can live up to 1 040 years. Due to their very hard and tough wood, these giants can withstand drought and fires. Their skeletons can remain standing for years after the tree has died. Examine the canopy shapes to distinguish between leadwood, marula and knob-thorn. Notice the distinctively coarse, **granulated bark** of the leadwood and, if you happen to visit between November and March, you may see the yellowish **cream-coloured flowers** or the **four-winged seedpods** once the flowers have disappeared. Because the **hard wood** is highly resistant to decay, dead tree trunks are often used in buildings. Notice their use in many of the buildings in the rest camps.

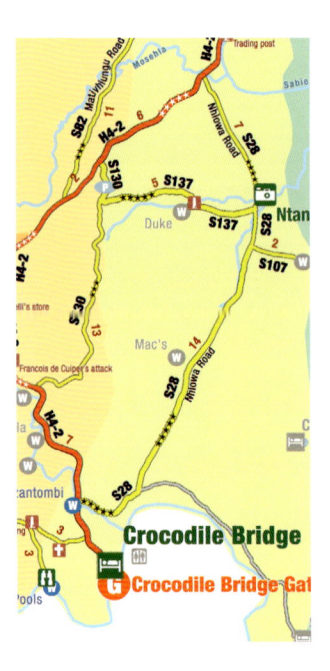

The open nature of the savanna offers extremely good visibility and is suitable habitat for scarce cheetah; here, they have enough space to run down their prey – impala, duiker and steenbok.

The occasional herd of elephant may be encountered anywhere along the S28, but more common are the lone bulls, which stand out in the open landscape. White rhino and buffalo herds are often seen, as well as lion and hyena that tend to follow buffalo herds. Look out for black-backed jackal in the vicinity of leadwood trees. The four-winged seedpods attract many rodents, which in turn are food for jackal.

Birding is particularly good for terrestrial species and there is a better than average chance of seeing ostrich, bustard, francolin and spurfowl.

Lion cubs, S28

S29
MLONDOZI ROAD

★★★★ ★★★★ ★★★ ★★

18 km; narrow dirt road; becomes slippery when wet; traverses one major ecozone

The open woodland on vast grassy plains offers excellent visibility.

The S29 branches off the H10 soon after the Sabie River bridge. The road winds through sweet grassland dotted with knob-thorn and the occasional marula and leadwood in the distance. It is the favoured habitat for white rhino, elephant, buffalo, zebra, blue wildebeest, steenbok and warthog. Stands of magic guarri indicate **clay depressions** where water gathers in summer to form muddy wallows. Low **termite mounds** are scattered over the plains.

Look out for hornbills, rollers and shrikes. There is also a good probability of seeing terrestrial birds such as ostrich, bustard, francolin and spurfowl.

Soon after the intersection with the S122, the **Muntshe Hill** looms and the S68 turns off to the picnic spot overlooking the dam.

Grey go-away-bird, S29

S30 SALITJIE ROAD

★★★★

★★★★ ★★★★ ★★★★ ★★★★★

- 18 km; narrow dirt road; traverses two major ecozones
- This road is a celebration of magnificent trees – tamboti, giant specimens of sycamore fig, Natal mahogany and jackalberry, marula, knob-thorn, leadwood, weeping boer-bean and silver cluster-leaf

The Salitjie Road is one of the best dirt-road drives in the southern part of the park. The probability of finding predators is extremely good. The trees and the river views are magnificent. The road is well worth taking.

At the northern end the Salitjie Road turns off the H12 immediately to the north of the bridge. In the south the S30 joins the S128.

From the H12, the road initially passes through **thorn thicket** and runs parallel to the northern bank of the Sabie River. Look out for klipspringer on the granite boulders and scan the riverbed for game. Predators such as lion or wild dog are often seen crossing the wide expanse of sand towards the water.

The northern section of the S30 is magical. **Several loops** lead from the main road, taking you closer to the riverbank. Take each one of them as they are all different. The anticipation of finding something special and unexpected around the corner is exhilarating.

The first loop on the northern section leads into a dense stand of huge **Natal mahogany trees**. Look out for nyala, which often feed on fallen leaves, fruit or seeds under the dense canopy. This antelope may be confused with the bushbuck. It looks similar, relies on similar food sources and also inhabits dense woodland and thickets along water.

One of the other loops leads to a dense stand of high **tamboti trees** with a fine jackalberry specimen amongst them. Notice the bark pattern of the tamboti trees – a good way to distinguish them from other trees. Spend some time here, as there may just be action at the river pool. Look out for drinking impala, crocodile, monkeys and waterbirds.

Another loop leads to an **open view** across the Sabie River** and large sections of the river can be scanned with binoculars. Floods have washed away much of the vegetation. You may see plenty of elephant, buffalo and even otter gambolling in the river.

Yet another loop leads to **giant sausage trees** on the riverbank. When these trees are in flower, monkeys, baboons and antelope enjoy eating the blooms.

Towards the south the landscape changes as the road turns away from the Sabie River and becomes more park-like with short, sweet grass. This is typical of **thornveld** on underlying rock foundations of **gabbro**. Here and there are clay depressions where **pans** form after good rains. Stands of magic guarri give an indication of clay soil areas. On hot days wallowers frequent the pans to find relief from the heat and cover their bodies with mud to get rid of parasites. At the seepage lines halfway down slopes, the **silver cluster-leaf** is common, but their leaves are seldom browsed. The dense stands are attractive in their grey attire and add a special ambience to the bush.

This is good **lion country**. The sweet grass attracts herds of grazers. Browsers are attracted by the buffalo-thorn, teak, marula and knob-thorn. Elephant and giraffe can be expected and kudu are prolific. Small antelope such as duiker feed on shoots and fresh leaves of low shrubs. Impala herds are abundant. Look out for cheetah where the landscape opens up.

Marula and leadwood trees are abundant. Scan the tree-tops for bateleur. These eagles are regularly seen in this area and often perch in pairs on dead branches. At the far southern end of the road there is a low bridge over the dry **Mafotini Stream** before the S30 joins up with the S128. Note the fine specimens of jackalberry, weeping boer-bean and sycamore fig on the stream bank.

Birding is good along the entire road. Look out for fish eagle, turaco and flycatcher.

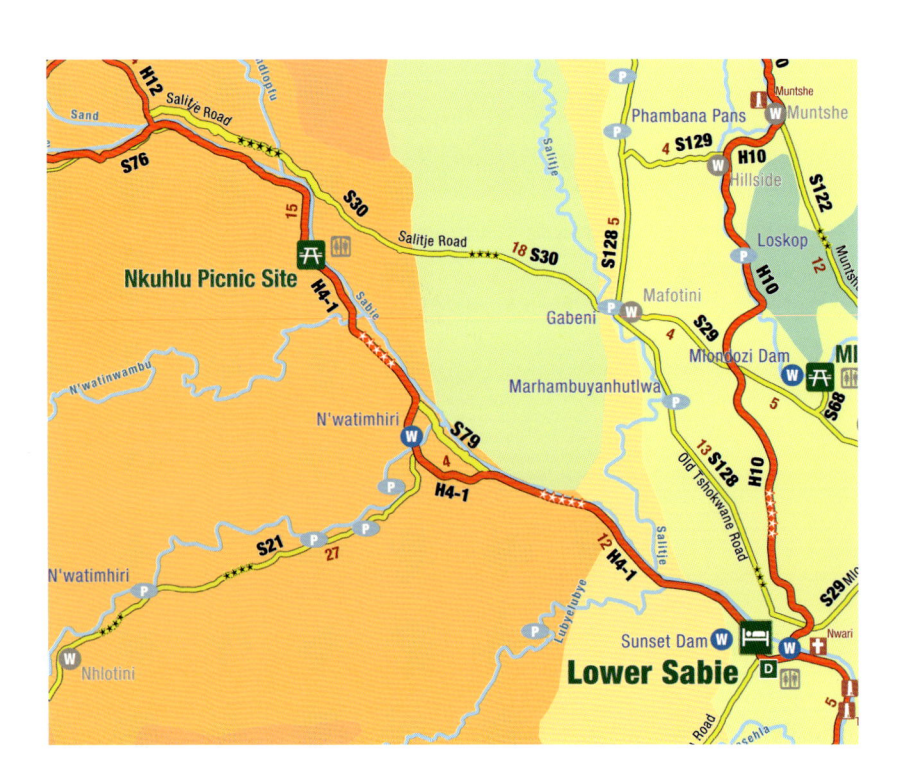

Female leopard and cub, S30

S32
ORPEN DAM LOOP

★★★★

★★★★ ★★★ ★★★★★ ★★★★

- 7 km; dirt road; corrugated sections; traverses one ecozone
- The low causeway over the N'waswitsontso Watercourse; Orpen Dam

If you need a pleasant surprise, drive this scenic dirt road that has extremely good game-viewing potential.

Before the intersection of the H10 with the H1-2, the S32 turns off the H10, leads to the **Orpen Dam** and continues along the **N'waswitsontso watercourse** until it joins the S35. The road passes through fertile **knob-thorn and marula savanna** on basalt soils with sweet grazing and access to permanent water in the Orpen Dam.

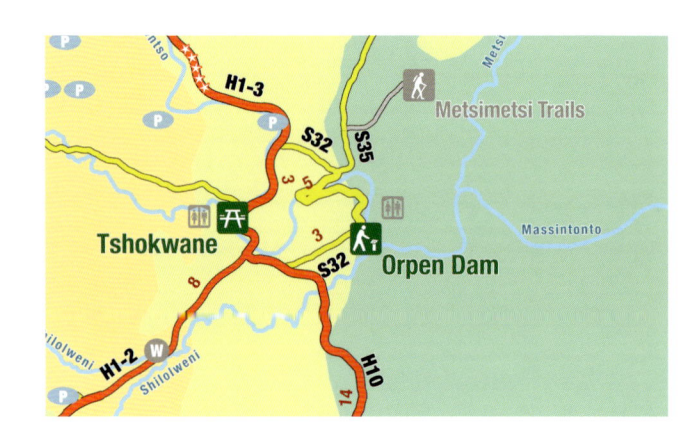

The **Orpen Dam Lookout** is a 'get-out' point worth visiting. A lovely shaded structure offers a fine view over the dam and enough seating for several people to spend a comfortable hour or two scanning the hills beyond for game. Take your picnic basket and binoculars. The views are pleasing and offer generally good visibility.

Expect to see white rhino, waterbuck, kudu, impala, hippo, elephant, giraffe and, if you're lucky, predators.

A variety of bird habitats offer good birding. Bushveld birds are abundant around the lookout and along the rest of the route.

Orpen Dam, S32

★★★

S33
VUTOMI ROAD

★★★ ★★★ ★★★★ ★★★

- 17 km; narrow dirt road; usually in a fair condition; traverses three major ecozones
- Sandstone outcrop

The Vutomi Road offers a welcome link between the H1-3 and the S36.

From the eastern entrance, this scenic road starts off with a small section of **knob-thorn and marula savanna**. Soon it enters a section that leads through **thorn thickets** dominated by many-stemmed false thorn and Delagoa thorn, with magic guarri in clay depressions. Here, the underlying geology is part of **a narrow band of Karoo sediments** that divides the predominantly granite formations of the western half of the park and the predominantly basalt formations of the east.

The road meanders along the course of the seasonal **Ripape River**, which is fringed with **riverine vegetation** – apple-leaf, river thorn, jackalberry and the occasional sausage tree. Elephant are attracted to the thickets along this part of the road, while white rhino prefer the more open parts of the landscape. During the peak rainfall season, when the grass to the east of the park grows too high for short-grass feeders such as blue wildebeest and zebra, these species are attracted to these parts of the park where the grass is shorter and sparser.

You will probably encounter impala but may also see kudu, giraffe, warthog and buffalo. Note the sandstone outcrop east of the **Tinhongana watering point** (usually dry). Rhino middens along the way indicate the presence of quite a number of these giants. At the time of writing the **Vutomi Dam** was broken and empty.

The western section of the Vutomi drive is much drier and passes through typical **granite geology** with vegetation dominated by **bushwillow and silver cluster-leaf**. The open broad-leafed savanna is very pretty but game densities are generally low.

This is one of the better birding routes in the central part of the park. Look out for common bushveld birds but the riverine vegetation also offers suitable habitats for many of the riverine tree species.

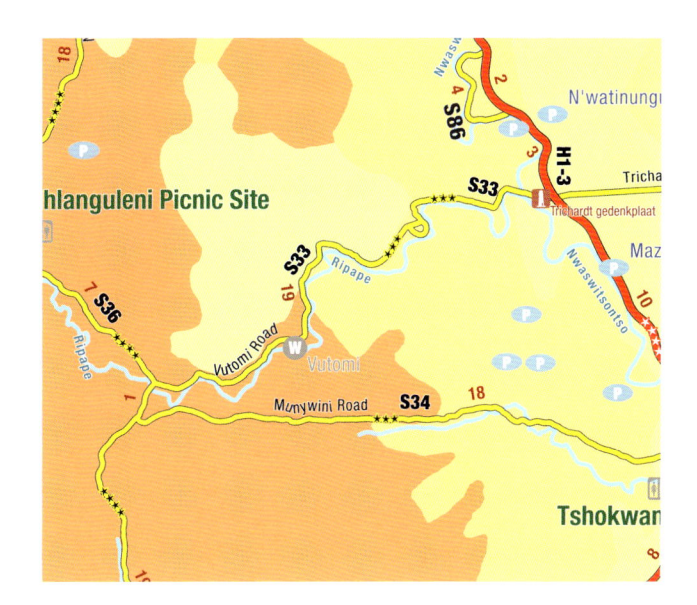

Southern yellow-billed hornbill with prey, S33

S34
MUNYWINI ROAD

★★★

🦁 ★★★   🦌 ★★★   🦅 ★★★   🌳 ★★★

19 km; narrow and intimate dirt road; traverses two major ecozones

The Munywini Road is a link between the H1-3 and the S36.

The eastern part of the road traverses typical **Delagoa thorn thickets** and visibility is somewhat restricted. This is a rather flat landscape where Karoo sediments (Ecca shales) underlie the vegetation. Water does not penetrate the soils easily and **many pans** tend to form. The grass here is generally short and sweet. The road crosses the partly dry **Munywini River course** twice. Look for bachelor buffalo on the stream banks where the vegetation is lusher. This part of the road generally offers good game viewing. Look out for both white and black rhino, as well as giraffe. Lion sightings are often reported.

The vegetation towards the western part changes gradually into **mixed bushwillow woodlands** where the underlying rock is **granite**, the savanna is more open and visibility improves. The grass along the drainage line is extremely palatable and attracts grazers. Kudu, giraffe and elephant can be expected anywhere.

This road may not be as popular as the Vutomi road but has just as much potential. Birding is average and any of the common bushveld species can be expected.

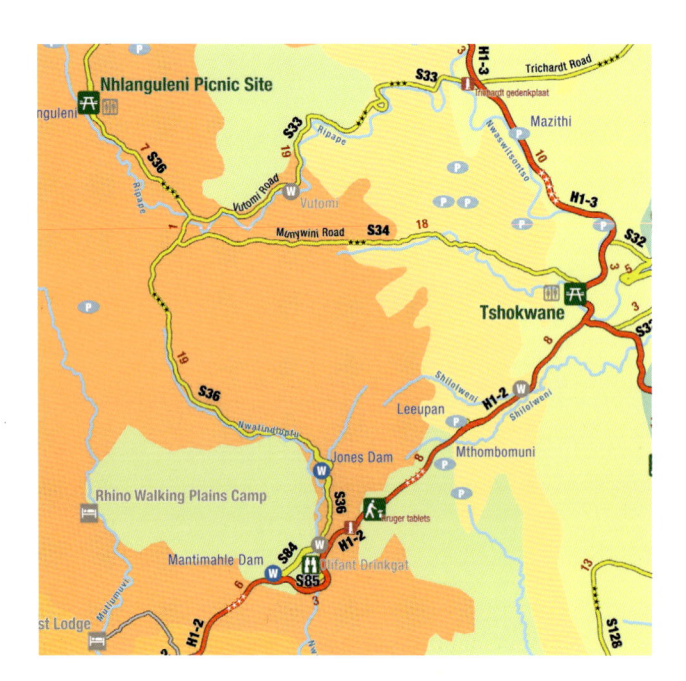

Giant plated lizard, S34 — Phil Muller

African buffalo, S34 — Callum Evans

★★★
S35
LINDANDA ROAD

🦁 🦌 🦅 🌳
★★★ ★★★ ★★★★ ★★★

- 20 km; narrow dirt road; traverses one major ecozone
- Harry Wolhuter Memorial

The S35 is less often travelled, which is a real pity since it traverses beautiful park-like plains where visibility is good. The narrow track is intimate and brings the bush up close.

At the museum in Skukuza, a lion skin and sheath knife are evidence of the true story of one of the early rangers of the park. In 1903, **Harry Wolhuter** was attacked and almost killed by a big male lion that pulled him from his horse while he was on patrol. It dragged him by the shoulder for almost 100 metres into the bush. He managed to take his sheath knife from his belt and stab the animal in the chest. When the mortally wounded lion dropped him, a second lion appeared. Wolhuter's brave dog kept barking at this lion, which distracted it from his master. The rest of the party was able to rescue the injured man and carry him to Komatipoort, which took four days, from where he was taken to Barberton where he recovered after several weeks in hospital. Wolhuter's nickname was **Lindanda**, and this name was later given to the road. The attack took place at the confluence of the **Metsimetsi and Banyini Streams** and the place is clearly signposted.

Duiker, kudu and warthog are around while herds of impala, zebra and blue wildebeest can be expected, especially in summer. Unfortunately animals along this track are not used to vehicles and tend to move away as you get closer.

Towards the southern end of the road **leadwood skeletons** are scattered across a big open plain. It feels quite eerie and one wonders what disaster – perhaps fire or flood – led to their death.

The S38 to the N'wamuriwa Hill is closed. Look out for white rhino on the lower slopes of this hill where they are quite prolific. Look for dry grassland birds.

Plains zebra, S35

S36
NHLANGULENI / MUZANDZENI ROAD

★★★★

🦁 ★★★ 🦌 ★★★ 🦅 ★★★★ 🌳 ★★★

- 48 km; gravel road with corrugated stretches; traverses one major ecozone
- Jones Dam; Nhlanguleni Picnic Site; Shimangwaneni Dam; Muzandzeni Picnic Site

This road has a little bit of everything – dams containing water and others that are dry; well-developed broad-leafed vegetation on the crests of the undulating landscape and thorn trees in the drainage lines; high termite mounds and sandy soils; common grazers, browsers, rare antelope and a sprinkling of predators.

The S36 is the **closest, shortest link** between the Orpen Gate and Skukuza. Two very popular picnic sites ensure that there is enough opportunity along the way to get out and stretch one's legs. The northernmost picnic site is called **Muzandzeni**, which has a watering point for game and offers good views over a marshy depression.

The southern picnic site called **Nhlanguleni** is just north of the **Airforce Dam** (which at the time of writing was broken) in the catchment area of the **Nhlanguleni stream**, which joins the **Ripape tributary** of the **N'waswitsontso** further south. This site also offers views over the surrounding grassland and the **Nhlanguleni Waterhole** in the far distance.

Mixed bushwillow and silver cluster-leaf woodland is predominant in the western parts between the Sand River in the south and the Timbavati River to the north. On the watersheds the soils are generally sandy to sandy-loam with sodium-saturated clay soils in the depressions. This is therefore typical broadleaf country. Visibility is mostly not too good and there are some rather monotonous stretches along this road, which does not mean that the area is devoid of game.

Although **game densities are generally low**, this is home to some of the **rare antelope** in the park. Sable antelope have a patchy distribution in South Africa but the largest natural population is presently in the Kruger National Park. Their distribution is dependent on cover and availability of water. They prefer open woodland, with adjacent wetlands or grassland with medium to high stands of grass. They avoid areas where tree density is high and grass is short and overgrazed.

Cheetah are often sighted towards the southern end of the S36. Elephant can be anywhere. Giraffe favour acacias in the drainage lines. Both of these two species usually browse no more than seven kilometres from a water source. Waterbuck however stay much closer to water – look out for these at **Jones Dam**.

At the northernmost section of the S36 and the far southern section up to Jones Dam the vegetation is slightly different with **sweet grazing and thorn trees** such as knob-thorn, buffalo-thorn, umbrella thorn, tree wisteria and marula. Grazers such as white rhino, buffalo and impala should occur and browsers such as giraffe and kudu are likely to be sighted. It is said to be the preferred habitat for a few scattered herds of roan antelope that occupy the western half of the park. Not many sightings had been reported during reconnaissance for this book in 2015.

The S36 runs along the **major migratory route for wildebeest** and, to a lesser extent, zebra in the lower western central section of the park. What happens is that during the rainy season these grazers prefer the sweet grazing north of the H7 and the **Timbavati River** (Hartebeesfontein Dam and as far up as Red Garten). As the water sources dry up towards autumn and winter, they are driven south. Wildebeest and zebra have to drink regularly; in the south, the perennial Sabie and Sand Rivers, as well as the Nhlanguleni Waterhole and often the Ripape River, can provide a reliable source of water throughout winter. This

Leopard cub, S36 — Dustin van Helsdingen

Sable antelope, S36

attracts the wildebeest and zebra to migrate southwards with the onset of winter.

There are also other year-round water supplies after a good rainy season, such as the pans at Leeupan, Manthimahle and Olifantsdrinkgat. The area around Talamati is one of those grazed during both the summer and winter, and some of the grazers will remain there throughout the year. Although this is a migratory route, the migration is not at all as spectacular as it is in East Africa. It's interesting that more than **80% of all wildebeest and 40% of all zebra** in the park **occur north of the Sabie and south of the Olifants Rivers.**

African elephant stripping bark, S36

African fish eagle fishing, Jones Dam, S36

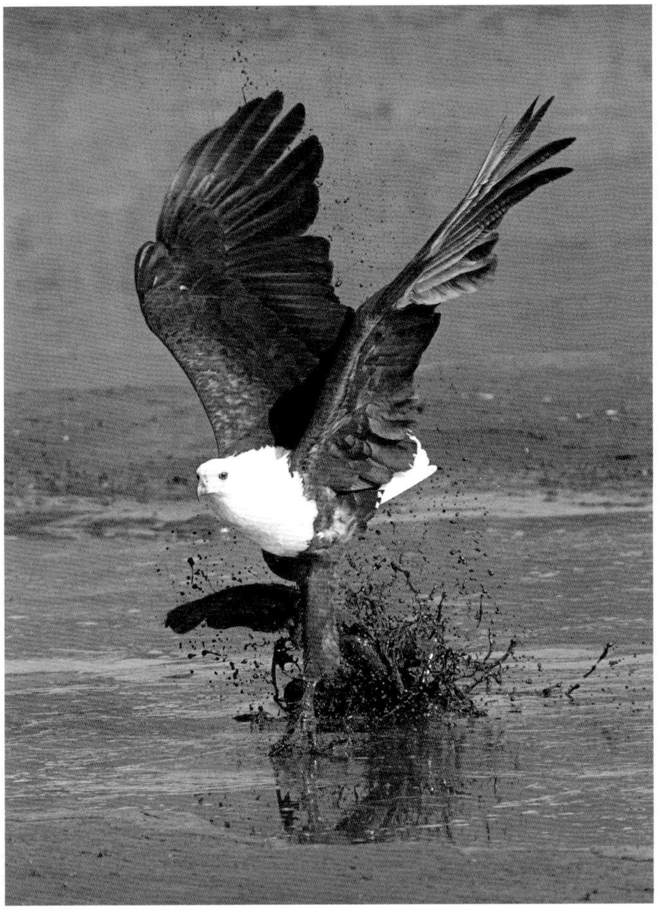

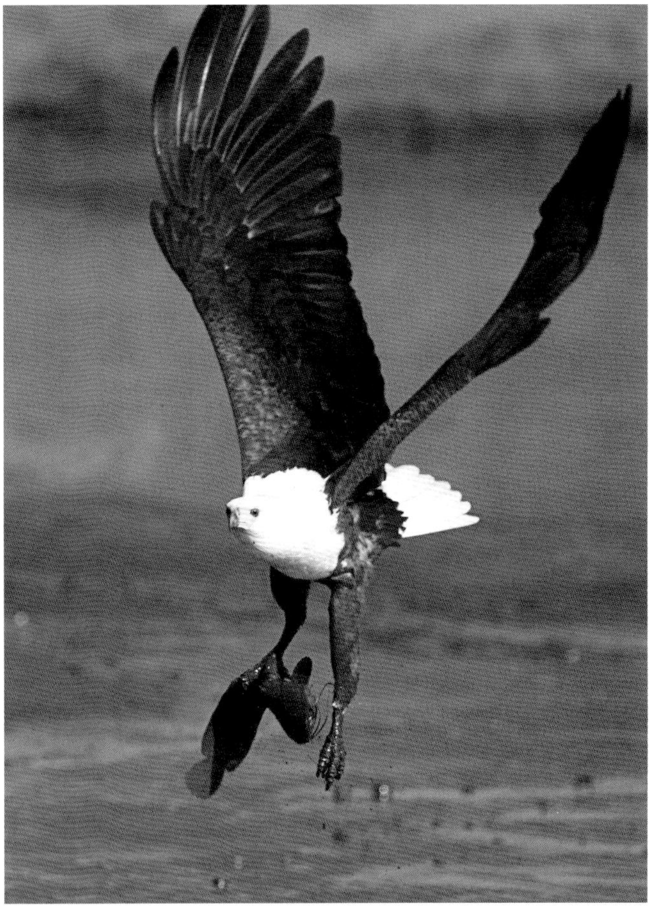

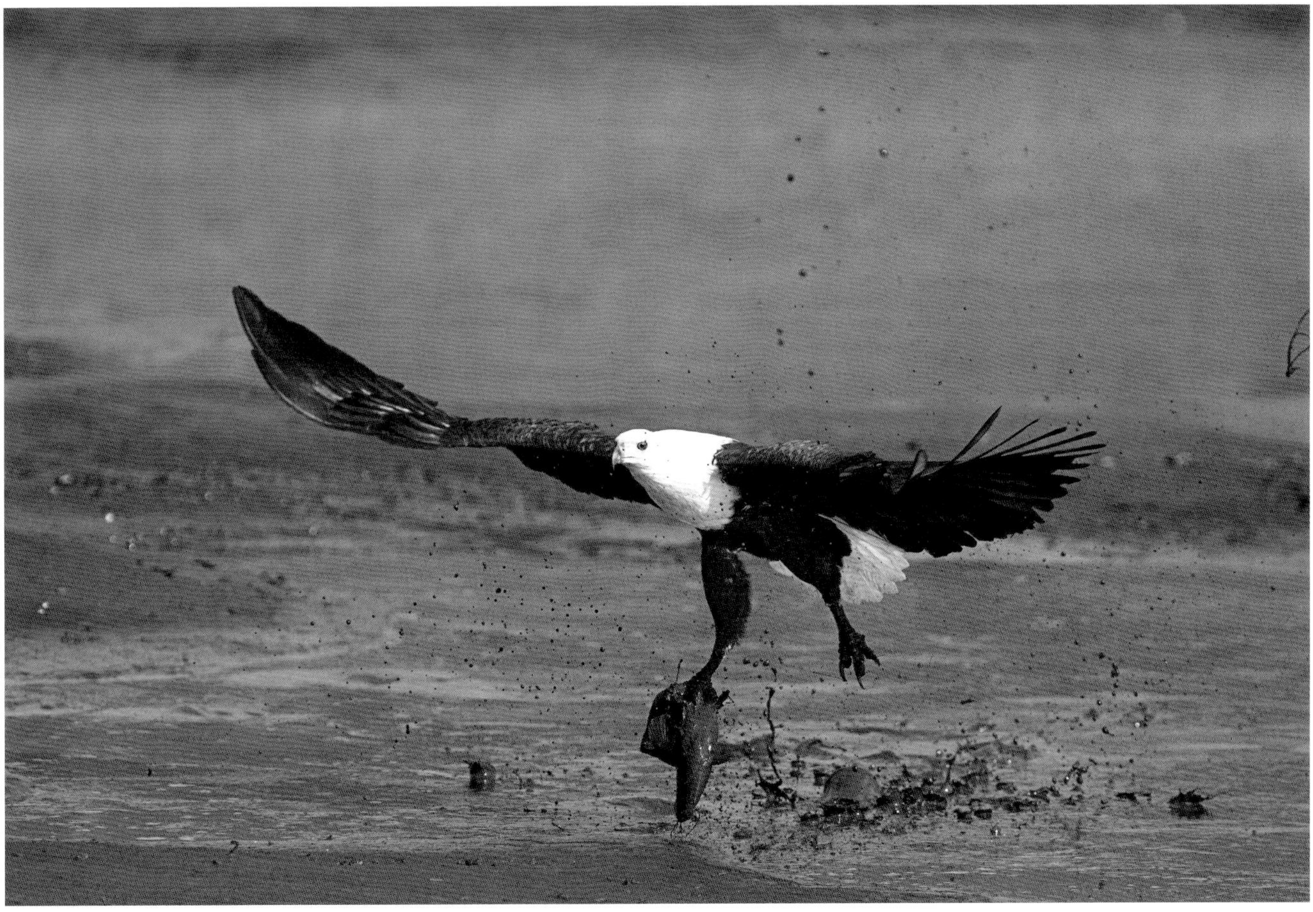

S37 TRICHARDT ROAD

★★★★

★★★ ★★★ ★★★★★ ★★★

- 36 km; narrow dirt road; traverses one major ecozone
- Sweni Hide

Red-billed queleas, S37

The scenic Trichardt road runs more or less parallel to the H1-3 but skirts the Lebombo Mountains. The northern end of this road is the more exciting end and probably deserves a slightly higher rating, but the rest of the road may, at times, be below average for game viewing.

The hotspot is the **Sweni Hide** situated on the banks of the **Sweni River** at the northern extremity of the road. The hide is an extremely popular destination in itself since it is ideal for watching hippo and animals coming down for water. Elephant, giraffe, zebra and blue wildebeest frequent the vicinity of this hide. Baboons are also regularly seen. Note the huge **leadwood tree** just before the entrance to the hide. This is an opportunity to touch one of these giants and to look at its bark and other features to enable you to recognise others from a distance.

Birding from the hide and the low-water bridge over the Sweni **is excellent**. Storks, kingfishers, moorhens, geese, jacanas, herons, ducks and crakes are but a few of the regular visitors.

Another interesting feature on the northern end is the **exposed rock face** of the **Lebombo mountain range** in the vicinity of the Sweni Hide. The Lebombos are composed of **rhyolite**, which is an igneous rock rich in silica. This is a form of lava that originated close to the surface of the magma during volcanic eruptions many aeons ago. The silica content makes the rocks hard and resistant to erosion. The basalt plains also originated from lava, but are more basic in origin, weathering more easily, forming fertile, black, clay soils.

The central plain between the S37 and H1-3 is known as the **Lindanda Section**. In the dry season the entire area along this road is generally dry, with no watering points and therefore almost completely devoid of animals except for the occasional steenbok, a tiny antelope not dependent on drinking water. During the wet season the seasonal **Makongolweni Spruit**, a tributary of the Sweni, provides drinking water for the grazers.

Large bare and brackish areas to the south retain water and minerals, forming **pans during the rainy season**. Look out for warthog here since they are often seen foraging for roots and rhizomes on such brackish flats, or rolling in the mud to get rid of parasites and cool down.

Because more than 80% of all wildebeest and 40% of all zebra in the park occur north of the Sabie and south of the Olifants Rivers, during the **summer** months after good rains these plains may be scattered with wildebeest and zebra as they tend to migrate northwards or southwards during the year in search of better grazing.

The migration starts from the south of Muntshe Hill and continues north to the area of the Sweni River. This usually happens in spring after the first good rains. The instinct to migrate northwards is very strong and the event takes place within a few days. Along the way the animals will drink from seasonal pans or pools in seasonal streams. It seems as if the only cue to start the migration northwards is sufficient rain in the summer grazing area they are heading for. But how do they know?

The movement from the north back to their winter grazing is more gradual and less driven. It appears as if motives for the southward migration are more deeply rooted in their distant past when the animals were dependent on the perennial Sabie River. Sufficient water supplies in the north, in rivers or in any artificial watering points, now keep them back there. Perhaps they are enticed by the better grazing in their winter grazing areas.

Any of the other general game species may seasonally occur, but most, such as impala, giraffe, buffalo, white rhino

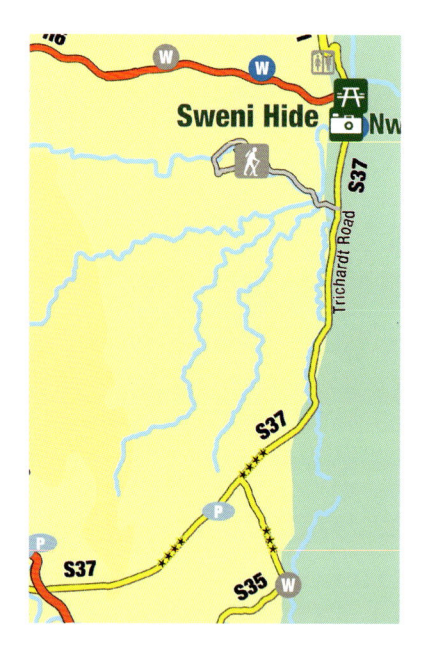

Cheetah and red-billed queleas, S37

Red-billed queleas, S37

Sweni Hide, S37

and elephant, are water-dependent and will move away when the surface water dries out.

Although this can be an exhilarating game drive, it is not rewarding in terms of game during the dry season. The **scenery**, **solitude** and **intimacy** of the bush experience however make taking this road worthwhile. Imagine what it must have been like to travel this route on an ox wagon – perhaps with a sick child, or somebody suffering from malaria?

The road was named after the Voortrekker leader **Louis Trichardt** who trekked along this route as far back as **1838 in search of a trade route to Delagoa Bay** (present-day Maputo) in Mozambique. He was a remarkable man

Yellow-billed stork, Nile crocodile and hippos, Sweni Hide, S37

– courageous and inspiring – with a clear vision of *ubuntu*, forging friendships and bonds with local communities rather than hostility and antagonism. Unfortunately this epic journey that started full of hope ended in tragedy and grief. The Lowveld was rife with **malaria-carrying** mosquitoes, tsetse flies (carriers of **nagana** or sleeping sickness) and ticks (carriers of several diseases e.g. **redwater fever** and others). More than half the party, with most of their livestock, succumbed to some of these diseases.

Trichardt's legacy to the Kruger National Park was his keen observation, his logical interpretation and his **accurate record-keeping in his journals**. This contributed enormously to knowledge of the geography, topography and climate, the grazing potential and animal distributions, the indigenous people and prevalent diseases of that time.

Instead of an ox-wagon track, the park today has an excellent road system, and knowledge of the geography helps to keep this gem safeguarded for the future.

Egyptian goose, Sweni Hide, S37

S39
TIMBAVATI ROAD

★★★★

★★★★★ ★★★★ ★★★★ ★★★

- 60 km; dirt road; good after grading but corrugated in the dry season; traverses six major ecozones
- Timbavati Picnic Site; Piet Grobler Dam; Ratelpan Hide

This is one of the most popular river roads in the park, with a special ambience. It meanders along the non-perennial Timbavati River slightly northeast of Bobbejaankrans and ends in the north a few kilometres from its confluence with the Olifants River.

The **Timbavati Picnic Site** is roughly at the centre of this long route. The northern section is generally more rewarding than the southern half, but all along it remains a route full of surprises and pleasing scenes.

The southern half initially runs through mixed **thornveld on gabbro** where the grass is sweet and attracts grazers. Look out for plains game but also for kudu and impala. Gradually the thornveld changes to **mixed bushwillow savanna** on granite soils and more sour grasses. On the river side of the road, the **riverine vegetation** is well developed with weeping boer-bean, river thorn, jackalberry, buffalo-thorn and date palm. Note the huge apple-leaf trees. On the riverbank the grass tends to be sweeter and game often congregates here. If game is sparse, feast your eyes on the beautiful trees and try to identify some of them. Don't ignore the loop roads that lead to viewing points over the riverbed, as elephant, buffalo and other game are often seen here. Make frequent stops and drive slowly. Leopards are masters of camouflage and are easily overlooked.

After the 2014 floods, huge **sandbanks** accumulated in the riverbed, but there are still some permanent or semi-permanent pools that hold water for a long time after the summer rains have stopped. Elephant often dig for water in the dry season. White rhino middens along the road are testimony to the presence of these endangered giants. Leeubron is a dry waterhole, but the area in the vicinity of this former watering point is popular with all kinds of grazers since the grass around it is sweet and palatable.

The **Timbavati Picnic Site** is a favourite with visitors. A huge baobab extends a welcome at the entrance road that leads to the picnic area further on. Restrooms and braai facilities are available with tables and chairs arranged around a huge jackalberry tree.

The picnic site is situated on the southernmost tip of rugged veld vegetation where soils are stony and the terrain rough. The road continues meandering northwards through **rugged veld** vegetation until the first mopane trees make their appearance. In the rugged veld the underlying geology is basalt with high concentrations of limestone concretions, while the soils are dark-brown, shallow and stony. Because of the basalt, most grasses along this section of the road are sweet and palatable and attract more game than the sour veld along the southern section of the S39. It is however a particularly dry part of the park, often receiving much less than 500 mm rain per year.

The popular **Ratelpan Hide** overlooks the upper reaches of the **Piet Grobler Dam**. At the hide you can leave your vehicle at your own risk and spend a peaceful hour or two watching birds and animals coming down to drink. Crocodile and hippo can usually be seen and water-associated birds abound, especially in the dry season when water is scarce elsewhere.

Although game densities remain low as you travel north, the diversity of species is surprising. Predators seem to be more abundant and you will probably come across lion or even leopard. You are sure to see elephant and impala. Look out for waterbuck near the water. Steenbok may be seen foraging among the low shrubs on the dry side of the road. Zebra and wildebeest favour the open spaces and the brackish depressions.

In the vicinity of **Roodewal**, the vegetation changes and the southernmost mopane vegetation becomes evident. Soon after the **Goedgegund Waterhole** the road turns away from the Timbavati River to join the tarred H1-4.

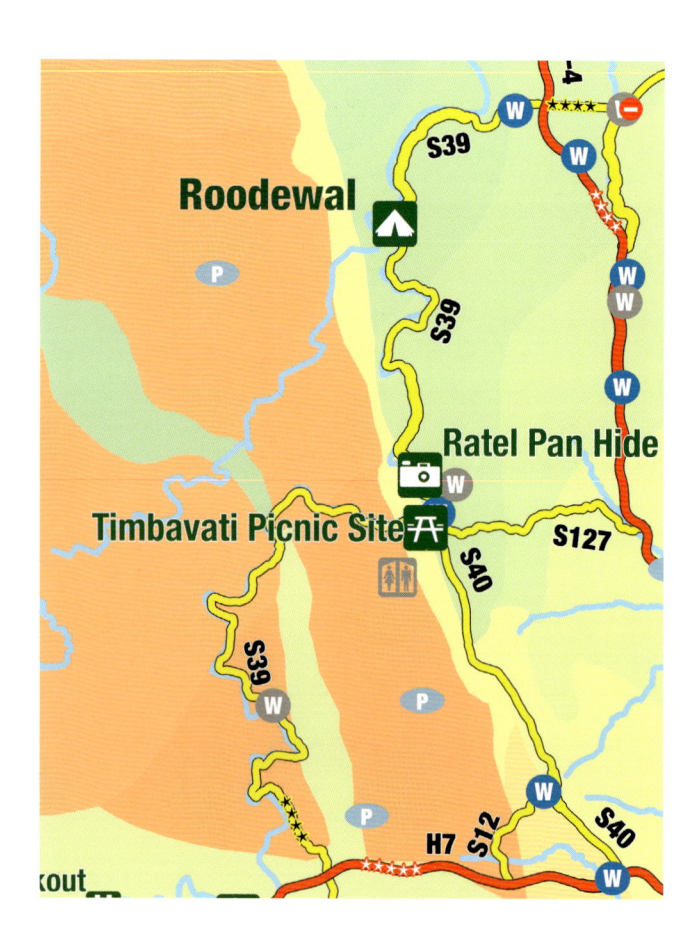

African elephants, S39

African elephant bull, S39

S40
NSEMANI TO TIMBAVATI PICNIC SITE ROAD

★★★

🦁 ★★★★   🦌 ★★★   🦅 ★★★   🌳 ★★★

- 16 km; dirt road; often corrugated; traverses four major ecozones
- Baobab tree; Timbavati Picnic Site

Sighting reports on this road are good and include waterbuck, elephant, white rhino, kudu, giraffe and steenbok, as well as buffalo, wildebeest and zebra. Then, of course, there are the predators that follow the herds – mainly lion and jackal, but also the occasional cheetah.

The road traverses or borders **four ecozones** – all of them with sweet or at least mixed grazing. This results in a diverse selection of habitats in which to find animals. The underlying geology at the southern end of the road is part of a narrow band of Karoo sediments that divides the predominantly granite formations of the western half of the park from the predominantly basalt formations to the east.

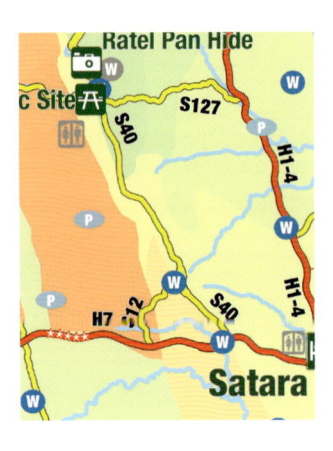

This road carries **heavy traffic** and is often corrugated and dusty, but if you want to picnic at the popular **Timbavati Picnic Site**, you almost have no choice but to follow this road. The other direct access road from the H1-4 tarred road to the picnic site is usually equally corrugated. The best plan is to slow down, find animals to watch and take the drive at a leisurely pace.

After the intersection with the S39 the road passes a huge **baobab tree** and ends at the Timbavati Picnic Site. Cold drinks can be purchased and gas barbeques hired. The picnic tables and chairs are arranged under big, shady trees overlooking the bed of the dry **Timbavati River**. Begging starlings and hornbills welcome visitors but should not be fed. The same applies to a group of bushbuck and the occasional duiker. These have also become habituated to people and started begging.

Large pride of lions, S40

Elmar Venter

Greater kudu, S40

S41
GUDZANI ROAD

★★★★★

🦁	🦌	🦅	🌳
★★★★★	★★★★	★★★★★	★★★★

- 29 km; dirt road; usually in good condition; traverses two major ecozones
- Gudzani Dam, S90 and S41 intersection

The entire S41 is a pleasant and scenic road for a game drive. The sweet grassveld in the knobthorn and marula savanna attracts grazers and browsers alike – many impala herds as well as zebra, wildebeest and kudu. The road roughly follows the Gudzani watercourse all the way from the north until it joins the N'wanetsi River close to the N'wanetsi Picnic Site.

The road leaves the S90 at the **Gudzani Waterhole**. Waterbuck are usually found in the swampy area close to the waterhole. Giraffe, white rhino, buffalo, zebra, wildebeest and impala graze and browse in the area and lion sightings are regularly reported here.

Quite interesting is that **badgers** are sometimes seen foraging in close proximity to the road. The reason is probably not that there are more badgers, but rather that the visibility is better than elsewhere. Badgers are relatively small animals and not easily noticed. They feed mainly on rodents, insects, snakes, lizards and honey. These tough little mammals are always on the move, sniffing and digging in search of food. They are however mainly nocturnal but are sometimes active during the day.

Another good sighting would be to come across the **ground hornbills** that are often encountered on this road. These huge terrestrial birds with their booming call, conspicuous red throats and faces, and pitch-black bodies are a threatened species and very special. They are omnivorous and feed on tortoises, snakes, insects, berries and fruit. They use very large holes in trees to breed, but unlike other hornbill species, they do not seal up the hole with mud while in the nest.

Towards the middle, the S41 gets more scenic. The crossing over the Gudzani stream is pretty and water is usually present. Stands of **magic guarri** indicate brackish depressions and these attract herds of impala and warthog. Look out for **oxpeckers** on animals. Drive up slowly and watch. These quaint little birds feed on ticks that pester giraffes, buffalo and antelope. They climb all over them with remarkable agility, their very short legs and sharp claws helping them to hold on to the animals while they prop themselves against their hosts with stiff tail feathers. Using their laterally flattened bills they shear ticks from the hides in scissor movements. Oxpeckers are well tolerated by their hosts even when several birds work simultaneously about their heads, probing into ears, nostrils and around eyes. The birds used to be plentiful and widely distributed but since the effective use of pesticides to combat ticks on cattle, their food source has diminished. They are now threatened and almost exclusively restricted to game reserves, especially the Kruger National Park.

The Gudzani River is dammed a few kilometres downstream and the huge **Gudzani Dam** offers a permanent water supply for the large numbers of game in the area. Look out for fish eagles, herons, geese and other waterbirds. The dam also hosts a healthy pod of hippos and a good number of crocodile. Waterbuck are particularly plentiful around this dam – these antelope are always seen in close proximity to water.

South of the intersection with the S100, the road **crosses the Gudzani** again and runs parallel with it for a while until it joins the **N'wanetsi River** on its way to Mozambique. The low-water bridge serves as a weir and a big permanent pool usually houses some hippo. Look out for the date palms and the river thorn on the banks.

Close to the southern end of the S41, the road crosses the **Shishangeni Stream**. Sometimes a semi-permanent pool forms and little fish and water organisms are trapped there. Check for kingfishers on the perches around the pool. Birds that rely on water organisms for their food are extremely opportunistic. If you spot one bird here, stop and see if there are others around. It is interesting to watch different species of heron, stork, goose, kingfisher and hamerkop all utilising the food supply offered by a small drying-up pool, each one having a different feeding method and thus not directly competing with each other.

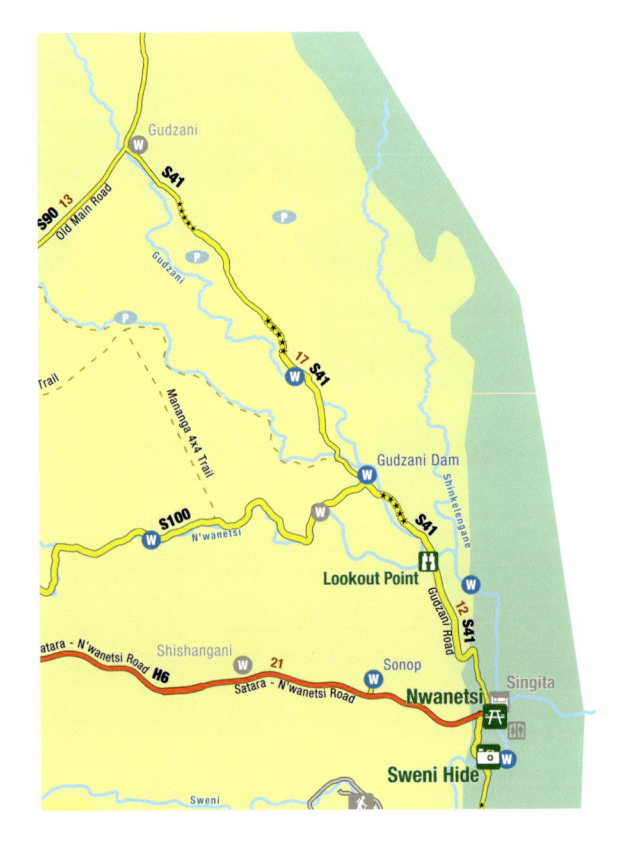

Waterbuck with calf, S41

S42
LAKE PANIC BIRD HIDE AND INDIGENOUS NURSERY

★★★★★

🦁 ★★★   🦌 ★★★   🦅 ★★★★★   🌳 ★★★★

- 4 km; narrow dirt road; traverses two major ecozones
- Lake Panic and the hide; indigenous nursery

Lake Panic is an emergency reservoir for the water supply to the Skukuza Camp. In times of severe drought the park staff involved with water supply used to say there was no need to panic since this dam still had enough water, hence the name Lake Panic.

Hidden within thorn thickets and riverine bush, Lake Panic is like a sparkling jewel. The **hide** overlooking the dam has become popular for both birders and photographers. It is easy to spend the entire morning sitting in the hide, watching and marvelling at the antics of the nesting herons, weavers, diving kingfishers, jacanas, crakes, cormorants, darters and grebes. In the water below the hide huge **barbel (catfish)** lazily linger while the resident **crocodiles** snoop around. On the opposite bank, more crocodiles may be basking in the sun, changing their position only now and again, soaking up sun energy for the day. The dam is deep enough for **hippo** and these can be seen taking it easy in their waterbed in the distance. For the shy **bushbuck** it is the ideal drinking place with lots of bush cover allowing them to approach unseen. Even **leopard** visit regularly for a drink. The hours simply fly by when watching the theatre of the bush. A visit to this place is not to be missed.

From the turn-off to the bird hide, the road continues past the Skukuza Golf Course to the **Skukuza Indigenous Nursery**. This is another magic place for birders. A wooden walkway was built to meander through the woodland and reedbeds around the nursery. This is also the place to do your shopping for indigenous shrubs and trees to plant back home in your own indigenous garden.

African jacana, Lake Panic

African darter with fish, Lake Panic

S44
OLIFANTS MOUNTAIN ROAD

★★★

🦁 ★★   🦌 ★★   🦅 ★★★★   🌳 ★★★★★

- 14 km; dirt road; rough and stony; traverses two major ecozones
- Splendid views over the Olifants River valley from the top of the hill

No other road in the park can quite match the scenic splendour and magnificent views of the S44. But there is a downside too. Sedan vehicles may find the road rough on their suspension and should take it very slowly.

The narrow and stony road winds its way along the rocky hill above the Olifants Camp until it reaches the lookout over the **Olifants River** far below. Far away to the south, the rugged veld of the **Bangu Flats** is visible. To the east, the **Letaba River** joins the Olifants River before it cleaves its way through the Lebombo range. Elephants can often be seen making their way towards the water, while kudu and other antelope linger close to the river. All in all, magical views.

The vegetation along the road is varied and exciting – on the mid-slope there are the cluster-leaf trees and shrubs with their purple pods, the abundant knob-thorns, the russet bushwillows with their winged fruits and, finally, the stately white syringa and candelabra trees on the crest. Down in the valley, fringing the river, are clearly distinguishable sycamore figs, leadwoods and fever trees.

The bird life is abundant and exciting. Look out for the cliff chat on the rocky outcrops along the road.

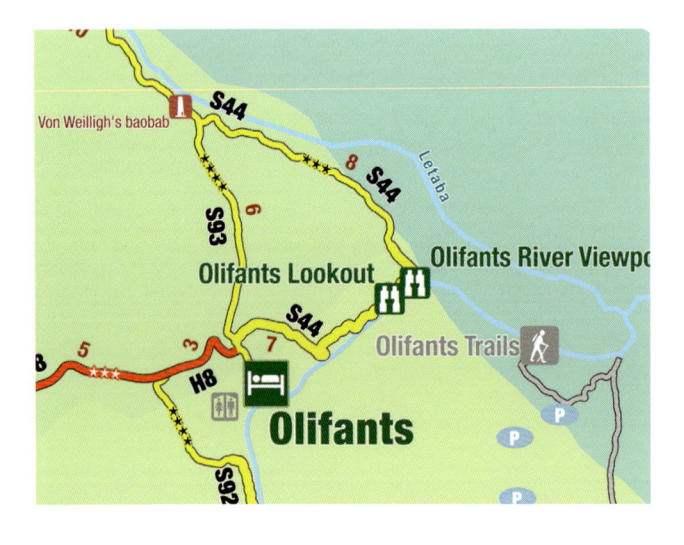

Olifants River, S44

★★★
S46
LOWER LETABA RIVER ROAD

★★   ★★   ★★★★   ★★★

- 21 km; dirt road; corrugated in the dry season; traverses one major ecozone
- Views over the Letaba River

The S46 leaves the tarred H1-5 and makes a loop along the Letaba River. The first section (south) is not very exciting, but as the road nears the Letaba River there may be increased game activity.

The river road along the Letaba should be rewarding, but it is often extremely slow, not revealing much of the animal life one would expect here. Nevertheless, pleasant surprises may await those who travel slowly and are willing to take their time.

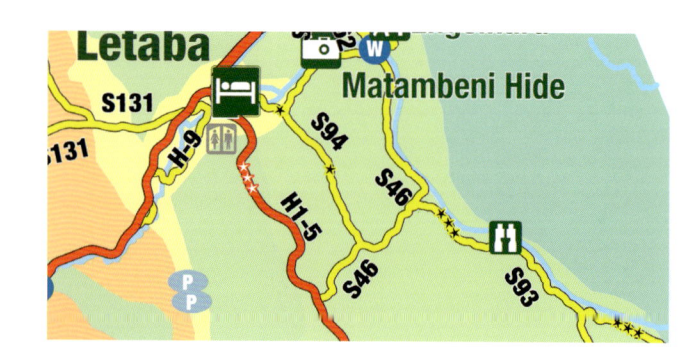

Floods in 2014 caused havoc in the river, washing away trees and piling up new **sandbanks**. Some of the familiar pools disappeared while new ones formed elsewhere. Reeds took over parts of the riverbank, spoiling the once good visibility over the river.

Look out for hippo, buffalo and elephant in the riverbed. Kudu and giraffe may be found browsing the riverine vegetation. Impala are the good old faithfuls. Lion, hyena and leopard may be skulking around. Baboons and monkeys frequent the riverbanks.

Southern yellow-billed hornbill at nesting hole, S46

★★★
S47
MINGERHOUT DAM LOOP

★★★ ★★★ ★★★★ ★★★★

29 km; dirt road; traverses four major ecozones

Letaba River

In mopane veld, the best drives are those that follow a river course. Not only are these roads particularly scenic because of the variety of trees along the river, but also because more animals, and especially predators, may be encountered.

Bushbuck and nyala occur on the riverbanks, as do baboons and monkeys. Kudu and giraffe are always present. Elephant and buffalo pass the road on their way to water or browse and graze amongst the mopane. Waterbuck often linger in the riverbed while smallish herds of impala browse and graze on the road verges. Look for the smaller antelope, duiker and steenbok. Most predators are opportunists that will use as little energy as possible to pursue their prey. For them, it is energy-effective to intercept prey animals that are on their way to drink.

Game viewing **varies with the season and time of day** and can be very quiet. The best time of the year for river roads is in the **dry season** when temporary pans have dried up and animals are dependent on the permanent water in the river. While the Letaba River does not flow strongly all year round, there is always water in it. Take note of the game paths into the riverbed. Take the lookout loops towards the river for wonderful views. Look for the big apple-leaf trees with their gnarled trunks.

The river road stretches from the H1-6 and ends at the demolished **Mingerhout Dam**. Unfortunately it is not possible to get close to the dam, but the weir and huge expanse of water where it dams the **Letaba River** is visible from the road. Look out for klipspringer on the granite dyke that stretches all the way into the river.

The dam is named after the Afrikaans word for the **matumi tree**. The boulders of the dyke provide the perfect substrate for these trees as they only grow on rocks within or along permanent rivers. The matumi tree is one of the biggest single-trunk trees in southern Africa and can grow up to 20 metres or more in height. The branches tend to grow upwards to form a moderately dense, irregular crown. The leaves also tend to grow upwards like fingers, or the leaves of a pineapple.

The other half of the road passes through three different landscapes before it joins the S131 close to the **strip of sandveld** near the Letaba Camp. In the proximity of the Mingerhout Dam the underlying geology is basalt – the same as in the eastern parts of the road opposite the river vegetation. It then traverses a narrow section of sandveld that acts as a corridor between the eastern basalt soils and the granite soils in the west. See if you can identify the sandveld corridor. Look for a change in vegetation.

The longest stretch of the route runs through **mopane and bushwillow woodland**. Silver cluster-leaf is found along seepage lines and knob-thorns are dotted in between. The mixed grass is well grazed by buffalo, zebra, wildebeest and impala. Look out for big elephant bulls and their companions.

Birdlife is quite plentiful all along the route. Look out for spurfowl, hornbills (especially the grey hornbill), babblers and sandgrouse.

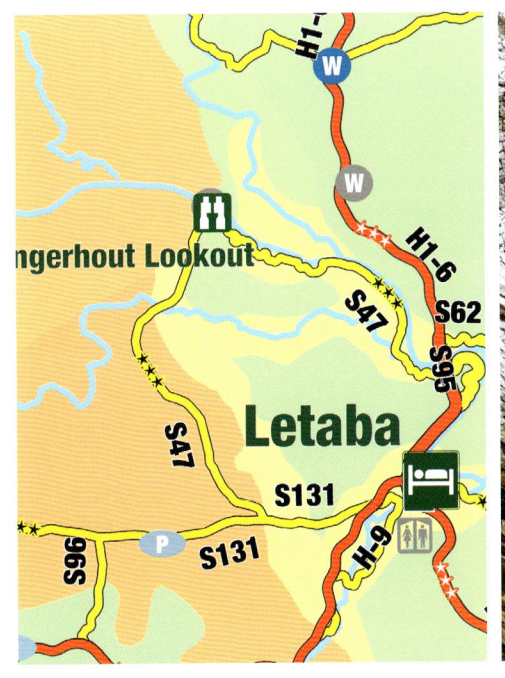

Woodland kingfisher at nesting hole, S46

Isak Pretorius

★★★
S48
TSENDZE LOOP

★★★ ★★ ★★★ ★★★★

🌀 17 km; dirt road; traverses two major ecozones

🚩 Tsendze Riverbed

The Tsendze Loop is popular not necessarily for its abundance of wildlife, but rather for its special ambience and scenic beauty.

The intimate gravel road meanders along the riverine vegetation on the banks of this seasonal river that eventually drains into the perennial Letaba River in the south. To the east of the road, scrub mopane is well developed but rather monotonous. The underlying basalt geology yields clay soils. During the rainy season pans develop in the depressions and attract impala and zebra.

A very special sighting would be the small **Sharpe's grysbok**. The reasonably thick bush habitat along this road is ideal habitat for them. The grysbok differs from the steenbok in that it has a grizzled appearance, but it has the same reddish-brown base colour. It is usually solitary; the male has straight, short horns while the female is hornless.

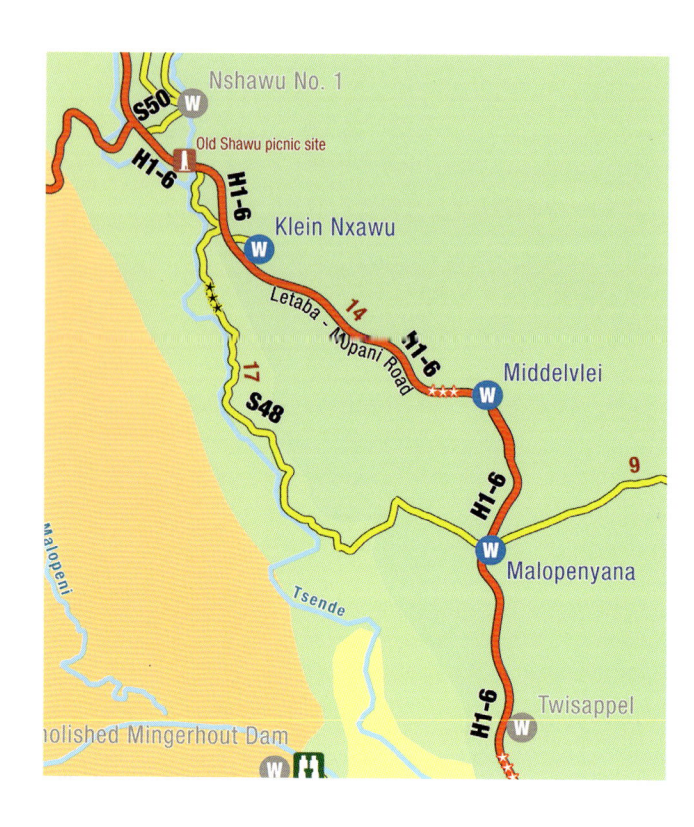

Red-billed oxpecker on buffalo, S48

★★★

S49
MOOIPLAAS LOOP ROAD

★★ ★★★ ★★★★ ★★★

- 11 km; dirt road; traverses one major ecozone
- Mooiplaas Wetland

The Mooiplaas drainage line that eventually spills into the Tsendze River is a good example of the marshy areas that form in flat landscapes located on basalt.

Mooiplaas means 'beautiful place' in Afrikaans. This is certainly what Mooiplaas is – a beautiful place in a sea of mopane. It is almost a shock when the mopane shrub suddenly gives way to open grassland, reminiscent of the Serengeti Plains though very much smaller. Towards one end is a typical concrete dam, and in summer there is a lovely little pan right next to the road.

The **atmosphere** is amazing when one arrives here early on a misty morning. There are always zebra and impala loitering. This is excellent waterbuck and reedbuck habitat. Serval cats are mainly nocturnal but may still be around hunting for rodents in the marsh early in the morning. It is exciting to scan the flats for the yellow tell-tale twitch of their ears amongst the grass. Visibility is good and **predators often lurk**.

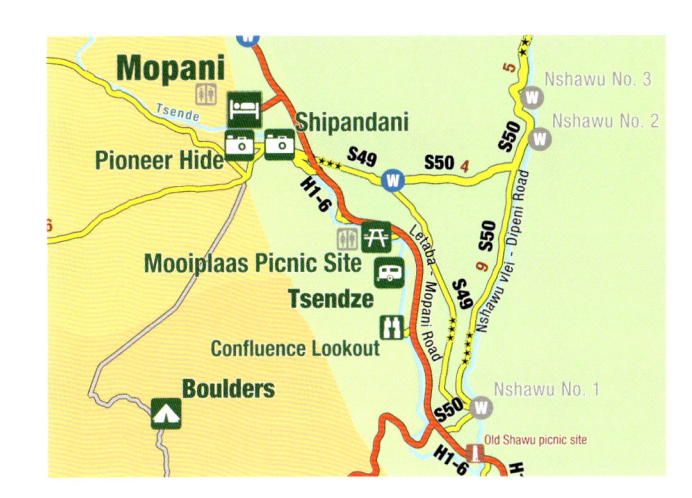

As in most marshes, birding is good. Open water may reveal herons, storks, geese or any other waterbird. On the exposed soil patches close to the dam, lapwings are usually found. Look for bustards as you leave the plain and enter the mopane shrub again.

The entire area east of the H1-6 is sweet veld on basalt soils, and therefore fertile and rich in minerals.

African buffalo, S49.

S50 PART 1
DIPENI ROAD SOUTH OF GROOTVLEI

★★★

★★★ ★★★ ★★★★ ★★★

- 32 km; dirt road; traverses one major ecozone
- Nshawu drainage line; Grootvlei Dam

The S50 is an amazing road that is full of surprises. As it is such a long and varying road, the information is given in two parts. This part deals with the road south of the Grootvlei Dam.

Martial eagle, S50 — Bruce Crossey

Permanent watering places along the eastern section of the park are generally sparse. The great distance between the Shingwedzi and Letaba Rivers makes the **Grootvlei Dam** an important **halfway water source**, especially during the dry season. For visitors staying at Mopani Camp it is usually worth the long drive as the dam attracts huge herds of buffalo and elephant. Waterbuck as well as impala and zebra are often seen. Hippo and crocodile are present and kudu come down to drink. Birding is good. Expect to see swallows, doves, larks, thick-knees and herons. **Easy access to good viewpoints** makes it a pleasure to spend time just watching and enjoying the solitude and the sounds of the bush.

The road runs parallel to the eastern border of the park and the last outlying hills of the Lebombo Mountains. **Shibavantsengele** (489 m) is one of the last high hills and a narrow, short 1.4 km road leads to the Shibavantsengele **Lookout**. The **Shilowa Hill** (382 m) to the south lies on the Tropic of Capricorn.

Southwards, the road follows the **Nshawu drainage line** that eventually spills into the Tsendze River. In summer, after the first rains, water from the foothills of the Lebombo and surrounding plains drains into the Nshawu system to form various **wetland areas** along the way. The most extensive marsh is near the S143 turn-off. Then follows a big pan (broken dam) and several other smaller marshes and pans. Eventually the Nshawu stream joins the **Tsendze River**. The road along the Nshawu drainage line is a welcome change after traversing featureless mopane veld. Big apple-leaf trees and others to the east of the road indicate the marshy nature of the substrate. A baobab has established itself here but is still young – it is only a couple of hundred years old.

Several **loop roads** lead closer to the marsh. Expect to see elephant and perhaps buffalo. Reedbuck sightings are also often reported and there may even be a sprinkling of tsessebe. Steenbok are common and usually seen in the drier mopane veld.

Birding is good around the marsh and several special species may be sighted here. Pratincole are reported to breed here. This is one of the few places in the park where the Kittlitz's plover occurs and it is also a good place to see quailfinch. Look out for rufous-winged cisticola in the reed beds. Among the commonly occurring species, magpie shrikes are plentiful along this part of the road. Good grassland birding can be enjoyed at Nshawu No. 1.

★★★★

S50
PART 2
DIPENI ROAD NORTH OF GROOTVLEI

★★★★ ★★★ ★★★★★ ★★★

- 36 km; dirt road; usually in a reasonable condition but dusty; traverses two major ecozones
- Shingwedzi River frontage; Grootvlei Dam

The S50 is a particularly long road and is an alternative route to the tarred road between Shingwedzi and Mopani Camp in the south.

Most people staying at Shingwedzi Camp do this game drive only up to the Grootvlei Dam and back, and this description only deals with the northern section.

From the **Shingwedzi Camp** the road closely follows the river until it enters Mozambique at the **Dipeni Outpost**. Since the entire Shingwedzi River is prone to regular **flooding**, the riverbed is constantly changing. Pools that seem permanent this year may be displaced to another location by next year. The same applies to sandbanks. Huge trees have been washed away. Overhanging trees and undergrowth on the riverbank that used to block the river view have suddenly gone – as has the wall that formed the **Kanniedood Dam**. River reeds are washed away during floods but there is quick regrowth because their rhizomes are well established in the riverbed. Changes are a part of natural cycles and so are floods.

The road meanders through **climax riverine vegetation**. Huge trees are part of the Riverine Community – mainly jackalberry, nyala tree, apple-leaf, river thorn, sycamore fig, leadwood, huge tree mopane and umbrella thorn.

Extensive **floodplains** exist along the entire catchment area of this major river of the north. The rich **alluvial soils** that are deposited stimulate new growth and development. Notice how the vegetation on the floodplains differs from the rest. Floodplains have their own specific ecology. The same ecology is evident on the Luvuvhu floodplains. Look out for the typical **fever-berry croton** (heart-shaped leaves) and **narrow-leaved mustard tree**.

The road is not only scenic but game is relatively abundant. Birding is particularly good along this route. A **bird hide** on the banks of the Shingwedzi offers good views over the water. Birds usually found near water are abundant. Hippo and crocodile can be seen in the deeper pools or basking on the banks; reeds attract old buffalo and elephant bulls and a great variety of birds. Impala are abundant but zebra less so; bushbuck and nyala are in competition for the same food source and both of these occur close to the river. Look for steenbok in the drier mopane veld; the rare and shy Sharpe's grysbok may surprise you in thick bush near the river. But best of all is that **leopard** sightings are regularly reported, as are **lion** encounters. Don't forget to scan the opposite bank for these predators.

At Dipeni Outpost the road turns away and roughly follows the **Mozambique border**. The first highlight on this part of the road is the **Nyawutsi Bird Hide**. A deep, permanent pool in the **Hlamvu Stream** offers a quiet hour of birding and maybe game viewing. It is not often visited and may be a bit overgrown. But the water is there and in the dry season it may be rewarding.

Look out for the dusky lark on the way to Grootvlei Dam. This is a summer visitor and is quite abundant in the dry mopane savanna. Kori bustard is another regular sighting.

Elephant bull, S50

S50

Giraffe and plains zebra drinking, Grootvlei Dam, S50

Elmar Venter

Hippos, Grootvlei Dam, S50

Elephants cooling down, Grootvlei Dam, S50

S51
SABLE DAM ROAD
★★★★

★★★★★ ★★★★ ★★★ ★★★

- 8 km; narrow dirt road; traverses one major ecozone
- Sable overnight hide and dam

This loop road out of the H9 skirts the Sable Dam, built just downstream of the source of the Tshutshi spruit that eventually drains into the perennial Olifants River.

The **Sable Dam** is a lovely expanse of water in the dry mopane veld and best known for the **overnight hide** built on its banks. (Bookings are made at the Phalaborwa Gate.) It is rather special to experience the night sounds and animals drinking after dark. During the day the hide serves as a bird hide accessible to any visitor. **Waterbirds** frequent the area, but during the dry season the edge of the water recedes rather too far for comfortable viewing. Nevertheless, herons, ducks and geese are old favourites. The dam wall is within easy viewing distance of the hide. Impala, buffalo and elephant are probably the animals most often seen here. Although the dam is named after the sable antelope, you are unlikely to get a sighting of these rare antelope since the surrounding area is not the kind of habitat they prefer. Predators drink at the dam and are frequently seen at dawn.

Elephant, Sable Dam, S51

A rather large pack of **wild dogs** often frequents the area. The movements of these animals are erratic and it is difficult to predict whether they will be sighted.

Look out for steenbok and kudu. They are browsers often seen where bushwillow occur. Steenbok get their moisture from the leaves they browse and seldom drink water.

Plains zebra drinking, Sable Dam, S51

★★★★
S52
SHINGWEDZI RIVER LOOP

★★★ ★★★ ★★★★ ★★★★

- 68 km; loop; dirt road; corrugated in the dry season; traverses three major ecozones
- Red Rocks; Tshanga Lookout

The Tshanga Road is one of the very special and fascinating drives around Shingwedzi Camp. It is a rather long route that loops on itself and closely follows the course of the Shingwedzi River.

Driving from the camp most visitors prefer to enter at the northern end, which initially traverses fairly open country that permits easy game viewing. The riverbanks are steep and the riverbed is mostly dry, but several pools attract all kinds of game throughout the year.

Huge **riverine trees** roughly fringe the river. Serious flooding is part of the Shingwedzi River system and the banks form big **floodplains** in places. Alluvial deposits are rich in nutrients and the fine structure of the sand particles forms flat, clayey surfaces. The **narrow-leafed mustard tree** has a pale bluish-grey colour and is common on and restricted to floodplains. Look out for these sprawling multi-stemmed shrubs and add another tick to your tree list. Away from the river, well-developed **mopane and bushwillow woodlands** are the norm.

Notice that **lala palms** are also plentiful on these flats. There are always small herds of impala, zebra and warthogs. Waterbuck are often seen resting in the shade of the mustard trees. Game birds are particularly abundant.

As you approach the **Red Rocks**, look out for the white-fronted bee-eaters that are usually around, probably roosting close by in a steep bank. When the big aloes on the bank are in bloom you may see go-away birds, orioles, white-eyes and, of course, sunbirds feeding on the nectar. Look out for mongooses since this is prime habitat for them. The slender mongoose will be on its own while banded mongoose move around in groups.

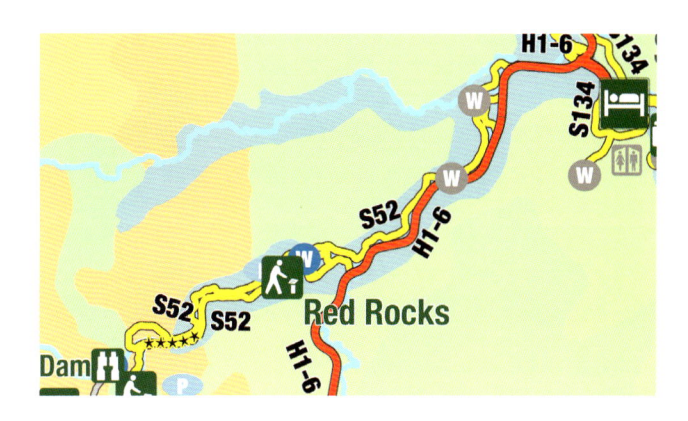

After the turn-off to the causeway across the river, the road continues and the riverine bush becomes thicker. This is a good section for finding **baboons**. They use some of these big trees for sleeping and are often seen here, foraging and sunning themselves. If you come across a troop, spend some time watching the interactions.

Watch out for **elephant**. Some of the big tuskers frequent this area. These giants have no natural enemies, have a high reproductive rate and adapt to any of the habitats in Kruger, but they are much more **prolific in the northern parts of the park**. Their numbers are a worrying aspect, since over-population does a lot of harm to the big trees in the park. The elephants cannot disperse as they are constrained by the limited size of the park. Elsewhere in Africa their numbers are dwindling because of poaching, while the Kruger National Park has to face the challenge of over-population.

At the western end the road crosses the **Shingwedzi River** over a low-water bridge. This causeway is a good birding spot since water birds are often found in this area. Look out for herons.

Red Rocks, S52

Leopard, S51

Leopard and cub, S51

The lookout on **Tshanga Hill** is a popular breakfast get-out point. Make sure you have packed your basket with coffee and rusks, as this is a place to spend time gazing over the large expanse of the bushveld. With your binoculars you may pick up some game activity at the **Tshanga Waterhole** down in the valley.

The rocks and boulders of the Tshanga Hill originate from gabbro. Shallow soils occur in pockets between the loosely stacked boulders, providing a habitat for **rock-loving plants**. See if you can find the **brown-and-yellow-striped plated lizard** that lives on those rocks.

The southern banks of the river are somewhat different from the north. **Take all the loops** that present themselves. Leopard is often encountered and so is lion. Look out for the rare Sharpe's grysbok.

Notice the dense stand of **tamboti trees** at the Red Rocks causeway. It is a good idea to cross the river and come back again. The riverbed always offers something unexpected – even if it's a rare bird such as the saddle-billed stork or an ordinary water monitor.

The **Red Rocks Lookout Loop** is worth following. The views over the river and the mopane woodland are exquisite, especially in August or September when the mopane leaves show rich autumn colours even though spring is approaching. Here, the river crosses a **sandstone shelf** (part of the Clarence formation) of an unusual brick-red colour. Water erosion has created a series of potholes where prospectors once panned for gold. Fortunately, this was not very successful and this beautiful place remained pristine and undisturbed.

Leopard and cub, Red Rocks, S51

Mohammed and Sarifa Jinnah

★★★
S53
NKULUMBENI LOOP

★★★   ★★★   ★★★★   ★★★

- 3 km; loop; narrow dirt road; traverses one major ecozone
- Nkulumbeni drainage line

This short loop crosses the seasonal Nkulumbeni Stream.

The road passes through a stretch of wetland, which is usually rewarding in the rainy season. Visibility is good. The stream drains into the Mphongolo system, which in turn joins the **Shingwedzi River** lower downstream.

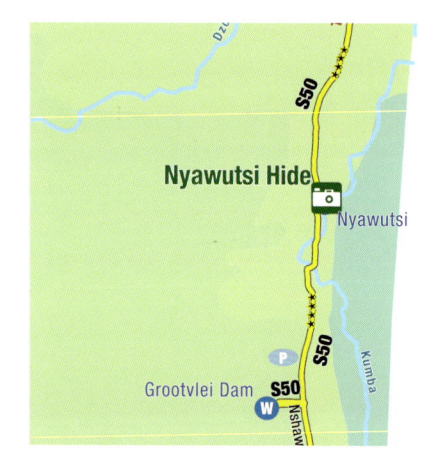

★★★
S54
NYAWUTSI BIRD HIDE ROAD

★★★   ★★★   ★★★★   ★★★

- 2 km; narrow dirt road; traverses one major ecozone
- Nyawutsi Bird Hide

Scene at Nyawutsi Bird Hide, S54

★★★
S55
LAMONT LOOP

🦁 ★★★   🦌 ★★★★   🦅 ★★★   🌳 ★★★

- 3 km; narrow dirt road; traverses two major ecozones
- Lamont Waterhole

This short loop is well worth taking. At the southern entrance it passes the confluence of the Shingwedzi and Mphongolo rivers before it turns away to follow the Mphongolo River course up to the Lamont Waterhole.

Elephant and buffalo herds often cross this road to the water in the **Mphongolo River**. Giraffe are not abundant in the north but they do occur along rivers where they feed on the knob-thorn. A lookout place enables you to get a **riverbed view** from your vehicle.

The open area around the **Lamont Waterhole** attracts impala and zebra, while buffalo bulls often congregate here to graze the sweet grass in the depression. Look out for rock monitors often seen in this area. **Predator sightings** are often reported on this road.

Birding is average as there is not a great variety of habitats. A few thorn trees and leadwoods provide good perches for hawking birds and the occasional raptor. Look for oxpeckers on animals near water.

African buffalo pair, S55

S56
MPHONGOLO LOOP
★★★★★

🦁 ★★★★ 🦌 ★★★ 🦅 ★★★★★ 🌳 ★★★★

- 20 km; narrow and meandering dirt road; traverses two major ecozones
- The loops onto the riverbank; Babalala Picnic Site

The S56 follows the course of the seasonal Mphongolo River and is rated as one of the best drives in the north.

Yet, as with any other drive, you may be extremely lucky and see a lot of game or perhaps nothing at all. But there are always plenty of bird species and **some of the best wildlife encounters** have been reported along this route.

Impressive trees fringe the Mphongolo. The most outstanding of these are the **huge nyala trees** and the **massive jackalberries**. Both these have huge trunks and cannot be missed. The nyala tree is found along the Sabie River, but is only common in the northern parts of the park (especially along the Mphongolo River) where it grows on **alluvial soils** along riverbanks. The **trunk is gnarled and crooked** with clusters of **branchlets and leaves** growing directly from it. The leaves are small and compound. Monkey and baboon, as well as a wide variety of birds, feed on the **grape-like fruit**. Elephant and antelope will pick up fallen fruit. Fruits ripen in March but are borne on the tree for most of the year.

The jackalberry trunk divides into a few large trunk-like branches that spread out close to their origin. They **often grow on termite mounds**. Look out for green pigeons, brown-headed parrots, grey hornbills and purple-crested turacos when the trees are in fruit (September to October). Kudu, impala, nyala and jackal eat the fallen fruit. Elephant, kudu and eland browse the leaves. It is easy to identify jackalberry trees in spring when some of the leaves turn yellow while young reddish-brown leaves appear simultaneously. The tree is never entirely without leaves.

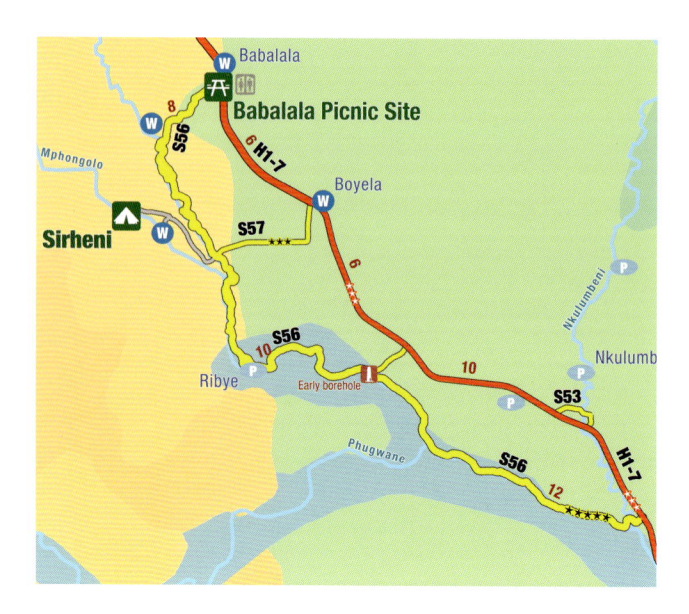

Sycamore figs and apple-leaf trees are as impressive while groves of tamboti trees with their characteristic bark pattern are also present.

Some of the **mopane trees** are well developed to form **high-branching, single-trunked trees** as opposed to multi-stemmed shrubs. Mopane trees are stunted where the soil is shallow, but in deeper soils and near watercourses they can grow to a substantial height.

Numerous loops lead closer to the riverbank. Take your time on these. Apart from the remarkable views, you may spot herds of buffalo or elephant on the opposite bank or in the riverbed. The route offers prime habitat for lion and leopard, although with lower game densities comes lower predator densities.

The rare **Sharpe's grysbok** is often seen on this route. Look out for this shy antelope that may easily be confused with steenbok. They occur in slightly different habitats but both feed on fallen leaves, flowers and fruit.

A large **permanent river pool** among impressive rocks is hidden away from the road but can be seen from a nearby river loop. Many animals use this source of water and it's well worth spending some time around that area.

Birding is excellent for terrestrial, fruitivorous and common bushveld species. Even waterbirds often congregate in the pools of the riverbed. Consider raptor sightings as very special, because raptors are increasingly endangered.

The **Babalala Picnic Site** marks the end of this pleasant route.

Tree squirrels, S56

Juvenile leopard, S56

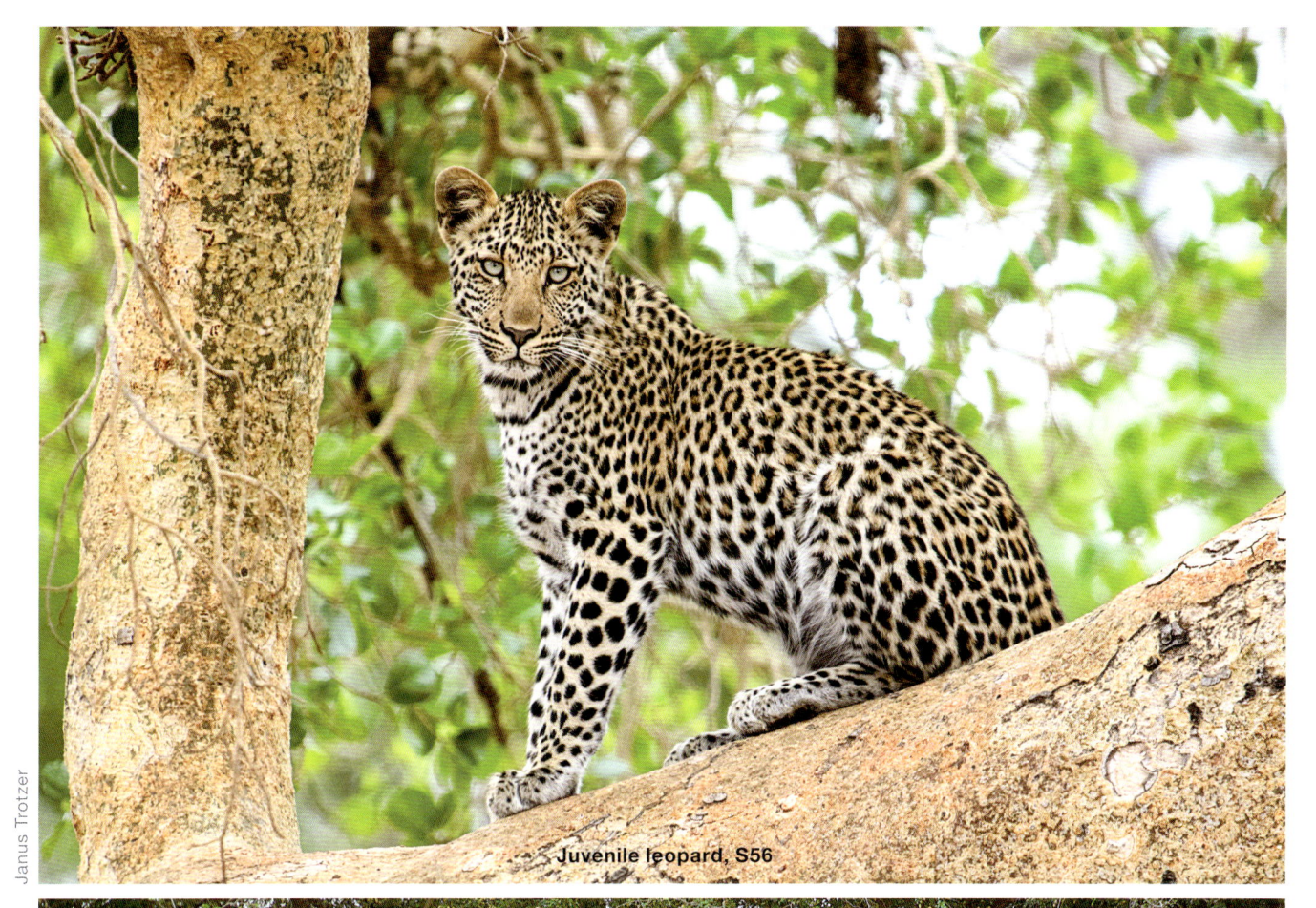

Impalas under nyala tree, S56

★★★
S57
BOYELA ROAD

🦁 ★★★   🦌 ★★   🦅 ★★   🌳 ★★

🛣 5 km; narrow dirt road; traverses one major ecozone

This short link road offers quick access to the Sirheni Bushveld Camp from the H1-7 tarred road.

It passes through **mopane shrubveld** on basalt (therefore sweet grazing) with well-developed, medium-height mopane, stunted apple-leafs and bushwillow. Adjacent to the tarred road there is a marshy area where waterbuck and impala are often seen.

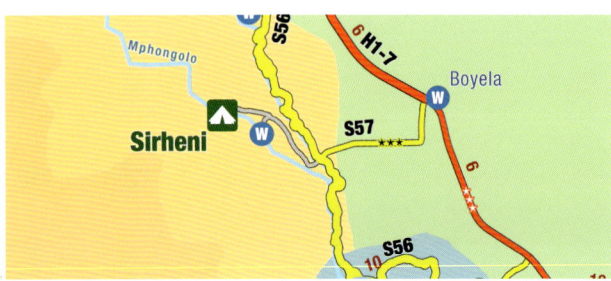

Brown-headed parrot, S58

★★★★
S58
DZUNDZWINI LOOP

🦁 ★★★★   🦌 ★★★   🦅 ★★★★★   🌳 ★★★

🛣 9 km; narrow dirt road; traverses two major ecozones
🚩 Dzundzwini Hill; the Shisha Wetland and natural spring

The S58 loop offers an intimate game drive experience. At places the road is simply a track meandering through mopane forest, but it opens up towards the Shisha Stream where a natural spring forms a huge wetland area. In the wet season the stream flows, but it gets drier as the season advances until only a trickle from the natural springs provides water for game.

From the northern entrance the road initially traverses **mopane woodland** on Ecca shale that yields clay soils. Towards the **Dzundzwini Hill** the substrate becomes stony and the vegetation changes to **mopane shrubveld** with sweet and mixed grazing. A short cul-de-sac leads up the Dzundzwini Hill (600 m), which is one of the highest points in the north, with a view over the far eastern bushveld as far as the distant Lebombo hills in the south.

At the foot of the hill a huge **sausage tree** indicates where **JJ Coetser** had his first temporary camp when appointed ranger of this area in **1919**. The natural spring provided water for his party. The camp **Punda Maria was named after his wife**. Jackalberry, boer-bean and apple-leaf add to the variety of beautiful trees.

Big herds of elephant are often seen quenching their thirst from pools in the wetland. Impala, kudu, nyala, buffalo, zebra and warthog are regular visitors. This is a good spot for predators – leopard and lion may be lurking around the periphery of the wetland and marshy areas are the natural home for serval cats.

Habitat diversity offers niches for a variety of bird species. Look out for spurfowl, shrike, oriole, parrot and pigeon.

Southern yellow-billed hornbill pair, S58

S59
MANDADZIDZI LINK ROAD

★★★

🦁 ★★ 🦌 ★★ 🦅 ★★★ 🌳 ★★

- 6.4 km; narrow dirt road; traverses two major ecozones
- Mopane woodland

This is a short link road between the H1-8 and the popular S60. Shrub mopane with sweet grass allows good visibility in the east; towards the west, the mopane grow into sizeable shrubs and trees.

Tamboti often grow in association with tall mopane trees. Look out for **Arnot's Chat** in the tree mopane. Hornbills are common and notice that mainly two species occur. The **grey-billed hornbill** usually perches high up in the mopane trees while the **southern yellow-billed hornbill** tends to perch lower between feeding sessions on the ground. Scan the higher trees for raptors.

Look out for elephant, buffalo, kudu and impala. You may be lucky to see a skittish herd of eland in this area. Most herbivores prefer the sweet grass and open spaces to the east and avoid the **denser mopane woodland**. Lions often follow buffalo herds and although this might seem to be ideal lion territory, their numbers in the north are low in comparison to the central parts of the park. The chances of encountering lion are therefore not great.

African elephant bull, S59

African buffalo, S60

★★★
S60
GUMBANDEBVU ROAD

🦁 ★★★   🦌 ★★   🦅 ★★★   🌳 ★★★

- 16 km; dirt road; corrugated due to heavy traffic; traverses three major ecozones
- Gumbandebvu Hill

Visitors staying at the Punda Maria Camp and travellers using the Pafuri Border Post generally use this shortcut on their way to Pafuri. It is a scenic road and well worth taking.

At the western end of the road, **magic guarri stands indicate a brackish area**. Impala and zebra are often seen here, as the sweet grass is nutritious and the open terrain makes it easier for them to see predators approaching. The occasional warthog may be seen digging for rhizomes and bulbs while buffalo herds sometimes cross the road here on their way to water.

The road soon approaches the **Gumbandebvu Hill**, which the locals believe is haunted. Lovely specimens of leadwood, apple-leaf, weeping wattle and silver cluster-leaf can be seen along the foot of the hill. Note the large uniform groups of **dark-green trees** on the crest of the sandstone hill. These are **Lebombo ironwood** and occur only in the sandveld and on the **Lebombo Mountains**. Take your time driving along here, since game is rather abundant along the foothills. Look out for baboon, especially on the crest.

Past the hill, the road continues through the finest example of **mopane woodland** in the park. The underlying geology of Ecca shale yields a fine clay soil (turf) rich in minerals. These are ideal conditions for the mopane to grow into the **tree form**, which has a single trunk and is high-branching with a narrow canopy. As the road continues eastwards, the soil geology changes to basalt and the mopane become **multi-stemmed with a v-shape** and a round, poorly developed canopy. Note that the butterfly leaf is characteristic of all mopane.

Tamboti trees, with their characteristic dark bark neatly cracked into rectangles, often grow in association with the mopane trees, in groups of a few big trees.

Dense stands of mopane seldom offer excellent game viewing unless animals happen to be on the road. Even huge elephants vanish as soon as they enter the woodland. In August–September when the leaves are shed, visibility improves and more game is seen.

Look out for the **Arnot's Chat**, which is endemic to the mopane woodland. Both grey and yellow-billed hornbill are very common. Notice that the grey hornbill usually perches closer to the canopy while the yellow-billed hornbill prefers perching on the lower branches. Look out for raptors.

S61
KLOPPERFONTEIN LOOP

★★★★

🦁 ★★★   🦌 ★★★   🦅 ★★★★   🌳 ★★★★

- 7 km; narrow dirt track; traverses one major ecozone
- Klopperfontein Dam; Shikuwa stream crossing

As the S61 branches off the S60, the vegetation and ambience of the area undergoes a change. The landscape becomes more open, the mopane more stunted and the grassy areas allow for better visibility. The road runs along the Shikuwa drainage line. Huge leadwood trees give the scenery a park-like feeling.

Klopperfontein was named after the notorius ivory hunter **Dirk Klopper** who frequently camped near a spring in the **Shikuwa Stream**. The stream, a tributary of the Luvuvhu, forms a natural crossing close to this spring where Klopper and other hunters such as **Cecil Barnard** crossed with wagons on their way to hunting grounds in the north. A short detour leads to this famous drift (ford).

Klopperfontein is the main centre for game activity between Punda Maria Camp and the Pafuri area. There is always activity at the waterhole and visibility into the surrounding landscape is great. Many game tracks lead here and predators such as lion frequent this area.

The **Klopperfontein Dam** is a favourite place for spending quality time in your vehicle, soaking in the peaceful environment while watching waterbirds and game come and go. On hot days, elephants bath and splash to cool off after quenching their thirst. Huge elephant bulls are reported crossing the dam via the narrow wall. The dam wall is more like a weir – narrow, with water cascading all the way over it. How these giants balance their huge bodies walking this 'tightrope' is simply amazing.

Hamerkop and African buffalo, S61

Hennie Bignaut

S62
ENGELHARD DAM ROAD

★★★★

★★★ (lion) ★★★ (antelope) ★★★★ (bird) ★★★★ (tree)

- 15 km; dirt road; becoming stony and rough across the Makhadzi Stream; traverses two major ecozones
- Low-water bridge over the Makhadzi Stream; Matambeni Hide for birders; fever trees along the Makhadzi Stream

The route along the northern banks of the Letaba River is well worth taking. Not only does it offer magnificent river views, but it is also extremely rewarding for general game and its predators, as well as for birding.

This road is rated by some serious birders as the best birding road in the park. This is probably because of the abundant **breeding sites** along the river and the popular **Matambeni Hide** that overlooks the river. Floods have taken their toll and displaced the sandbanks and reed beds in front of the hide. This is evidence of the constant changes that take place in all the systems of the park. Conditions can even change from season to season: places that are good in summer may not yield much during winter; those that are excellent one year may be barren the next.

The **riverine vegetation** with its huge apple-leaf, sycamore and fever trees and knob-thorns is a pleasure to the eye. Make sure to **drive along all the loops**. The third loop is the longest. It follows the **Makhadzi Stream** up to its confluence with the **Letaba** and continues a little way further along the river. In summer the Makhadzi is usually a flowing stream with crocodiles and hippos in the deeper pools. **Fever trees** line the way with their lovely yellow-green trunks and branches covered with a yellow powdery substance and peeling layers of paper-thin bark. They only grow where there is permanent water, whether it be rivers, swamps or pans. Look out for weaver birds that often build their nests in the branches of these trees, possibly because the formidable thorns give some protection against snakes and other predators.

The low-water **causeway** across the Makhadzi Stream is a favourite as waterbirds and others forage in the standing pools. Look for herons, storks, hamerkops and other waterbirds.

Elephants with young prefer to drink in the pools upstream of the Makhadzi for the safety of their offspring. Waterbuck, kudu and nyala may be around. Look out for **water monitor** – these reptiles can reach a length of up to two metres and are the largest of the lizards in the park. Their young are yellow and black but fade to olive green or grey-brown when mature. Water monitors are often seen in permanent bodies of water with enough vegetation in and around them. The pool upstream of the causeway is exactly the kind of habitat this reptile prefers. It is an excellent swimmer and will vanish into the water when it feels threatened.

Across the stream the substrate of the road changes and becomes rough and stony. Sedans may find the road difficult and turning space becomes more and more restricted. For those with high-clearance vehicles however this may be an adventurous trail leading up to a **viewpoint over the bushveld plains**.

The S62 route is **good for predators**. Sightings of lion and leopard are regularly reported. Big brackish sites are indicated by magic guarri. This is where herds of impala and zebra often congregate. **Visibility along this route is as good** as it gets in the mopane veld.

Bateleur, S62

Saddle-billed stork female, S62

Saddle-billed stork male, S62

S63
PAFURI LOOP ROAD TO CROOK'S CORNER

★★★★★

★★★ ★★★★ ★★★★★ ★★★★★

- 23 km; dirt road; alluvial substrate causing fine, penetrating dust so drive slowly; traverses one major ecozone
- Crook's Corner; Pafuri Picnic site

The highlight of this loop road is the confluence of the Luvuvhu and Limpopo Rivers. This is however right at the end, where the two arms of the S63 meet. It is probably best to take the second arm first (the one that leaves the H1-8 at the bridge). This part of the road, with its river frontage, is not tarred.

Alluvial deposits are rich in nutrients and the fine sand particles form flat clay surfaces. Look for the **narrow-leafed mustard trees** that are particularly abundant and restricted to floodplains. This is a pale, bluish-grey, sprawling, multi-stemmed shrub. Another species restricted to floodplains is the **fever-berry croton** (heart-shaped leaves).

Passing the numerous **tree skeletons** evokes sadness for these giants that had to succumb to the forces of nature. Regrowth is already taking place however, and within a few decades the riverine vegetation will hopefully restore itself. The worrying part is overbrowsing of the young growth by too many elephants.

The **Pafuri Picnic Site** is one of the highlights of the area, offering an air of peace and tranquility and excellent opportunities for birding. Several loops lead on to the riverbank and offer good views over the wide expanse of the **Luvuvhu**. Hippo and crocodile are abundant, as are waterbirds. In the woodlands on the floodplains, nyala, impala, waterbuck, baboon and the occasional zebra may be found. This is also the only place in the entire park where the **Sykes' monkey** is likely to be seen. These primates are restricted to a forest habitat and at Pafuri the riverine forest meets their habitat needs. **Leopard** is probably more abundant than lion and sightings are reported from time to time.

In the rainy season, parts of this road may be flooded or too muddy to be driven on. Enquire at your camp before you attempt the long drive. The fever tree forest on the southern floodplain took a severe beating during the 2014 floods. Regrowth does take place but a contributing factor to their decline may be, as with some other tree species, overbrowsing by elephants.

Crook's Corner is probably one of the most notorious places of years gone by, before the era of the National Park. A small triangular tongue of land, wedged between three countries at the confluence of two rivers, was exploited by poachers, gun-runners, fugitives and others who were avoiding the law. Law enforcers were far away and ivory poachers took advantage of this. When based at this intersection it was easy to move over the border whenever police from one particular country approached, placing oneself out of legal reach.

Today the **Pafuri Border Post** is responsible for law enforcement and allows legal entry to and from Mozambique and Zimbabwe. The road between the H1-8 and the border post is tarred.

All in all, this is a magical river road along one of the few perennial rivers of the park giving access to the heart of the only corner of South Africa **within the tropics**.

Female nyala with suckling young, S63

Red-billed firefinch, S63

Melanistic gabar goshawk, S63

Wahlberg's eagle in flight, S63

S64
NYALA LOOP ROAD TO THULAMELA ARCHAEOLOGICAL SITE

★★★★

★★★ ★★★ ★★★★★ ★★★★★

- 7 km; narrow dirt road; traverses one major ecozone
- Thulamela Archaelogical Site – book a guided tour at the reception of your camp

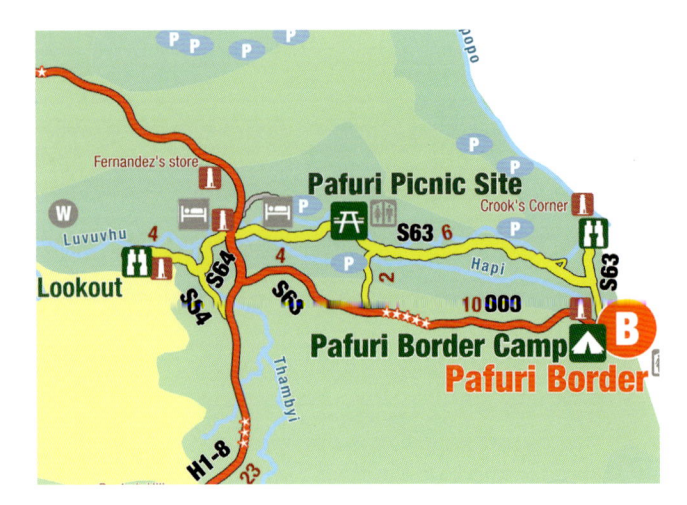

The loop road to the west of the H1-8 is scenically spectacular.

Hidden within thorn thickets, the century-old **baobab trees** evoke an eerie atmosphere of unreality. Animals such as nyala, bushbuck, waterbuck and impala are fairly common; here, they seem to move about the flat floodplains as if in a trance. Of course this is not true, but this is what a vivid imagination under certain conditions does to you. Being a floodplain, it happens that the best part of the road with the biggest baobabs is sometimes closed due to flooding or damage to the road or the causeway over the drainage line. It's really bad luck if your visit coincides with such a closure.

This is also the road that leads to the **archaeological village of Thulamela** that was established almost **500 years ago** on the **Thulamela Hill**. The finely crafted stone walls and other artefacts indicate that it must have been a **royal village**. Imagine that as far back as the 13th century a well-trodden **trade route** already existed between Sofala and Inhambane on the east coast and the interior. The Thulamela inhabitants and others exchanged ivory, gold, copper, tin and slaves with Arab traders for beads, ceramics, cloth and implements. Who were these people and where did their wealth come from? Were they related to those of the ancient **City of Zimbabwe** and **Mapungubwe**? If these questions fascinate you, arrange at the Punda Maria or Shingwedzi Camp for a **guided tour** of these ancient ruins.

The **best view of the exceptionally beautiful Pafuri scenery is from the top of Thulamela Hill** where you can look out over the valley of giants. Most of these baobabs were already mature trees during the reign of the Thulamela dynasty. You must be on the guided tour to go to this hilltop view site.

Game viewing is average to good but it is an excellent drive to get up close to a giant baobab. You are sure to see impala and nyala and probably also a few zebra and the occasional elephant. The birding paradise continues and you should look out for special sightings.

Temminck's courser, S64

White-crowned lapwing, S64

Crested guineafowl, S64

S65
N'WASWITSHAKA WATERHOLE ROAD

★★★★

★★★★ ★★★ ★★★★★ ★★★

- 14 km; dirt road; traverses one major ecozone
- N'waswitshaka Waterhole

There is plenty of wildlife activity on this road, with regular leopard sightings being reported. The road's biggest attraction is the crossing over the seasonal N'waswitshaka River and the N'waswitshaka Waterhole with the small dam nearby.

The **Sihehleni inselberg or koppie** (380 m) is one of the many granite outcrops in this part of the park and is home to klipspringer. Although this is a very dry and sandy part of the southern Kruger, the vegetation contributes in a big way to make this a particularly attractive route. The stands of silver cluster-leaf, tamboti and magic guarri with occasional elegant tree wisterias are pleasing to the eye.

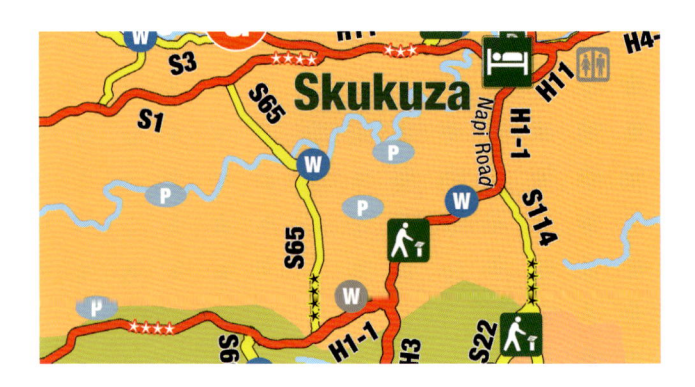

The **river crossing** is one of the **most scenic in the park**. On the northern bank there is an inviting forested area exuding a mystical ambience. The low-water bridge offers a lovely view with wide white sandbanks and deep pools in places after rains. However, this is also one of the many seasonal rivers of the park.

The waterhole is a **good afternoon viewing site**, but grazers tend to drink during the mid-morning and predators often early in the morning. Herds of impala and zebra frequent the grassy sections, but the area also abounds with kudu and giraffe.

Good birding can be done in the vicinity of the waterhole and dam. This is a good road for looking out for less common bushveld species.

Marsh terrapins on hippo, S65

★★★
S68
ACCESS ROAD TO MUNTSHE OR MLONDOZI PICNIC SITE

★★★   ★★★   ★★★★   ★★★

- 2 km; narrow dirt road; traverses one major ecozone
- Mlondozi Dam

For a shortcut to the Mlondozi Dam, take the northern S29 turn-off from the H10, 10 km north of the Lower Sabie Bridge.

The **Mlondozi Dam** is a get-out point and picnic area not to be missed. With binoculars in hand, a picnic basket and a steaming cup of coffee next to you, spend a few enjoyable hours here and watch game from an excellent vantage point. In the dry season, grazers visit the dam in great numbers. The surrounding area is the **winter grazing ground for zebra and wildebeest** and they may come down in large numbers to drink. Following in their wake are the predators.

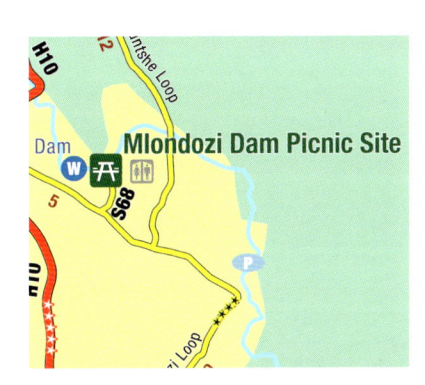

A personal experience is appropriate here, because this is the place where our family once witnessed an amazing lion kill. The entire story unfolded before our eyes. We watched three lionesses approach; saw how they grouped themselves for an ambush; waited patiently with them for about two hours before the right moment for an attack presented itself; saw them focus on an individual and move in for the kill; saw the wildebeest being overpowered and suffocated by one lion while the others helped to hold it down. After about five minutes, they pulled the carcass into nearby shade and rested before starting to feed. What intrigued us was that after the kill, the rest of the wildebeest herd stood nearby, watching the drama unperturbed, as if they knew that they were now out of danger.

Look out for elephant, rhino, waterbuck and hippo. Waterbirds steal the show when the mammals are absent. Find the resident plated lizards baking in the sun on nearby boulders. Take the opportunity to look at the different shrubs and trees on the hill behind the picnic spot.

Mocking cliff chat, S68

★★★
S69
NHLANGANINI LOOP

🦁 ★★★ 🦌 ★★ 🦅 ★★★ 🌳 ★★★

- 8 km; dirt road; loops out of the H9; traverses one ecozone
- Nhlanganini Stream

The Nhlanganini Stream is seasonal, but semi-permanent pools along the stream bed attract animals. That is why the S69 is a good loop road to follow since the narrow nature of the dirt road allows an intimate game drive experience.

The road traverses a short stretch of **sandveld**. See if you can recognise the sandy soil and the change in soil colour and vegetation – almost no mopane shrubs occur but look out for silver cluster-leaf and sickle-bush. The grass here is sweet and animals favour this. Look out for steenbok.

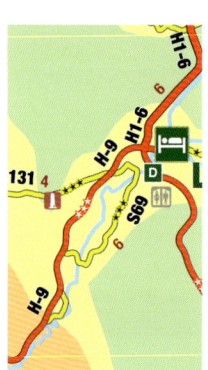

★★★★
S76
H4-1 LOOP ROAD

🦁 ★★★★ 🦌 ★★★ 🦅 ★★★★★ 🌳 ★★★

- 4 km; dirt track; traverses one ecozone
- The entire loop

The S76 is a dirt track winding next to and over the H4-1 several times at the Skukuza end. It is often worth taking since there is less traffic and it brings you intimately close to sightings.

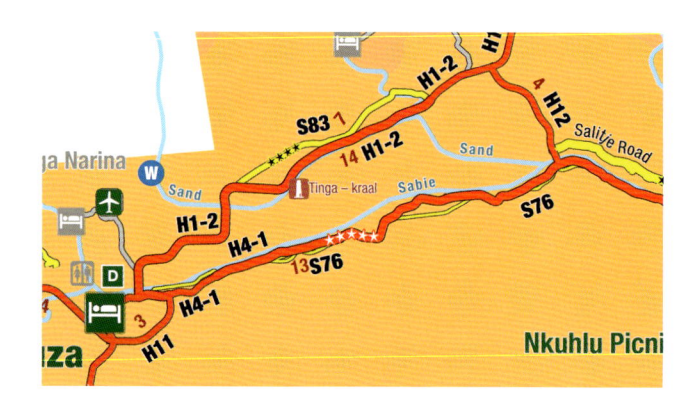

Giraffe browsing, S76

★★★★

S79
THE N'WATIMHIRI CAUSEWAY

★★★★ ★★★★ ★★★★ ★★★★

- 4 km; dirt road; traverses one ecozone
- N'watimhiri Stream crossing

The S79 loop leads to a low-water bridge over the N'watimhiri watercourse, which feeds into the Sabie River. This is a very worthwhile drive.

Steenbok foraging, S69

★★★

S82
MATIVUHLUNGU LOOP

★★★ ★★★ ★★★ ★★★

- 10 km; dirt road; often corrugated; traverses two major ecozones

This is not the most exciting road in Kruger yet people have encounters with predators here from time to time.

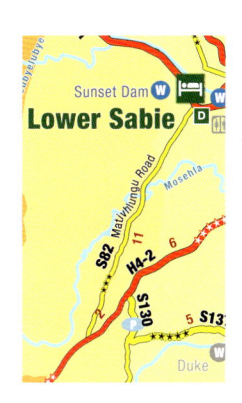

The southern section passes through **Delagoa thorn thicket** on clay soils but the far northern section gradually becomes more open and changes into **knobthorn and marula savanna**.

Although both ecozones support abundant game, the **bush is dense** and **visibility is restricted** to a few metres from the road. Giraffe and elephant are regularly seen, while dung middens betray the presence of rhino. At the southern entrance of the road there is a bare, ovegrazed patch where warthog often forage.

White-backed vultures, S79

★★★★
S83
MARULA LOOP

★★★★ ★★★ ★★★★ ★★★

- 7 km; dirt road; traverses one major ecozone
- Mutlumuvi watercourse

Soon after crossing the Sand River from the south, the Marula Loop makes a detour from the H1-2 tarred road. This intimate dirt road leads into drier, dense bush, eventually joining up with the tarred road again.

The thorn thickets are however quite dense in places and visibility is low. The road crosses one of the Sand River tributaries, the **Mutlumuvi**. Good lion, leopard and hyena sightings are often reported from this area. A popular drive.

★★★★
S84
MANTIMAHLE DAM

★★★★ ★★★★ ★★★★ ★★★★

- 3 km; dirt road; traverses one major ecozone
- Mantimahle Dam

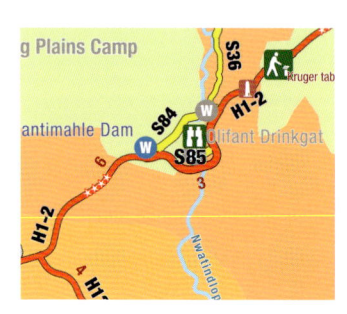

The area around the Mantimahle Dam is extremely good for game viewing. Lions favour the dam wall as a vantage point for watching game come and go across the savanna below.

This dam has changed face recently. It is a **bit overgrown** and, when there is water, it is far away from the road that leads to the viewpoint. It is nevertheless a pleasant **open stretch of savanna with marula and knob-thorn trees**. Look out

Giraffe, S83

for impala, zebra, kudu, waterbuck and giraffe approaching the water.

The turn-off to the Mantimahle Dam is also the first turn-off to the alternative route to the north along the **Hhlanguleni road (S36)**. The entire area around the Mantimahle Dam, and 4 km north on this road, is extremely good game country because of the underlying gabbro that yields soils rich in minerals. The grasses here are sweet and the vegetation consists mainly of thorn trees such as large knob-thorn and buffalo-thorn, but also marula and round-leafed teak that are favoured by elephants. Drive slowly and be vigilant. Predators are regularly encountered in this area.

Elephant pair, S84

★★★★
S85
OLIFANTSDRINKGAT

★★★★ ★★★★ ★★★★ ★★★★

- 1 km; dirt road; traverses one major ecozone
- Olifantsdrinkgat and watering point

The turn-off to Olifantsdrinkgat (Afrikaans for 'elephants' drinking place') is soon after the S84/36 signpost off the H1-2. It is a short dirt track but worthwhile exploring.

At a small dam you may encounter buffalo, elephant, white rhino, giraffe, zebra and predators in their wake. Note the vegetation at the end of the track. The prolific evergreen shrubs with the dark-green, simple leaves are **magic guarri**. Wherever you see these shrubs in the park you can be sure of **clay soil, sweet grass and possible pans** in the rainy season. Sweet grasses attract grazers; they in turn attract predators.

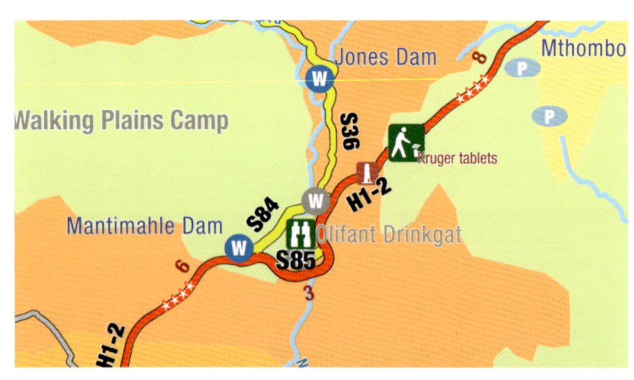

Butterfly, S85

★★★★
S86
N'WASWITSONTSO LOOP

★★★ ★★★ ★★★★ ★★★★

- 4 km; narrow dirt track; traverses one major ecozone
- Pools in the seasonal N'waswitsontso River

The N'waswitsontso loop is only a short detour off the H1-3 tarred road and is often overlooked or confused with the link road called N'waswitsontso Road (S125) further north. This detour is well worth taking. It is intimate and not often travelled.

Look out for elephant along this road, as well as giraffe, kudu and, of course, impala. The track **leads along the river** and **the riverine vegetation** is ideal habitat for lion and leopard.

The **N'waswitsontso River** is not perennial but usually has many standing pools along its way as it meanders down to the **Orpen Dam**. From there, it cuts through the Lebombo range and enters Mozambique. It is therefore an important source of drinking water for the game in the area north of Tshokwane. It enters the park west of the Talamati Private Camp and tourist roads follow its course from its entry into the park to the Orpen Dam.

Warthog male, S86

★★★★

S89
NGOTSO WEIR ROAD

🦁 ★★★   🦌 ★★★   🦅 ★★★★   🌳 ★★★

🛣 8 km; dirt road; traverses one major ecozone

🚩 Ngotso drainage line

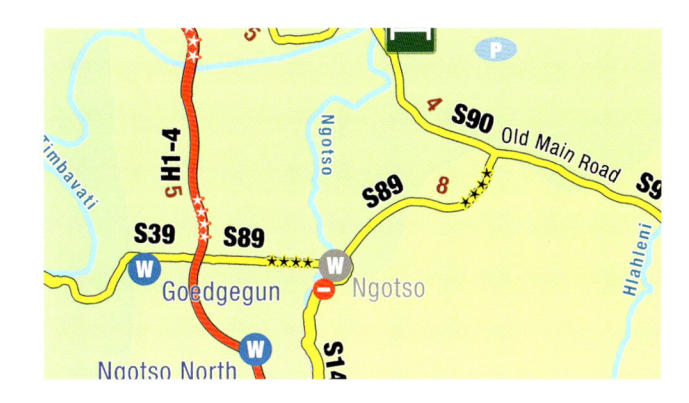

This link road between the tarred H1-4 and the Old Main Road S90 is the main access road to the Balule Camp on the banks of the Olifants River. It is scenic in places, especially where it crosses the Ngotso stream.

The lush vegetation along the stream is home to several bird species. Look out for leopard in the vicinity of the bridge. There used to be a weir damming the Ngotso stream, but it has now been demolished. The seasonal Ngotso stream flows into the Olifants River.

If you are passing the S89/H1-4 intersection early enough in the morning, you may be surprised by the resident hyena family that lives in one of the culverts under the tarred road. The adults are often encountered on the dirt road as they make their way back to their pups and the den.

Hyena are generally believed to be scavengers but research shows that in the Kruger National Park, they **kill more than they scavenge**. They are the second major group of predators and kill more animals than leopard and cheetah together. They hunt by night and when they scavenge they are great chancers, and are fearless. They hunt alone or in packs and pursue their prey at a steady pace over a long distance until it succumbs to exhaustion. On their own they go for baboon and any other smaller animal, even birds. In packs they will take on wildebeest, zebra and kudu. They may even go for buffalo.

Elephant bull, H1-2

S90
OLD MAIN ROAD

★★★★

- 38 km; dirt road; often corrugated; traverses two major ecozones
- Mavumbye Stream crossing; Gudzani crossing; Bangu pan when it contains water

From Satara and the H1-4, the S90 takes you on to the old main road to the north.

The southern section from the H1-4 to **Gudzani** traverses extensive open plains with only a few larger **knob-thorn or marula trees** scattered around. The sweet grassland attracts wildebeest and zebra in great numbers. Towards the **Mavumbye watercourse** congregations of mixed herds, including several grazing species such as impala and waterbuck, are often seen. Baboons often forage amongst the other game, and sleep in trees in the riverine vegetation.

The **open plains** provide a special feast for the eye from October to December after the first rains. **Bulbous river lilies** grow in waterlogged parts of the grassland. They are a delightful sight, with their huge, bell-shaped, pink flowers. The abundant bulbs of the **ground lily** (also called tumbleweed) grow in clumps in open, often brackish, patches near pans along the road. They attract attention with their bright, silvery-pink flower heads. All kinds of other **wild flowers** appear from nowhere – morning glories, wild foxgloves, violets, yellow cleome, wing-seeded sesame and many others. They are especially abundant closer to the Mavumbye Stream where the grass cover has been removed by heavy grazing. These flowering plants prepare the bare soil for grasses to re-establish themselves.

This is also a **good** stretch of road for **birding**. Grassland birds abound – guineafowl, thick knees, francolins and queleas. Look out for korhaans and, in summer, for coursers. Termites in the winged stage emerging from the ground after rain attract raptors such as steppe eagle, lesser spotted eagle and harriers such as the Montagu's and Pallid harrier. In late summer, huge quelea colonies descend on these plains.

Before the intersection with the S41 the road passes through a swampy area in the **Gudzani Watercourse** before it gets to the closed **Gudzani Waterhole**. Look out for waterbuck that are often seen in this area. Buffalo, white rhino, giraffe, kudu and lion are regularly seen here.

The stretch from Gudzani to Balule is not particularly exciting. The road traverses large plains with **dwarf knob-thorn savanna**. Steenbok abound – these small antelope are not dependent on drinking water since they derive enough moisture from what they browse. Game is generally sparse except for impala and kudu that are abundant but skittish.

Beautiful kudu bulls with exceptional horns are often seen browsing in small groups. For most of the way, open water is not available until the **Bangu Waterhole**. As the road gets closer to the Bangu watercourse, the landscape gets more attractive, with larger trees. Although the Bangu Stream is mostly dry, **seasonal pools** remain where animals go for water. Giraffe, zebra, impala and buffalo often congregate here. Game viewing here is unpredictable, though, despite the large herds that are often encountered. During the rainy season this is quite a scenic area.

The S90 ends at the low-level crossing over the Olifants River close to the Balule Camp. The bridge was seriously damaged in the 2012 and 2013 floods. This crossing is the highlight of the S90.

African wild cat, S90

Honey badger, S90

S91 and S92
OLIFANTS RIVER LOOP ROAD

★★★★

🦁 ★★★ 🦌 ★★★ 🦅 ★★★★ 🌳 ★★★★

- 5 and 7 km; dirt road; traverses one major ecozone
- Olifants River views

These two linking roads follow the course of the Olifants River along its northern bank. They are roads well worth travelling, as they offer good game viewing.

North of the **Olifants River** the underlying geology is still basalt and the soils generally shallow and stony. The vegetation is a **mix of bushwillow, knob-thorn and mopane**, but closer to the riverbank typical riverine vegetation is found.

The Olifants River has a **permanent water flow**, which makes it ideal for hippo and crocodile. The river is shallow and slow-flowing in places and all kinds of waterbirds can be seen feeding on what it offers.

This road warrants a slow drive. Most animal activity north of the Olifants River is close to rivers and one can expect this route to be rewarding. Elephants and impala are sure to be encountered, but also look out for buffalo, zebra and kudu.

The main predators in the area are lion and hyena, although leopard is often sighted.

Elephant bull, S91

S93
OLIFANTS CAMP TO LETABA RIVER ROAD

★★★

🦁 ★★ 🦌 ★★ 🦅 ★★★★ 🌳 ★★★

- 16 km; dirt road; corrugated in the dry season; traverses two major ecozones
- Von Wielligh's Baobab

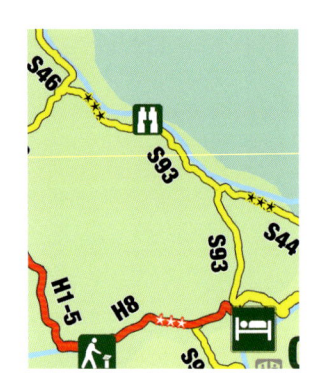

The two sections of this road are quite different from each other and together they offer a pleasant drive.

The southern part passes through dry **rugged veld** while the northern section is a **scenic river road** skirting the **Letaba River**. The S93 leaves the H8 close to the Olifants Camp. The first important stop is at a small pan where the S44 turns away from the S93. Unfortunately this pan contains no water in the dry season. Giraffe are often seen here, as are impala and other general game species. In the **rainy season** this scenic watering point is a **popular sundown dam,** ideal for a peaceful final hour of daylight, and close enough to the camp for you to be back before the gates close.

The road passes through hilly terrain with knob-thorn, cluster-leaf, leadwood, mopane and round-leafed teak. Soon after the S44 joins the S93 again, a huge **baobab** named **Von Wielligh's Baobab** looms ahead. It was named after the **surveyor general** of the old Zuid-Afrikaansche Republiek (i.e the Transvaal), **Gideon Retief von Wielligh**, who carved his name into the tree trunk in **1891** after setting up his camp here. He was responsible for surveying the border between the Transvaal and Mozambique.

Downstream from this point is the **confluence** of the **Letaba and the Olifants Rivers** (not visible from this road). With the Letaba River in close proximity to the road, game viewing should theoretically be good but the **game density is low** and excellent sightings are not regularly reported. As this is elephant country these giants can be expected anywhere along this road. Look out for waterbuck close to the river. The most likely predators to occur here are leopard and lion.

Von Wielligh's baobab, S93

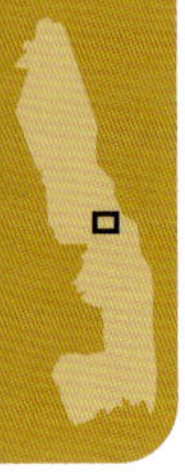

S94
LINK ROAD

🦁 ★   🦌 ★   🦅 ★★   🌳 ★

🛣 7 km; dirt road; traverses one major ecozone

The S94 is a shortcut between the Letaba and Olifants Camps and avoids the longer river road.

The **mopane shrubveld** on the underlying basalt geology can be a little monotonous. However, it is still relatively close to the Letaba River and one may intercept a herd of buffalo on their way to water, or come across elephant. Although blue wildebeest are not plentiful in the north, a small herd or a territorial bull waiting to impress passing females may be encountered. They are dependent on a regular water supply and prefer sweet, short grass. Even a sprinkling of zebra may occur.

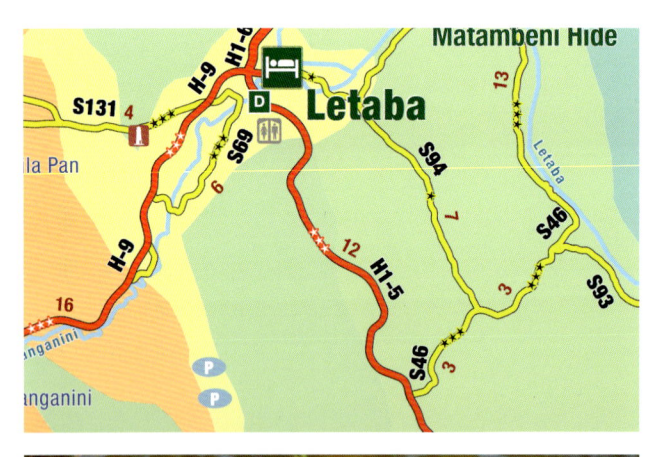

Hippo, S94

S95
LETABA RIVER ROAD BETWEEN THE BRIDGE AND THE CAMP

🦁 ★★★★   🦌 ★★★★   🦅 ★★★★★   🌳 ★★★★★

🛣 4 km; dirt road; traverses one major ecozone

🏁 Entire road

River frontages are centres of activity in the park – especially in the north. The first section of the H1-6 and the S95 are probably the most popular roads in close proximity to the Letaba Rest Camp.

There are magnificent views over the **Letaba River** and animals here seem to be less skittish and more used to traffic. This makes it possible to approach them closer than elsewhere. In the months when the pans have dried up, animals become even more dependent on visits to the river.

In the riverbed you are likely to see hippo – and lots of them. The **Letaba River** houses the **highest density of hippo** in the park. During the day they may be basking in the sun on the opposite bank. Look for crocodiles on the sandbanks. Old buffalo bulls may be feeding in the reeds. Waterbuck and impala often linger to graze the sweet grasses on the riverbanks. Elephants may be drinking or crossing the wide sandbanks. Buffalo herds and elephant breeding herds are often seen on the opposite bank as they come down to drink.

Be vigilant and look deep into the bush on both sides of the road for approaching game. **Predators** such as lion regularly intercept prey as they approach the river to drink and leopard sightings are regularly reported. So are hyena sightings in the early morning or late evening. During night drives this is the place to find bushbabies (galagos) and genet.

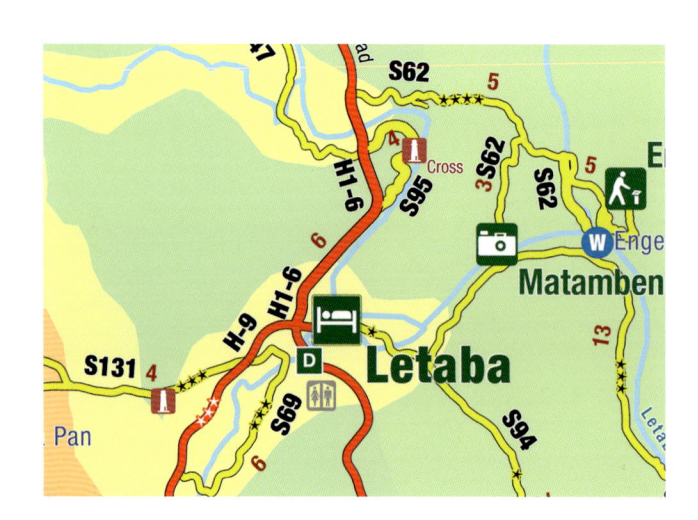

Little bee-eater, S95

In the **late afternoon** the reflections of date palms, sycamore figs, mopane trees, apple-leaf and fever trees across the river paint a pretty, constantly changing picture at sunset.

Look out for the lovely specimens of **umbrella thorn** (formerly umbrella acacia) with their distinguishing flattish crowns and tightly curled pods. The umbrella thorn is prolific on the brackish flats alongside the river road (both the tarred section and the gravel S95) where it is found in groups. The pods are particularly nutritious and a favourite with giraffe, antelope, monkey and baboon.

Giraffe are scarce north of the Olifants River, but those that do occur are usually encountered close to riverine vegetation since they prefer thorn trees (acacias) such as the umbrella thorn and the knob-thorn as fodder. Giraffe feed on leaves, flowers and pods.

The river road is also **excellent for birding**. Look out for raptors – especially fish eagle – and hornbills, bee-eaters (especially in summer when the migrants visit), rollers, herons, storks and geese.

★★★
S96
SHILAWURI LOOP

★★ ★★★ ★★★ ★★★

- 5 km; narrow dirt road; traverses one major ecozone
- Shilawuri inselberg

This pleasant and intimate link road is interesting and surprisingly rewarding. It passes the rugged granite Shilawuri inselberg with its associated vegetation.

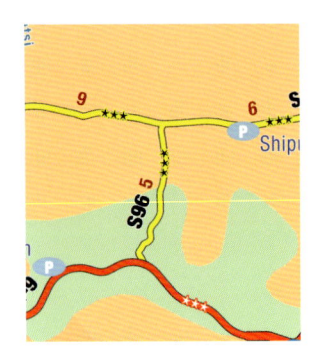

Birds are abundant along the way, particularly southern yellow-billed hornbills that attract attention. Since the **general grassland grazers and browsers** are well represented in the entire area, any of these can be expected. It is also a good road for hyena and jackal sightings, especially in the early morning. Two species of jackal occur in the park. The more common is the **black-backed jackal** while the **side-striped jackal** occurs widely but is less common. Both are nocturnal, but the side-striped is even more so and will only be seen on overcast days and very early in the morning.

Slender mongoose, S96
Bruce Crossey

★★★
S98
THULAMILA LOOP

★★★ ★★★ ★★★★★ ★★★★★

- 3 km; narrow dirt road; traverses one major ecozone
- Thulamila spring and magnificent sycamore fig

This short drive traverses an open, park-like landscape with magnificent trees. This is typical sandveld with well-drained soils and a complex plant community. A natural spring and wetland area along a drainage line attracts a variety of game. The road continues up an incline and offers a good view over the eastern bushveld and far hills in the distance.

This is a good road for **practising tree identification**. The easiest trees to recognise are the stately pod mahoganies (prominent bare trunk and huge umbrella-like canopy – a typical sandveld species), apple-leaf (gnarled trunks, pale green leaves), jackalberry (dense, roundish canopy), nyala trees (clusters of untidy leaves growing low down from a massive gnarled trunk), sycamore fig (yellowish trunk), marula (single trunked, high-branching, semi-circular canopy and distinctive bark) and leadwood bushwillow (very tall, high-branching, majestic with pale grey bark that breaks up into small regular snakeskin-like blocks). Other prominent trees are white kirkia (pale green, fine-leaved, feathery looking, spreading canopy), baobab (the so-called upside-down tree) and Natal mahogany (striking, large, roundish, dense, deep green, glossy canopy). Abundant small trees are sjambok pod and weeping wattle. Shrubs that are easy to recognise when in flower include the Pride-of-De-Kaap *(Bauhinia galpinii)* (peach-coloured orchid-like flowers in summer) and plumbago (blue flowers in summer). Bushwillow species can be recognised by their typical four-winged pods.

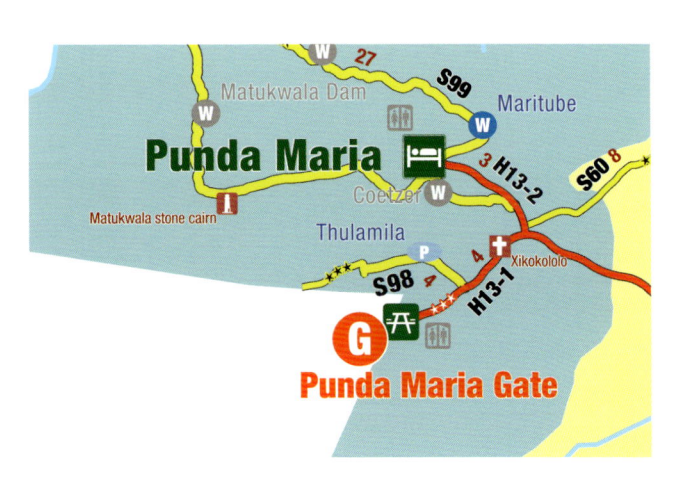

★★★★★
S99
MAHONIE LOOP

★★★   ★★★★   ★★★★★   ★★★★★

- 23 km; narrow dirt road; traverses one major ecozone
- The entire road

The Mahonie loop circles the hill on which the Punda Maria Camp is built and is renowned for plants and animals that are scarce elsewhere in the park. The road was named after the many specimens of pod mahogany in the Punda Maria area. But this is not the only majestic tree species along this road. The hill slopes support an astounding diversity and several are unique to the park.

In summer this is an extremely pleasant drive through a wonderland of different flowering shrubs and wild flowers. The Pride-of-De-Kaap scrambling shrubs offer cascading, orchid-like, peach-coloured flowers amongst their butterfly-shaped leaves. This is a close family member of the abundant mopane. The striking blue flowers of the plumbago shrubs attract butterflies and birds. Then there are the flame lilies, flame climbing bushwillows, wild heliotropes, violets, wild morning glories, vernonias, wild hibiscus and many more. The botanical diversity is simply amazing.

African buffaloes, S99

Broad-billed roller, S99

The easiest trees to recognise are the large-fruited bushwillow (large four-winged pods) and the stately pod mahoganies with their umbrella-like canopy. There is also apple-leaf with its gnarled trunk, jackalberry, nyala tree with clusters of untidy leaves which begin low down, sycamore fig with its yellowish trunk, the marula and its distinctive bark and the leadwood bushwillow with its snakeskin-like blocks of pale grey bark. Also worth looking out for are kirkia, baobab and Natal mahogany. The Lebombo ironwood is found only in the sandveld and on the Lebombo Mountains.

The animal numbers are not particularly high, but there are quite a few specials such as the Sharpe's grysbok and the suni that both feed on fallen leaves and fruit, and are extremely small and shy. Buffalo, impala and kudu are common, while elephant, zebra and nyala are represented. Predators are scarce, though leopard and lion do occur, and wild dog have been seen here on occasion.

A large number of habitats occur in a relatively small area, which yields a high diversity of bird species.

Even reptiles are abundant and diverse. Apart from the water and rock monitors and the usual snake species found elsewhere in the park, scarce species include the montane blind snake, rough-tailed girdled lizard and tigroid thick-tailed gecko.

Baobab, S99

Springhare, S99

Jackalberry, S99

Sharpe's grysbok, S99

S100
N'WANETSI RIVER ROAD

★★★★★

★★★★★ ★★★★★ ★★★★ ★★★★★

- 19 km; dirt road; popular, often dusty; traverses two major ecozones
- Loops to the pools in the N'wanetsi River

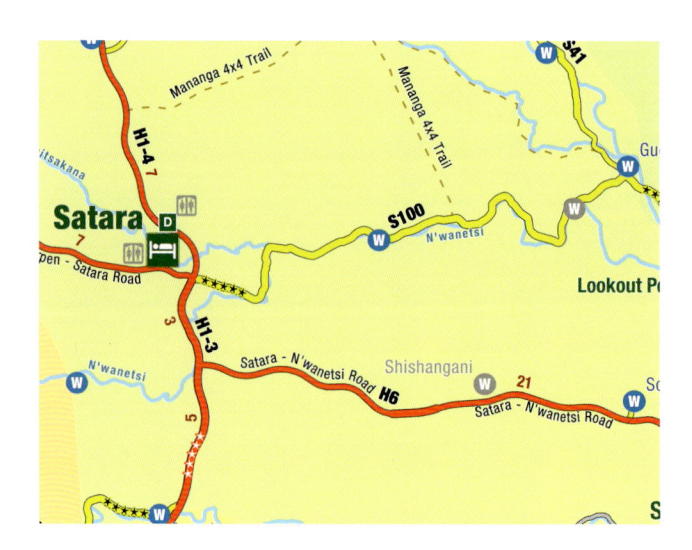

Many visitors rate this road as the best for game viewing in the Kruger. That may be so but even the most popular road may be devoid of visible game at times. However all the best conditions for game viewing are present and the chances of seeing game are better than elsewhere.

The road meanders close to the **N'wanetsi River**, which may not be flowing but still has permanent waterholes where game can drink. N'wanetsi means 'shimmering water' in Shangaan and probably refers to the lovely pools along this river. These attract game from the surrounding plains since most animals need to drink regularly.

The **riverine vegetation** is stunning and inspiring. Beautiful climax riverine vegetation lines the river road. The **grassland savanna** away from the river is open and **visibility is at its best**. Clay depressions can be recognised by stands of magic guarri where **shallow pans** form in the rainy season. The grass is sweet and rich in minerals. This is good grazing for species such as wildebeest and zebra. In spring when the first rains fall these species often move away from the fringes of the river and the crowded grassland.

The S100 is **supreme lion country** and often more than one group of these top predators may be encountered. Lions develop a preference for a particular prey species. Wildebeest are generally the favourite on the basalt plains, but some prides prefer to hunt buffalo, and others have learnt to overpower giraffe. Smaller prey such as porcupine and warthog are taken when the preferred prey is not available. It is interesting that lions neither favour nor avoid zebra, and seldom take impala.

This is also a **good road for leopard**. The preferred prey for leopard differs from that of lion and these two predators are often found in close proximity to each other. The size of prey animals depends on the body size of the predator. They kill their prey by delivering a bite at the base of the neck after stalking or ambushing it. Impala are the most common prey for leopard, followed by bushbuck, reedbuck and waterbuck, but they may take prey as small as rodents and even as big as a young wildebeest. Although leopards are the major enemy of baboons they seldom manage to catch one. Lions, being larger than leopards, are able to prey on larger animals such as adult wildebeest, giraffe, buffalo, waterbuck, kudu and others.

Buffalo need water daily and big herds on their way to the water are often encountered. Look out for herds close to the **Shibotwana and Nsasane waterholes**. Look carefully in the riverbeds since older bulls prefer juicy riverine vegetation. These old bulls are usually found in small groups since a solitary animal is an easy target for lions, and there is safety in numbers.

Birding is generally good and most of the common bushveld species may be encountered.

African buffalo, S100

Cheetah on lookout, S100

Phil Muller

Sunset scene, S100

S100

Lions interacting, S100

Lionesses with cubs, S100

Graeme Mitchley

Lion cub, $100

S101
SHIPIRIVIRHI LOOP TO THE SHINGWEDZI RIVER

★★★ ★★★ ★★ ★★★

3 km; narrow dirt road; traverses one ecozone

This short loop road leads closer on to the riverbank of the Shingwedzi where a deep pool attracts all sorts of game. The mopane shrubveld is well developed and visibility is not particularly good except at the lookout over the river.

Game density is generally low in mopane veld, except close to rivers. Sometimes kudu browse along the river's edge and the occasional impala and zebra may be seen as they make their way towards the water. This is elephant country and some of the biggest tuskers may be encountered. Predators keep close to the river to intercept potential prey on their way to drink.

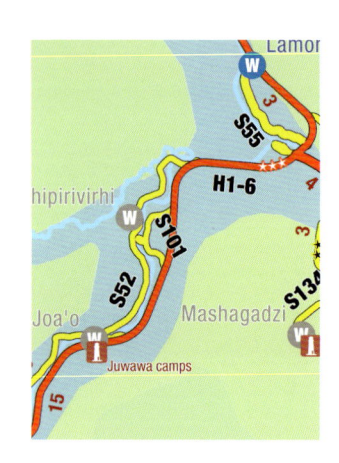

S102
MPONDO LINK ROAD

★★ ★★★ ★★★ ★★★

9 km; dirt road; often corrugated; traverses one major ecozone

The scenic S102 links the S26 with the H5 and is highly recommended.

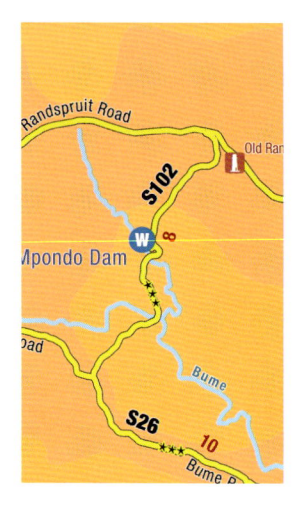

Buffeldorings Waterhole in the **Bume Watercourse** and the **Mpondo Dam** attract a fair number of game species. Since the surrounding **thicket vegetation** has good browsing, kudu are plentiful. This is good black rhino country, but unfortunately they are seldom seen due to their secretive nature. Lion sightings are often reported from this area. This road is **one of the less travelled gems** of the park and the best thing about it is that you can spend time on your own with a good sighting.

Lappet-faced vultures feeding, S101

Bruce Crossey

⭐⭐
S103
TO OLIFANTSBAD PAN

🦁 ★★★ 🦌 ★★ 🦅 ★★ 🌳 ★★

- 1.2 km; narrow dirt track; traverses one major ecozone
- The pan in the rainy season

This seasonal and overgrown pan attracts game when it has water.

Game densities are generally low in the north although elephant may be encountered. This is however a wonderful pan for game watching when conditions are favourable.

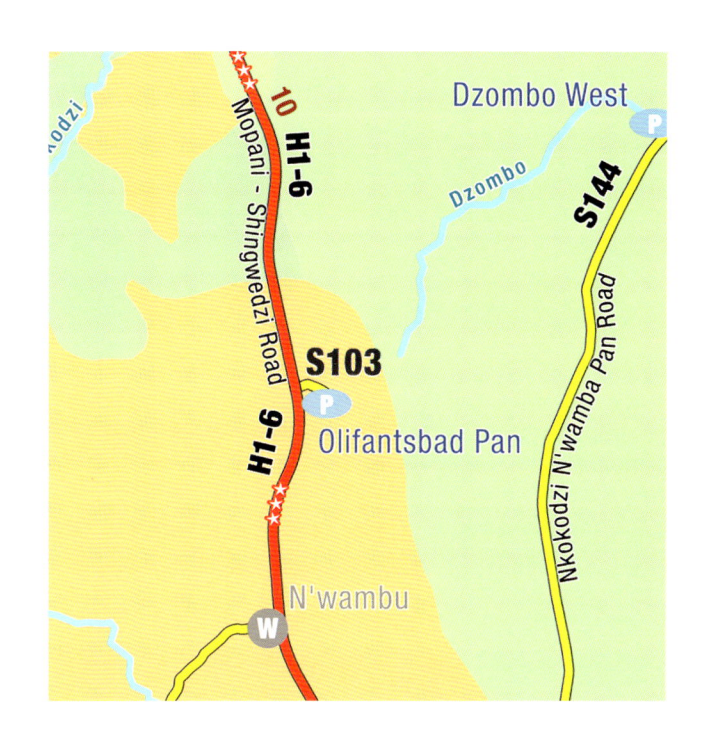

Olifantsbad Pan, S103

S105
TO NTANDANYATHI BIRD HIDE

★★★★

🦁 ★★★★ 🦌 ★★★ 🦅 ★★★★ 🌳 ★★★★

- 2 km; narrow dirt road; traverses one major ecozone
- Ntandanyathi Bird Hide

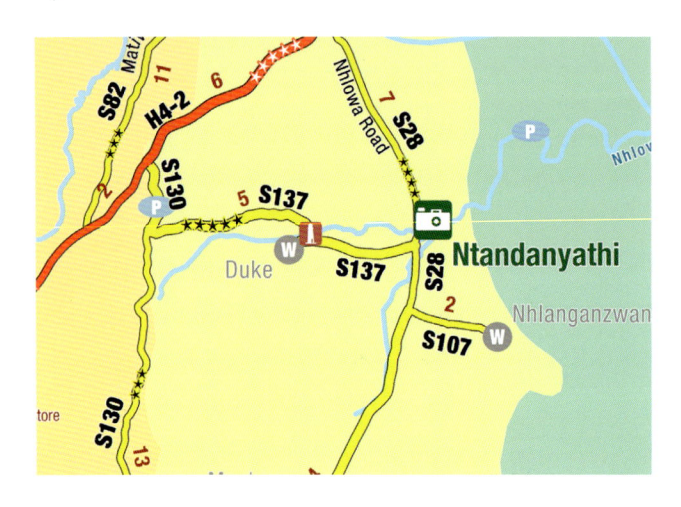

It is well worth visiting this bird hide on the banks of the Ntandanyathi drainage line.

A permanent deep pool is home to a pod of hippo, and birdlife abounds. Look out for heron, weavers, ducks and geese. Hawking birds make use of the big trees and some have even become used to tourists, forming a welcoming party at the parking area.

Banded mongoose pair, S105

S106
RABELAIS ROAD

★★★

🦁 ★★★ 🦌 ★★★ 🦅 ★★★ 🌳 ★★★

- 14 km; narrow dirt road; traverses one major ecozone
- Rabelais Hut

This loop road takes you past the historical Rabelais Hut that was once the entrance gate into the park.

Eileen Orpen donated seven farms (altogether 24 530 hectares in total) to the Kruger National Park. This extended the park westwards and the new gate was named in her honour. The **Orpen Gate** was opened in **May 1954**.

Another feature of this road is that it leads through typical **bushwillow woodland** on a geological bed of granite where the soil is sandy and coarse with mixed grasses. Look out for **bustard** next to this road. The bustard (formerly known as the korhaan) is a typical terrestrial bird about the size of a domestic fowl but with rather long, strong legs and a long neck. The overall colouring matches the surrounding grasses and because the bird tends to turn its back to any intrusion, the black belly is not always visible. When you come across one, stop, switch off the vehicle's engine, watch and wait. The males of these birds perform a rather **grand courtship display**. It starts by calling from a call site, uttering a series of clicks followed by a ventriloquial kyip-kyip-kyip. Then it suddenly flies 10–30 m into the air, throws itself backwards, seems to lose all control and plunges earthwards in a mad tumble. Just as one expects it to crash to the ground in a feathery explosion, it spreads its wings and glides away. A spectacular sight!

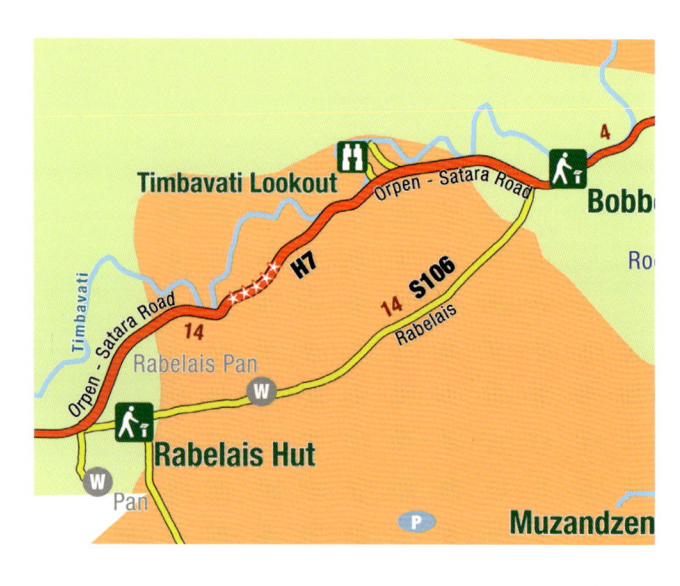

Red-crested korhaan calling, S106

S107
NHLANGANZWANE WETLAND ROAD
★★★★

🦁 ★★★★　🦌 ★★★　🦅 ★★★★★　🌳 ★★★

- 2 km; narrow dirt road; traverses one major ecozone
- Nhlanganzwane Wetland

The S107 cul-de-sac leads to the broken dam in the Nhlanganzwane watercourse.

It is a **wetland area** with longer grass where the dam used to attract reedbuck and waterbuck. Giraffe browse the knobthorns and zebra keep to the grassland areas. The open nature of the savanna is suitable habitat for the scarce cheetah since there is enough space to run prey – such as impala, duiker and steenbok – down.

The occasional herd of elephant may be encountered. White rhino and buffalo herds are often seen, as well as lion and hyena that tend to follow buffalo herds. Look out for jackal.

Birding is particularly good for terrestrial species and the probability of seeing ostrich, bustard, francolin and spurfowl is above average.

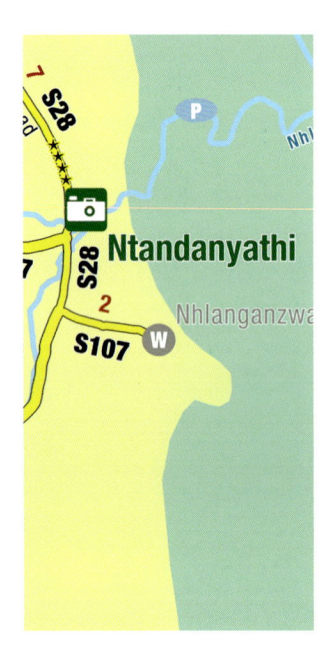

S108
LINK ROAD
★★★

🦁 ★★★　🦌 ★★★　🦅 ★★★　🌳 ★★★

- 4 km; dirt road; traverses one major ecozone

This is a short link road between the H5 and S25 and leads through well developed riverine bush along the Bume stream and drainage line.

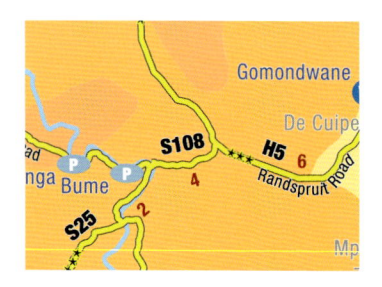

Giraffe licking calf, S108

S110
BERG-EN-DAL ROAD LOOP

★★★★

★★★★ ★★★ ★★★ ★★★★

- 9 km good tarred road; 13 km dirt road, corrugated in dry season; traverses one major ecozone
- Matjulu Dam on the gravel part of the road

The tarred part of the road from the H3 closest to the Malelane Gate leads to the Berg-en-Dal Rest Camp. It then continues as a dirt road and makes a loop to join the H3 further north.

The S110 traverses the heart of **Malelane mountain bushveld**. This is typical of the vegetation in the southwestern parts of the park where the terrain is mountainous, the soils coarse and the grass mostly unpalatable for much of the year. It is **an attractive landscape** as the road winds through several granite hills. To the south the **Khandzalive Hill** (839 m) is the highest peak in the park and is visible soon after the road passes the **Tlhalabye Hill** (630 m) on the northern side of the road. The road gradually descends into the **Matjulu valley** with the **Matjulu Hill** (627 m) rising in the distance.

The granite rocks underlying these hills are some of the **oldest rocks in the world** and were formed at least **3.6 billion years ago**. They are igneous, acidic, crystalline and slow-weathering. The resultant soils are sandy, relatively infertile and rich in silicon. Due to the higher rainfall and their age, the soils are leached and grasses that grow here are predominantly unpalatable and attract fewer grazers. Notice the tall yellow thatching grass that grows along parts of the road – this is a sure indicator of unpalatable, sour grass. Fine clay soils rich in minerals are produced in the weathering process but are eventually washed down the slopes into the valleys. This makes the valleys more fertile. Notice the size of the trees in the valleys; even the grasses here are sweeter and richer in minerals.

Although game densities are low, regular sightings along this road afford **unexpected game viewing pleasure**. Expect to find kudu and giraffe, but also impala and duiker, while small groups of zebra and often even a few wildebeest may occur seasonally. **Regular leopard sightings** add to the excitement, and it is also an area frequented by wild dog. Lions do occur but sightings are not regular. Look carefully in the valleys and along the lower slopes for white rhino. Elephant keep mainly to the lower contours and deeper parts of the valley but are regularly sighted. Herds of buffalo can be expected and are occasionally seen drinking at the dam below the rest camp and at Matjulu Dam.

Notice that the **mid-slopes** of the hills are covered with **broad-leafed bushveld**, mainly bushwillows. In the **valleys** plenty of knob-thorn as well as marula, jackalberry and magnificent specimens of sausage trees growing on termitaria occur. Other species are tamboti, magic guarri and weeping boer-bean. Many tree species uncommon to the rest of the park occur here. Two of these are the Cape chestnut and the wild pear. Mountain bushveld is not only diverse in vegetation, but also offers suitable habitat for a few special animal species. **Mountain reedbuck** do not occur in other parts of the park, but around Berg-en-Dal a small population has been re-established by translocation. However, for a time after they were moved they were not seen, and it was not clear whether they had survived. The mountain bushveld and hilly terrain is also suitable habitat for **klipspringer**.

The second part of the road is a dusty stretch through beautiful **rugged mountain scenery** and partly runs along the **Matjulu Spruit** with its lush vegetation. Soon after the camp, a loop road takes you to the **Matjulu Dam**. This is a pleasant game-watching place. White rhino prefer to drink in the late afternoons or early evenings. Wallowing in summer is a common ritual.

Birding is good in this area. Look out for barbets, hornbills, hoopoes, scimitarbills, rollers and shrikes, as well as raptors.

White-fronted bee-eater, S110

★★★★ S112
RENOSTERKOPPIES ROAD

🦁 ★★★★ 🦌 ★★★ 🦅 ★★★★★ 🌳 ★★★

- 6.6 km; dirt road; traverses one major ecozone
- Renosterkoppies; Shirimantanga

A series of inselbergs run in an east to west direction across central Kruger. This road skirts a group that is known as the Renosterkoppies (Rhino Hills). Shirimantanga, the boulders at the Stevenson-Hamilton Memorial, is part of this picturesque collection of huge boulders.

The mixed woodlands in the area of the granite inselbergs are generally **good for game**. White rhino are often seen and so are giraffe, elephant, zebra, kudu and impala. Predators such as lion and leopard are often encountered. Scan the granite boulders for klipspringer.

Birding is good as the variety of vegetation offers many different habitats. Both terrestrial and tree-living species are well represented.

★★★ S113
LINK ROAD BETWEEN S23 AND H3

🦁 ★★★ 🦌 ★★★ 🦅 ★★★ 🌳 ★★

- 3 km; dirt road; narrow; traverses one major ecozone
- Low-water bridge crossing over the Biyamiti River

This short 3 km road is a useful link between two popular routes.

Mixed woodlands are generally good for game. Visibility on this short link road is good. This is ideal habitat for cheetah. The causeway across the Biyamiti River offers the possibility of waterbird sightings.

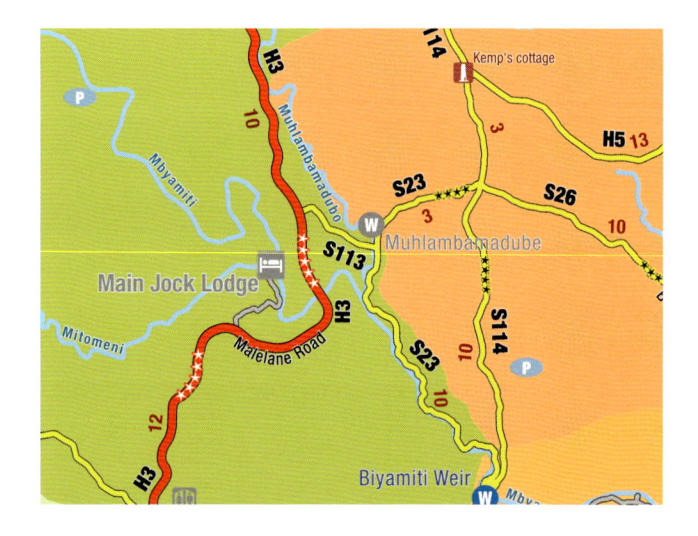

Cheetah, S112

Scene at Byamiti Weir, S114

★★★★

S114
ORIGINAL ROUTE FROM MALELANE TO SKUKUZA

★★★★ ★★★★ ★★★★ ★★★

- 52 km; dirt road; varying quality; traverses four major ecozones
- Renosterkoppies Dam; Biyamiti Weir, Mhlambane River/Stream crossing

Game drives are generally rewarding along the S114, especially the southern and northern sections. Although this road is often corrugated in places, it is worth taking. There are several escape routes to the tarred H3. Low traffic volumes and intimate encounters are well worth the dust.

The road traverses several ecozones. From the south, the first section is still part of the **Malelane mountain bushveld** landscape – mostly bushwillow shrubs and mixed grasses with a few patches of sweet grass and magic guarri.

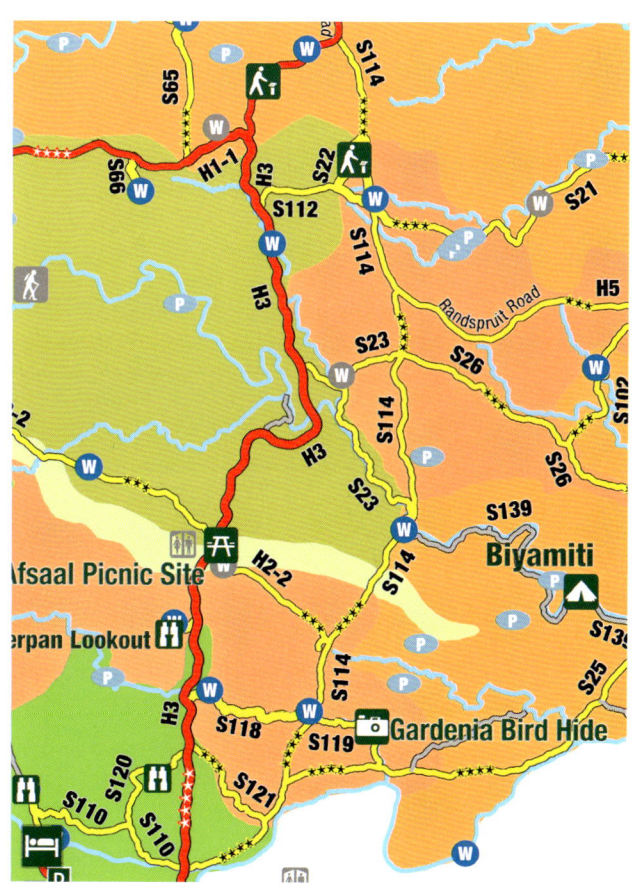

Giant kingfisher male, S114

The grass attracts grazers and the bushwillow browsers and when the guarri is in fruit, bird parties abound. Stunted impala lily shrubs grow in profusion on the stony flats close to the intersection. **Impala lilies** flower during the **winter** months. Spot the large-leafed rock fig on the low granite hillock.

As you approach the intersection with the S118 and S119 you enter the **Mhlambane River basin** on the way to the low-water bridge. Although it's a seasonal river, **pools** remain long after good rain and are regularly visited by most game. Before the **Biyamiti River** crossing, the road passes through a **dyke of gabbro** with extremely sweet grass. Be vigilant around here since you can expect good game sightings. The **Biyamiti Weir** is another favourite. The little dam above the weir usually has water and even hippo visit this pool. Look for kingfishers, lapwings, storks, cormorants and herons. Most of the time this is the only water in the area, popular with most of the game. Leopard sightings are often reported. Klipspringer inhabit the surrounding koppies.

The long stretch that follows passes through typical **mixed bushwillow woodland** up to the **Renosterkoppies**. The **Renosterkoppies Waterhole** is a popular drinking point for all game of the area. It is well worth waiting to see who visits to have a drink. As a rule, good numbers of wildebeest, zebra and warthog are present. It is also a favourite with elephant and white rhino.

North of the waterhole the vegetation changes to **dense thorn thickets** where visibility is often bad, particularly in the summer months. Find a wild gardenia bush in the thorn thicket savanna on the northernmost stretch of the road. The S114 meets up with the H1-1 close to Skukuza.

Birding is good all along. Watch out for lapwings, hornbills, shrikes, larks and starlings in the sparsely grassed areas.

Malachite kingfisher, S114

Leopard at Biyamiti Weir, S114

Leopard at Biyamiti Weir, S114

S118 — MHLAMBANE ROAD ★★★★

★★★★ ★★★★ ★★★★ ★★★★★

- 8 km; narrow dirt road; traverses one major ecozone
- Ampie's Waterhole

S119 — GARDENIA HIDE ROAD ★★★★

★★★ ★★★ ★★★★ ★★★★★

- 6 km; meandering dirt road; traverses one major ecozone
- Gardenia Bird Hide

The S118 and S119 are attractive river roads that are worth following. Good sightings are regularly reported.

The seasonal **Mhlambane River** winds its way down to the Crocodile River. It carries water from an **extensive catchment basin** during the rainy season and has water in standing pools even in the dry season.

Many **rhino middens** indicate the presence of both black and white rhino. Elephant, buffalo and impala droppings give away their presence. Elephant are often seen digging for subterranean water in the riverbed with their trunks. Lush **riverine vegetation** shows that there is adequate underground water even when the river is not running.

Drive slowly. With plenty prey animals around you may be surprised by leopard or lion, or even wild dog. At the eastern extremity the road ends at the intersection with the S114 and a **low-level causeway** that is often rewarding. At the western extremity it may be worthwhile lingering at **Ampie's Waterhole**. Just after the intersection with the H3, the tarred road crosses the river at a high bridge. Spend time scanning the riverbed in both directions.

The S118 continues as the S119 further along the Mhlambane River. Along the meander there are several loops closer to the river. Don't ignore these as they often offer good views over the riverbed.

Huge **riverine trees** fringe the riverbanks and offer good perches to **raptors**. Look out for the magnificent specimens of knob-thorn, weeping boer-bean, leadwood and sausage trees.

Away from the river on the southern end of the road, the landscape is covered by typical **broad-leafed vegetation** consisting mainly of bushwillow with the occasional torchwood. Find the fine specimen of torchwood where the S119 joins the S25.

Also along the southern end of the road, the **Gardenia Bird Hide** is not to be missed. In the rainy season this clay depression, surrounded by the evergreen magic guarri, forms a pan favoured by the local population of white rhino. It is an exhilarating experience to watch these giants from the safety of the hide as they drink or roll in the mud only a few metres away.

Male lion, S119 (Hamman Prinsloo)

★★
S120
STEILBERG MOUNTAIN DRIVE

★★ ★★ ★★ ★★★★

- 8 km; narrow and rough dirt road; traverses one major ecozone
- The lookout at the top of the hill

The S120 is rough on sedan vehicles but taken slowly it is worth the drive. The scenic beauty, extraordinary tree species and the possibility of klipspringer sightings are the biggest lure.

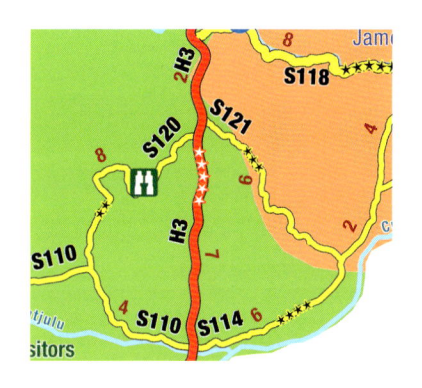

Game is however generally sparse on this road. Look out for the large rock fig on the eastern side of the hill right next to the road. Another tree species you may recognise is the mountain kirkia or syringa on the upper slopes. In autumn it is fairly easy to recognise this graceful tree due to the beautiful colours of its leaves. White rhino may be spotted in the distance down the lower slopes. Look out for leopard. Most of the more common bird species may be seen, but look out for typical mountain species.

★★★
S121
TIMFENHENI LOOP

★★ ★★★ ★★★ ★★★

- 6 km; dirt road; stony and often corrugated; traverses one major ecozone
- Vegetation along the seasonal Timfenheni Stream

The road roughly follows the course of the Timfenheni seasonal stream. This is a narrow intimate road passing through dense bushwillow woodland with a sickle-bush understorey towards the south.

Where the road runs closer to the stream, **clay depressions** are indicated by stands of magic guarri. Along the stream bank typical **riverine vegetation** is found with mature specimens of knob-thorn, jackalberry, apple-leaf and tamboti. It offers a home for vervet monkey populations.

Visibility is mostly restricted to a few metres from the road but being browsers, kudu find this vegetation attractive.

African wild dog, S121

African wild dogs, S121

S122
SKIRTING THE MUNTSHE HILL

★★★

★★ ★★★ ★★ ★★★

- 12 km; narrow dirt track; traverses one major ecozone
- Good after a fire when grasses sprout

This road provides a nice drive if you have time and love quiet roads. On the far eastern horizon the Lebombo Mountains vanish in the distance. Sparse tree cover allows for good visibility in all directions.

Although the track runs through sweet grassland plains where big herds of zebra and wildebeest often congregate, it is not always rewarding. The time of year is crucial. This is the winter grazing ground for zebra and wildebeest. As soon as the first spring rains fall in the central part of the park, the herds migrate northwards up to the Lindanda Plains south of the Sweni River. The migration is not as extensive as in central Africa, but happens nevertheless. If you happen to be there at the right time, a **grand game spectacle** may await you. **Take your chances**.

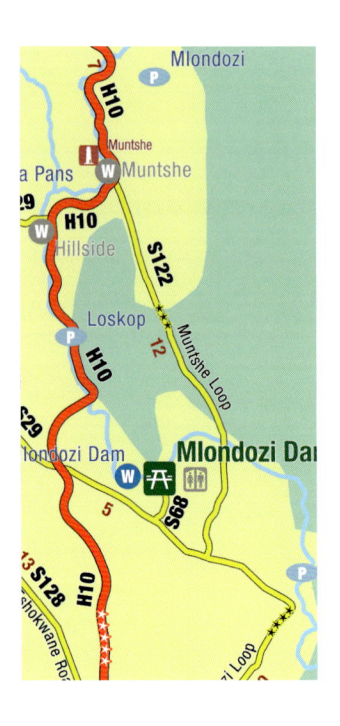

This is one of only a few tourist roads in the park that traverses **Lebombo Mountain bushveld**. This type of landscape includes the Lebombo range itself and is only represented in a narrow strip along the park's eastern boundary. The **Muntshe Picnic Site** and **Muntshe Hill** are all part of this landscape. The only other tourist access to this kind of landscape is the area around N'wanetsi.

The soils are generally shallow and stony. Along the Muntshe area the topography is more undulating than mountainous, except for Muntshe Hill itself. The **plateaus are extensive**. Note the prominent ridges and watersheds, and the different vegetation. Most general game species are represented here but scarce species may occur.

Blue wildebeest, S122

★★★★
S125
N'WASWITSONTSO ROAD

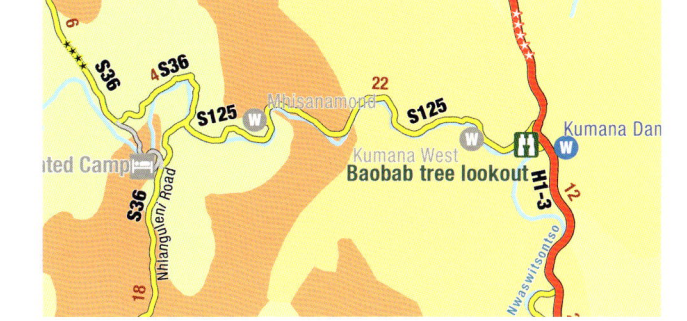

★★★★ ★★★★ ★★★ ★★★★

20 km; winding dirt road; traverses three major ecozones

The scenic S125 meanders along the non-perennial N'waswitsontso River. Despite the seasonal nature of the river, underground water is sufficient to support lush riverine vegetation along the banks while several pools remain well into the dry season.

The road traverses three different geological substrates. The underlying geology at the intersection with the H1-3 is basalt. Then follows a **narrow band of Karoo sediments** that divide the basaltic formations of the east from the granite formations of the west. The **Delagoa thorn thickets** are typical of the Ecca shales of the Karoo sediments. Note the **sandstone ridges** at places. Many-stemmed false-thorn and the trees, including magic guarri, around clay depressions, are typical of this ecozone.

The short, sweet grass attracts mid-sized impala herds, zebra and blue wildebeest. Look out for duiker and kudu. Rhino middens are an indication of their presence and elephant often keep close to the river.

Several loops towards the river allow better views of the riverbed. Lush **riverine vegetation** lines the riverbanks. Huge jackalberry, sausage tree, sycamore fig and tamboti add to the scenic nature of this route. The occasional nyala tree is also found. Look out for buffalo, leopard, lion and elephant on the sandbanks and in the riverbed.

The western section of the road passes through **broad-leafed savanna** with bushwillow, cluster-leaf and mixed grassland. Although game densities here are low, buffalo are often encountered.

Black-backed jackal, S125

S126
SWENI DRIVE
★★★★

🦁 ★★★★ 🦌 ★★★ 🦅 ★★★★ 🌳 ★★★★

- 22 km; dirt road; traverses three major ecozones
- Sweni and Welverdiend waterholes

This is one of the favourite game-drive roads for many visitors. The eastern section is usually particularly rewarding and you can expect good sightings.

Along the **Sweni River** the **riverine vegetation** is ideal habitat for leopard.

The Sweni drive traverses three landscapes as it runs along the seasonal Sweni River. The eastern end is the prettiest and also the most rewarding. The open nature of the savanna attracts all kinds of game, from herbivores to predators. Stands of magic guarri indicate sodic depressions in the vicinity of the first watering point. Warthogs, zebra, wildebeest and impala are usually seen around here.

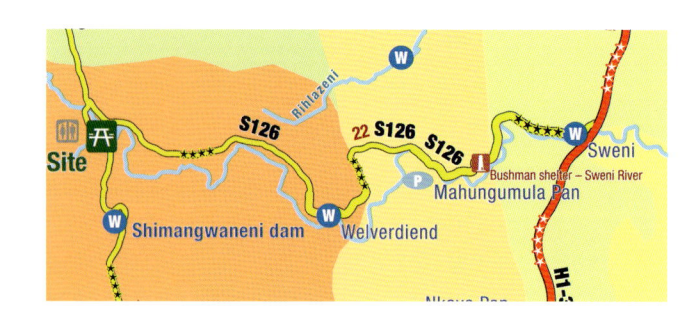

Note the **wild date palms** growing in profusion along the riverbank, with their big, arching, medium-green leaves. The other species is the **lala palm** with its silver-grey, fanlike leaves. It grows in abundance further away from the river on the clay substrate. Lala palms do not necessarily grow near water, but prefer basaltic clay soils. The fruit – hard, shiny, dark-brown balls – are borne in big spikes on the female plant.

As the vegetation changes to **Delagoa thorn thickets** with false thorn and magic guarri, sodic sites become more evident. These bare patches of soil that may look eroded are a natural part of this landscape. Clay soils retain water and minerals and form **pans** during the rainy season. Such pans become **temporary wallows** for rhino, buffalo and warthog. Grazers often congregate on such sites, partly because it is relatively safe since approaching predators can easily be spotted, but also because of the sodium content of the soil. The plants on such brackish sites are rich in sodium and animals crave this salt. Animals will even **lick the soil** to obtain salt.

The western section of this road passes through a much drier area with broad-leafed vegetation dominated by **bushwillow and clusterleaf**. At the **Welverdiend** short loop, visibility over the grassy plain is good and sometimes herds of game are seen in the distance. Giraffe and kudu usually occur. The far western section of the road is rather featureless and visibility is poor due to **dense broad-leafed bushwillow**. Animal densities are also much lower.

Light and normal-coloured male lions, S126

Juvenile giraffe portrait, S126

★★★
S127
NTOMENI ROAD

★★ ★★★ ★★★ ★★

🛣 9 km; dirt road; often corrugated; traverses one major ecozone

The road serves as a convenient link between the Timbavati River road and picnic site and the H1-4 tarred road.

From the east the road runs through dry **open grassland** dotted with **stunted knob-thorn**. It then gradually changes into **rugged veld** with low shrubs as it approaches the Timbavati River. The underlying geology is basalt with high concentrations of limestone concretions, while the soils are dark-brown, shallow and stony.

Expect to see impala, kudu, giraffe, zebra and wildebeest. The grass is generally short and palatable. There are no animal drinking points along this road.

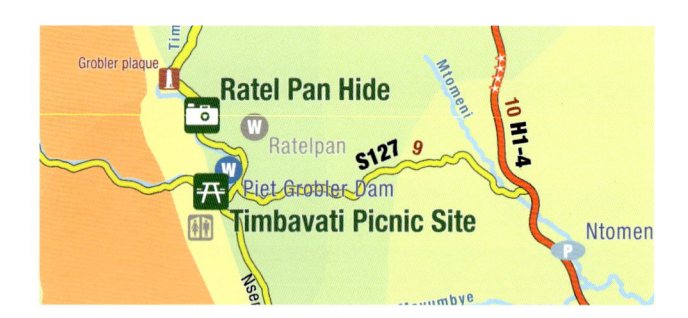

★★★
S128
OLD TSHOKWANE ROAD

★★★ ★★ ★★★ ★★★

🛣 31 km; narrow dirt track; traverses one major ecozone
🚩 Migrating zebra and wildebeest herds when they occur

The S128 was the original main track linking Lower Sabie and Tshokwane.

The southern section gives access to the popular Salitjie Road or S30. This part of the road is often corrugated since it is well travelled up to the S30 intersection. Towards the north (after the S30 intersection) the road becomes narrower and featureless with open, sweet grassland plains grazed by zebra and blue wildebeest. Shrubs are stunted and do not clutter the view. The sky seems huge, even overwhelming, and humans small and insignificant. This is a road to travel after the spring rains when wild flowers appear and the grass is short and green. Or when you wish to get away from crowds.

Impala nursery, S127

Cheetah with impala lamb prey, S128

S129
LINK BETWEEN S128 AND H10

★★

🦁 ★★   🦌 ★★   🦅 ★★★   🌳 ★★

🛣 4 km; narrow dirt track; traverses one major ecozone

Should you feel you've had enough of the S128, this is a quick escape road leading back to the tarred H10.

As it is narrow and intimately close to the veld, you are likely to come across various terrestrial bird species such as francolins, guineafowl and bustards. These birds can be fascinating to watch. Visibility is good. Shrubs are stunted and do not clutter the view. Here, one feels dwarfed by the vast sky.

Cheetah, S129

Villiers Steyn

S130
GOMONDWANE LOOP

★★★

🦁 ★★★   🦌 ★★★★   🦅 ★★★   🌳 ★★★★

🛣 13 km; narrow dirt road; traverses one major ecozone
🚩 Rainwater pans

The Gomondwane loop is as enchanting as the sound of its name. Visibility is not good, but the atmosphere is magic. It is well worth doing this drive if you enjoy roads with a special ambience.

Dense stands of **many-stemmed false-thorn** (v-shaped trees that are small to medium height) grow in association with **Delagoa thorn** all along this loop road. The finely granulated soils derived from Ecca shales or mudstone form a **clay substrate**. The area is **very fla**t and water does not penetrate the soils easily. False thorn grows exclusively in this kind of clay soil, which forms typical **seasonal pans** or depressions. The evergreen magic guarri serve as indicators of depressions where water gathers in pans.

Warthog and rhino often visit such pans to wallow. The very sweet grass, in association with enough browse, attracts impala all year round. **White rhino middens** are proof that a good number of these giants inhabit this area. Game abounds but is elusive because of the dense vegetation. Kudu, impala and elephant browse the dark-green foliage, while giraffe feed on the seed pods.

The changing foliage colours of the many-stemmed false-thorn make for an enchanting drive, whatever the season. It is red when young, dark-green when mature and yellow in autumn, with brown pods towards winter and smooth, bare, grey stems until spring.

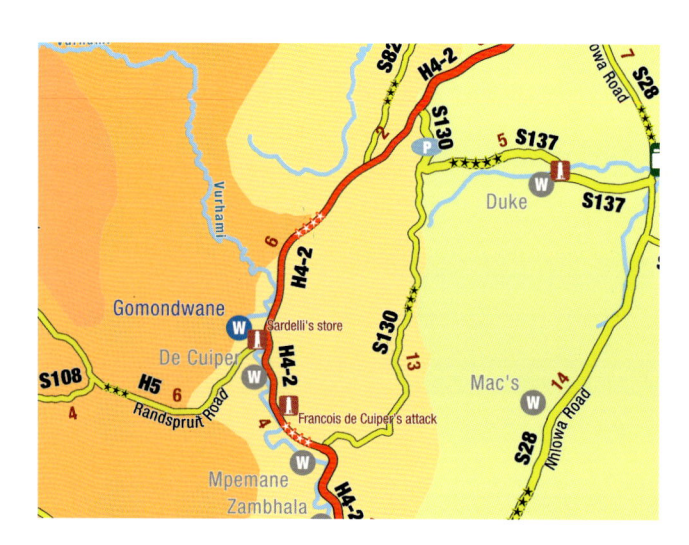

Vervet monkey, S130

S130

Spotted hyenas, S130

Gerhard Geldenhuys

Pride of lions at hippo carcass, S130

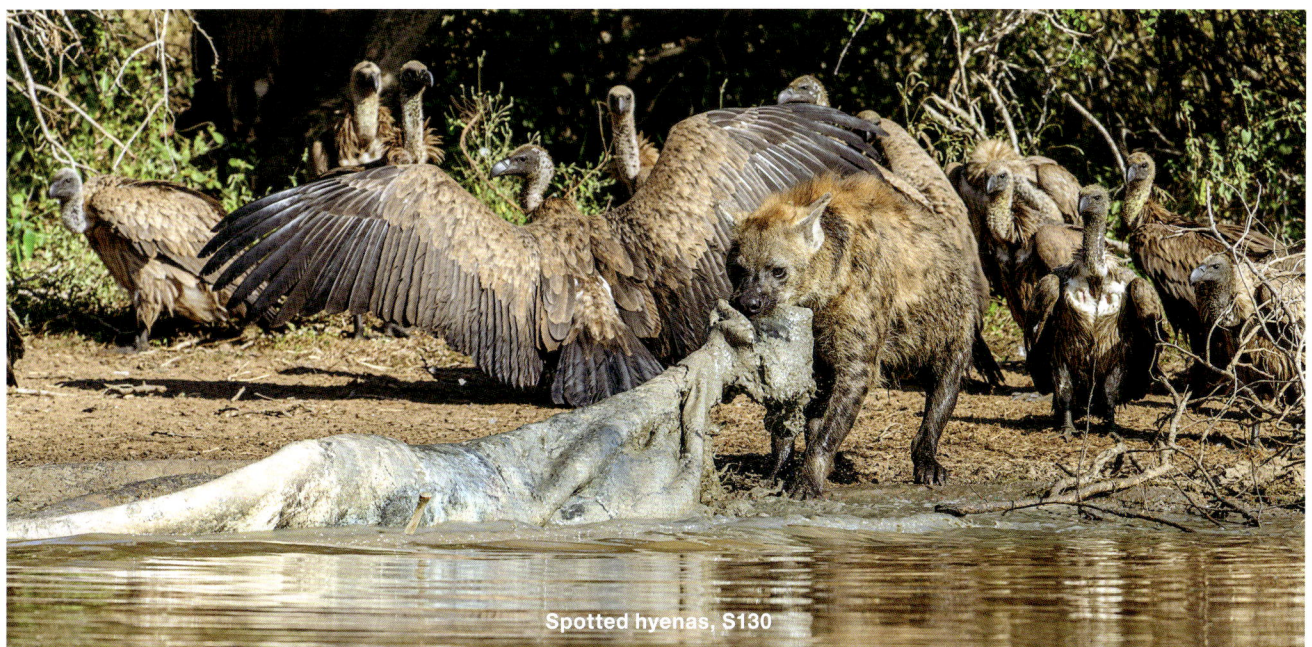

Gerhard Geldenhuys

Spotted hyenas, S130

Gerhard Geldenhuys

S131
SHIVULANI ROAD
★★★

- 46 km; narrow dirt road; often corrugated; traverses two major ecozones
- Mashangeni and Ngwenyeni watercourses; Shikumbu Hill

The best part of this road is the extreme western section immediately after leaving the Phalaborwa Gate where the S131 passes through the catchment area of the seasonal Mashangeni and Ngwenyeni watercourses that will eventually deposit their seasonal accumulation of water into the perennial Letaba River.

Common duiker, S131

This region is particularly favoured by elephant and zebra, but wildebeest are also well represented. Concentrations of impala occur close to the Ngwenyeni drainage line while baboons use the trees near the river course as their sleeping trees – huge apple-leaf, leadwood, sycamore fig and false marula are dotted along the drainage lines. Sizeable buffalo herds roam in pursuit of suitable grazing.

In summer, after the first good rains, a plethora of **wild flowers** appears along the road verges and the grasses between the mopane. Around the waterhole the **magic guarri** indicates clay depressions, which attract warthog and impala. All in all, the section between the H9 and the intersection with the H14 is a scenic road with a large array of game species.

Between the H14 and S133 the most exciting section is the part that skirts the northern slopes of the **Shikumbu Hill** (494 m). The typical Phalaborwa kind of **granite koppie** (hill) is scenically pleasing and one may find giraffe and other general game feeding on the lower slopes. The only watering point on this section of the route is **Shivulani**, where a **pan** forms in the rainy season and a wind pump and cement dam indicate underground water. There is a good lookout over the pan.

Between the S133 and S47 intersections, the road runs through **featureless mopane shrubveld**. Game densities are fairly low, although good sightings are reported from time to time. Look out for buffalo herds and predators that follow them. The **N'wanetsi Waterhole** is graced by two huge **apple-leaf trees**. A cement dam and wind pump indicate water, but again, animal densities are low around here. The N'wanetsi drainage line is usually dry but when it rains the accumulated water is deposited into the Letaba River system.

To the east, after the intersection with the S47, the road runs through a section of **sandveld** where the soil is coarse and water retention is low. Almost no mopanes are found here, but look out for silver cluster-leaf and sickle-bush. The grass on the sandveld area is sweet and animals favour this.

Several turn-off routes for four-wheel drive vehicles have been developed along this road. Enquire at any of the reception offices for details.

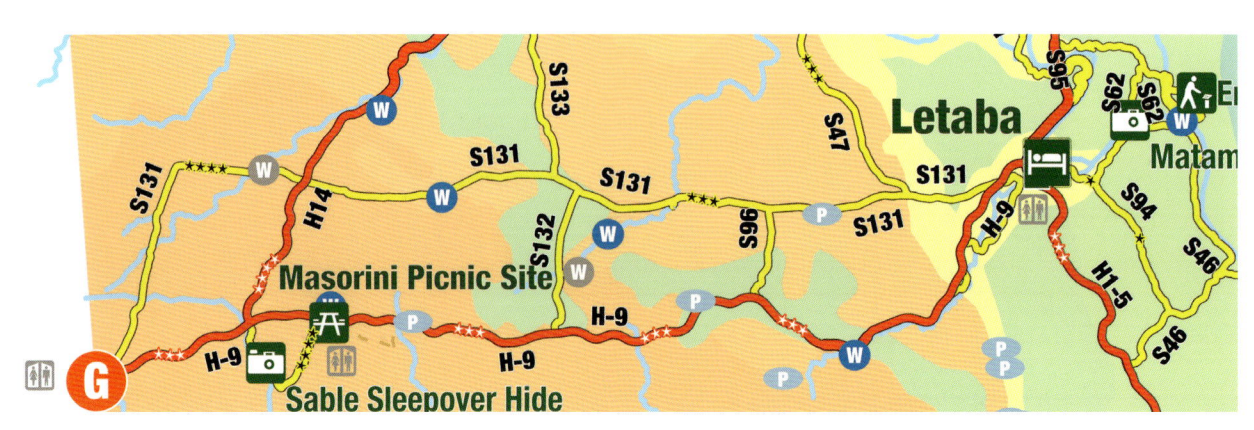

★★★

S132
MARHUMBINI LINK ROAD

🦁 ★★★ 🦌 ★★★ 🦅 ★★ 🌳 ★★

- 7 km; narrow dirt road; traverses one major ecozone
- Marhumbini Waterhole

This is a useful link road between the H9 and the S131.

The smallish **mopane trees** form sparse to **fairly thick stands**. Although the mopane veld supports a large variety of large mammals, **visibility** from the road is **not too good**. Even elephant may simply vanish once they move more than a few metres away from the road. Zebra and wildebeest are plentiful but do not occur in huge herds and are not necessarily seen. The closed **Marhumbini Waterhole** is fairly open and visibility here is much better than along the road.

Stands of silver cluster-leaf indicate a seepage line along the mid-slope around the waterhole. Good specimens of weeping wattle are prominent when they have bright yellow flowers in long drooping clusters during the summer months.

Sandgrouse are occasionally seen along this road. They move about in pairs, nest on the ground and feed on seeds. They favour the road verges where seeds often accumulate and are easy to find. The male is particularly handsome, with a double band of darker feathers across the chest.

★★★

S133
JUMBO ROAD

🦁 ★★ 🦌 ★★ 🦅 ★★★ 🌳 ★★★

- 9 km; narrow dirt road; traverses one major ecozone
- Jumbo Waterhole

This narrow road traverses typical mopane and bushwillow woodland. It is not often travelled and is a good road to take if you enjoy solitude and getting close to the bush.

As in most of this kind of habitat, **game densities are low**, making surprise encounters all the more special. The only watering point on this road is the **Jumbo Waterhole**, which lies in the **Shikome Stream** where it converges with the **Matrabowa Stream**.

The road enters the H14 just beyond the bridge over the **Shivulani stream** a few kilometres before the bridge over the Letaba.

Honey badger, S132

S134
MASHAGADZI LOOP
★★

★★ ★★★ ★★★ ★★

6 km; dirt road; traverses one major ecozone

S135
CAUSEWAY OVER THE SHINGWEDZI RIVER
★★★

★★★ ★★★ ★★★★ ★★★★

4 km; narrow dirt road; traverses two major ecozones

Causeway over the Shingwedzi River

This is a favourite last-minute drive before the gates close and is highly recommended.

The low-water causeway is popular for its mid-river ambience. Birding is good for waterbirds visiting the standing pools formed by the causeway, which is closed during heavy rains. Spectacular views up and down the riverbed help to locate animals. The biggest section of the road runs through dry shrub mopane where animals are often intercepted as they cross the road on their way to drink.

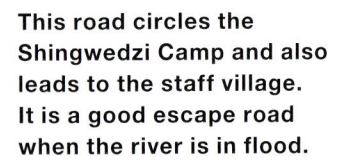

This road circles the Shingwedzi Camp and also leads to the staff village. It is a good escape road when the river is in flood.

It traverses typical **mopane woodland** but falls partly within the floodplain of the river. In recent years heavy floods have caused much damage to both the camp and the staff village.

About halfway along this road a short 2 km track leads to the **Mashangadzi Waterhole**, which is normally dry. Close to the intersection with the S50, a reasonably large **pan** forms during the rainy season, which holds water for a long time and is regularly visited by warthog and impala.

Spectacular sightings are seldom reported from this road, but birds are everywhere and you may be lucky enough to get a good sighting.

Saddle-billed stork pair, S135

Cape glossy starling, Shingwedzi Camp

Bennet's woodpecker, Shingwedzi Camp

S137
DUKE ROAD
★★★★

🦁 ★★★★ 🦌 ★★★★ 🦅 ★★★★ 🌳 ★★★

- 8 km; narrow dirt road; traverses one major ecozone
- Duke Road

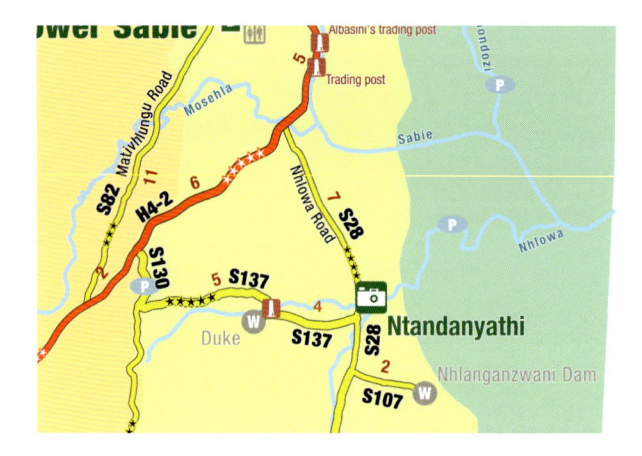

The S137 links the S28 to the H4-2 and is good for both game viewing and birding.

Both the demolished **Duke Dam and waterhole** are dry and offer less interesting game viewing than in the past. **Pans** form in the clay soil during the wet season, attracting birds and general game. Buffalo and elephant herds are often encountered on this stretch of road.

The open savanna is suitable habitat for the scarce cheetah since there is enough space to run down prey – impala, duiker and steenbok.

White rhino are often seen, as well as lion and hyena that tend to follow buffalo herds.

Birding is particularly good for the common bushveld species as well as for terrestrial species. The probability of seeing ostrich, bustard, francolin and spurfowl is above average.

S140
MAHLABYANINI ROAD
★★★★

🦁 ★★★★ 🦌 ★★★ 🦅 ★★★★★ 🌳 ★★★

- 19 km; dirt road; traverses one major ecozone

The full length of this road leads through mixed broad-leafed woodlands to the upper catchment of the N'waswitsontso River. It is the link between Orpen Gate and the popular Talamati Private Camp.

The mixed grassland supports the general antelope found in the western parts of the park as well as buffalo, elephant and giraffe. These in turn attract lions and good sightings occur on this road. It is a pleasant **sunset drive** for guests at Orpen, Tamboti and Marula Camps, as well as those guests with accommodation at Talamati itself.

The closed **Mahlahyanini Waterhole** is close to the camp and the road crosses the upper reaches of the **N'waswitsontso River** here. Good game sightings are reported on this last section of the road.

Hamerkop with fish prey, S142

★★★
S142
SHONGOLOLO LOOP ROAD

★★ ★★ ★★★ ★★★★

36 km; dirt road; traverses one major ecozone

Mtomeni Pan; Welgelegen Pan; the causeway over the Tzendze River and the Shipandani Hide

This is not a particularly rewarding road during the dry season but it is scenic during the wet season. Pans attract game when they have water. The loop to the Welgelegen Waterhole situated on the Shongololo Stream is worth taking.

A 'shongololo' is a millipede in African languages and the S142 is probably called this because it curls up on itself on the western side of the Mopani Camp almost in a way a millipede would do.

The entire area fringing this road is typical of **mopane and bushwillow woodland** with an underlying geology of granite. Soils are coarse, sandy and low in nutrients, and water drains from them easily. The landscape is slightly undulating and smaller sand particles are carried down the mid-slopes to accumulate in the lower-lying areas. Notice the many drainage lines crossing this road.

Where the sand meets hard rock, water seepage into the soil is stopped and runs down the rock, forming a **seepage line**. Notice that many patches of **silver cluster-leaf** occur along the way; these trees grow particularly well on seepage lines. Notice that there may be depressions close by. Finer clay particles are washed down into these depressions. Because these soils are so fine-grained, they lie close together, preventing water from seeping through. These areas can become very muddy and waterlogged in the rainy season and **pans** form. Some of these hold water for a long time into the dry season. They even have abundant growths of **water lilies**. The pans at **Outspan, Shongololo** (the beginning of the watercourse with that name), **Welgelegen** and **Mtomeni** are some of those that retain their water longest into the dry season.

This intimate road is particularly scenic and quite rewarding in summer, but yields few excellent sightings during the dry season when the animals have moved away to find better grazing closer to water. Big apple-leaf, leadwood, knobthorn, tamboti and a few tall mopane trees account for the diversity in vegetation that is pleasing to the eye.

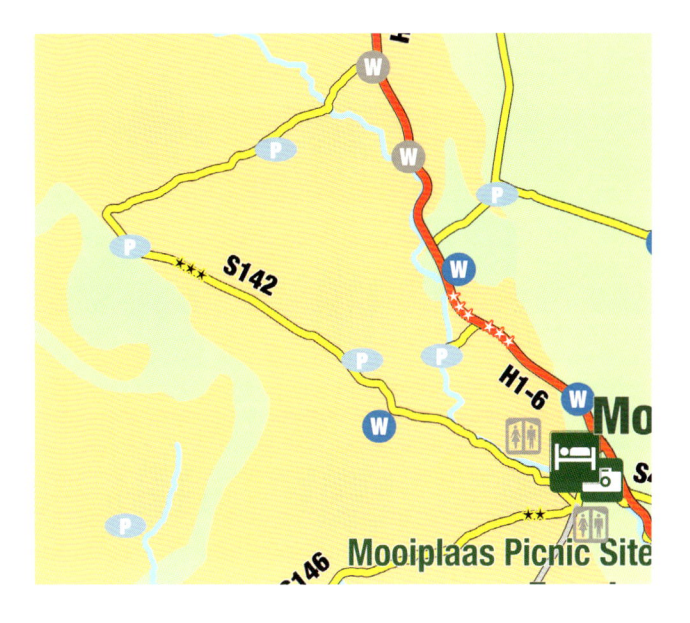

The turn-off to the banks of the **Pioneer Dam** is reached from the southern part of this road. The **Pioneer Hide** overlooks the dam and offers quiet time close to the bush. The better hide is the one lower down on the Tsendze River close to the low-water causeway. The **Shipandani Hide** also accommodates overnight visitors (apply at the Mopani reception) but is open for all during the day.

The best birding spot close to the Mopani Camp is the **low-water causeway** downstream of the hide. Look out for crocodile and birds amongst the reeds.

Juvenile green-backed heron with fish prey, S142

S143
TROPIC OF CAPRICORN LOOP

★★★ ★★★ ★★★ ★★★

14 km; narrow dirt road; traverses one major ecozone
Tihongonyeni Waterhole

The Tropic of Capricorn loop is one of the better roads for game viewing in the northern sector.

The road traverses **mopane shrubveld** typical of the northeastern half of the park. Gradually the mopane shrub becomes more stunted until it transforms into an **open plain** of grassland. Due to the underlying geology of basalt, the soils are fertile and the landscape flat. The sweet grass is palatable for most of the year and is favoured by the main grazers.

Sweet grass on its own is not enough to attract the plains game: **access to water** is of prime importance. Natural pans form after summer rains but do not provide enough water throughout the dry period, so the **Tihongonyeni borehole** helps to maintain the water level of the waterhole. Zebra and wildebeest do well, yet they occur in much smaller numbers than they do in the south. Other antelope are impala, steenbok, tsessebe and possibly even eland.

Impressive **big tuskers** are awe-inspiring when they approach the waterhole over the plains – the absence of trees makes them look even bigger. Sometimes they appear out of nowhere from all directions. Once they have quenched their thirst they may linger, interacting with each other, or take showers or enjoy a mud bath. Huge tuskers often have one or more younger companion bulls with them.

Ostriches are abundant. They also prefer these open places to the denser mopane woodland as they can see approaching danger more easily. They may have lost their ability to fly, but they can run at 60 km/h and defend themselves by kicking. Unfortunately they are vulnerable when they are breeding but they use camouflage when on the nest. The grey female incubates the eggs during the day while the dark male takes his turn during the night.

The three giants: elephant, common ostrich and kori bustard, S143

★★
S144
NKOKODZI N'WAMBA PAN ROAD

🦁 ★   🦌 ★★   🦅 ★★   🌳 ★★

- 33 km; dirt road; traverses one major ecozone
- Nkokodzi Waterhole

The old main road to Shingwedzi leads over extensive flat plains of basalt covered with mopane shrub. Since general game densities are low on the northern plains, this road is generally quiet.

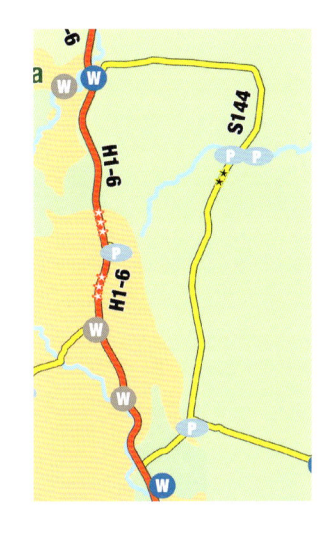

The road leads through sweet grazing amongst the mopane, but the biggest restrictive factor for game distribution is access to water. The only water source along this road is at Nkokodzi. Many animal tracks leading to the water suggest that good numbers of animals in the area visit this watering point regularly.

★★★
S145
TALAMATI ROAD

🦁 ★★★   🦌 ★★★   🦅 ★★★   🌳 ★★★

- 12 km; narrow dirt road; traverses one major ecozone
- River views

The main attraction of this road is the lush grazing on the banks of the N'waswitsontso.

In the afternoons large zebra herds, waterbuck and other game gather on the plains next to the N'waswitsontso River. The riverine vegetation is quite lush and is an indication of a healthy supply of subterranean water. The N'waswitsontso is mostly dry but is one of the important watercourses in the central part of the park. Its course can be followed by road down the S36 on to the S125 and then southwards along the H1-3 up to Tshokwane where the road crosses the river as it meanders towards the Orpen Dam. From there, the river passes through the Lebombo Range into Mozambique.

Flap-necked chameleon, S145

S146
STAPELKOP ROAD

★★

🦁 ★ 🦌 ★ 🦅 ★★ 🌳 ★★

- 16 km; narrow track; traverses one major ecozone
- Stapelkop Dam

The Stapelkop road leads to a rather large dam within a huge wilderness area in the western part of the park. It stores water from the upper drainage areas of the seasonal Mpofeni/Shipikana River, which eventually spills into the perennial Letaba River.

The road is a mere track in places, but gives one a sense of adventure and solitude. You are unlikely to come across many vehicles, if any, and your only companions will probably be elephants unaccustomed to traffic. It is therefore unwise to be lulled into complacency on your way through the sea of thick mopane bush. The road mostly follows the power line service road, which may be reassuring for the faint-hearted, but for the 'bundu basher' this may be an unwelcome reminder of civilisation.

Past the first granite hill with its young baobab, it is still a considerable way until you reach Stapelkop (meaning 'hill of piled-up boulders') and the dam. Once there, the disappointment is great when it is difficult to get a closer view of the water's edge or the dam. The positive aspect is that should you come across a special sighting, it will be all yours. Imagine sitting in your vehicle next to a pride of lions and having them all to yourself. But be warned – take no chances with elephants. There will be nobody around to rescue you.

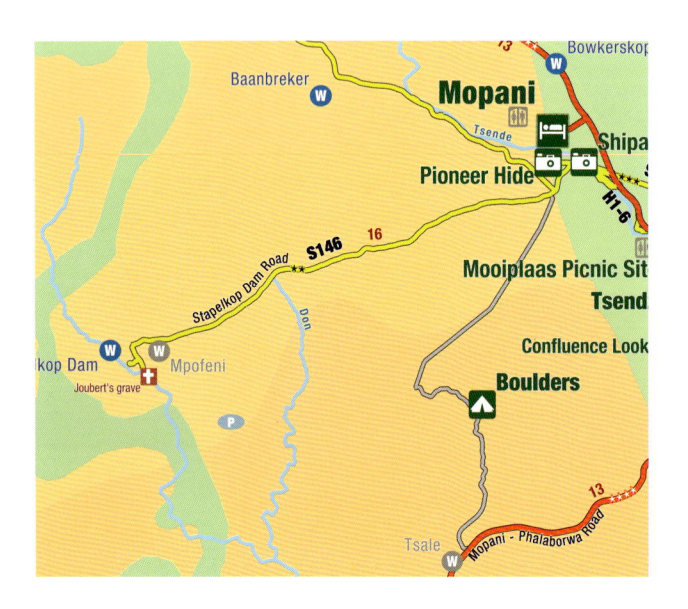

S147
NGOTSO LOOP

★★★★★

🦁 ★★★★★ 🦌 ★★★★ 🦅 ★★★★★ 🌳 ★★★★★

- 8 km; narrow one-way track out of the H1-4; follows the Tsendze stream
- The entire loop

The Ngotso loop is a welcome new addition to the roads in the park. It is not only scenic as it winds along the stream with its lovely riverine vegetation, but is also an excellent road for leopard spotting. Get there as early as you can, drive extra slowly and scan the stream banks and trees for the spotted cat.

Since the S147 is a one-way road, it must be entered from the H1-4 while it ends up at the S89. The track is narrow but has several loops that will take you closer to the stream. It can become slippery when wet and should be avoided during or after rain. One of the dry stream crossings make it difficult for low vehicles to navigate.

This is a drive where you can feast your eyes on typical lush riverine vegetation with age-old gnarled apple-leaf trees in the distance, golden fever trees on the banks, many mature sycamore figs hanging over the stream and several other favourites. Look out for raptors and ground hornbills.

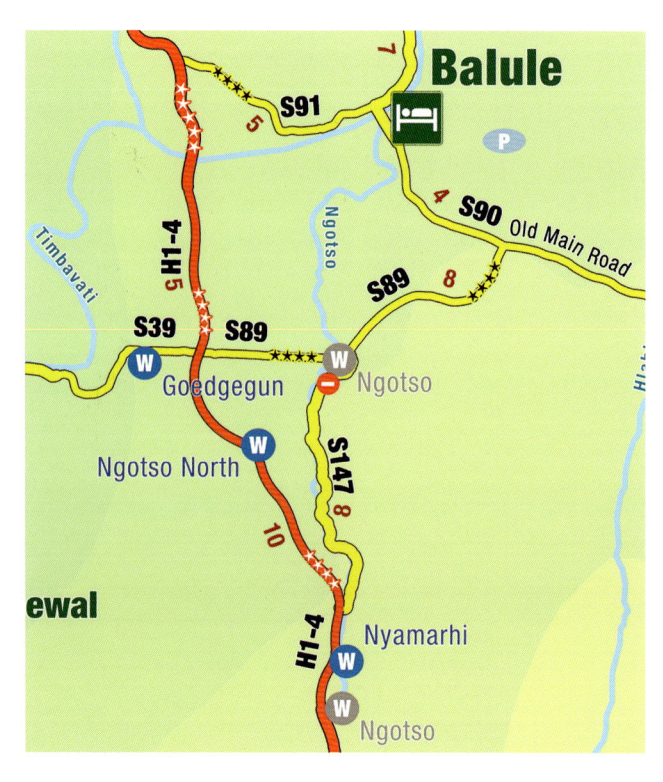

Western barn owl, S147

Lion pride, H3

Understanding Kruger

Leopard, S110

DYNAMICS OF THE SAVANNA

The Kruger National Park lies in the **Mixed Woodland Savanna Biome** characterised by a ground layer of grass in which scattered trees and shrubs occur. Within the broader concept of mixed woodland savanna, a diversity of **landscapes or ecozones** can be recognised. **Flora** differs according to the underlying **geology**, including rainfall, and other factors. Some landscapes (ecozones) have trees that reach up to 20 m or more where the canopies almost touch, while in others the trees are further apart with a ground layer of grasses. In others still, the tree layer is dominated by shrubs. And all this has a profound effect on the **fauna** that occurs in the area.

- The Savanna Biome has an extremely **high biodiversity** both in plants and animals and supports more large animals than any other biome in the world. Kruger National Park with a **surface area of 19 633 square km** or 7 580 squared miles, is home to an amazing abundance of flora and fauna.
- It is estimated that **1 990** or more **plant species** are found in the park.
- Of these, **404** are trees or shrubs, **224** are grasses, **18** are aloes and the rest are mosses, ferns, sedges, herbs, succulents, and lianas.
- The **mammal species** alone add up to **148** or more, **bird species** can exceed **500** including rare migrants, **reptile species** are estimated at **118** of which 51 are snake species, **amphibians** and **fish** amount to **35** and **53** respectively.
- Several factors influence the **dynamics of the ecosystem** – grazing, browsing and fire are natural factors, but so are season and climate. Ecozones differ in their composition – note how the variety trees, shrubs and grasses change as you travel through the park, as do soil types and topography. All this determines the animal distribution.
- The **rhyolitic** Lebombo Mountains form the entire eastern boundary with Mozambique. The extensive **basalt** plains support the largest concentration of grazers such as impala, blue wildebeest, zebra, buffalo, kudu, and waterbuck. The undulating landscapes with underlying **granite** have coarser-grained soils and sour grasses attracting less grazers, but support browsers. Clay soils originating from **Ecca shales** are characterised by natural pans in the rainy season, where sweet grasses attract a diversity of game. **Gabbro** landscapes have black cotton-type soils that become sticky when wet but support nutritious grasses with knob-thorn and marula trees. **Sandveld** occurs only in the far north and supports many flowering herbs and shrubs. Floods are a natural occurrence and leave behind deep alluvial and fertile soils on **floodplains**.
- The park is big enough to accommodate a strong population of the endangered **wild dog**. Rare antelope also find a home in the park. **Sable** antelope are generally more numerous in the more undulating, heavily wooded western part of the park. The **roan** antelope population has plummeted to no more than 50 individuals and are mainly confined to the north of the park. A small herd of **Lichtenstein's hartebeest** is the rarest of all antelope in Kruger. **Tsessebe** numbers have increased and there are now in excess of 200 in the park. The rare **Temminck's pangolin** is also found in the park but this illusive nocturnal animal is seldom seen.
- The extremely large and ever-growing **elephant** population is a matter of concern since elephants need extensive space, but careful monitoring and managing, help the park authorities find natural ways to curb population growth.
- **Predators** abound and lion, leopard, spotted hyena, cheetah and a variety of smaller ones are regularly seen on game drives.

Everything in nature is connected and interdependent. The living systems within Kruger National Park do not exist in isolation. What happens outside the park also affects ecosystems within the park and vice versa. Understanding Kruger is the power that comes from knowledge and consciousness of how living systems operate. Let nature be our teacher.

SUPPORTING FOUNDATIONS

The geology of the park is fairly simple, and knowing about it will enhance your game-viewing experience. The mostly hidden underlying geology of an area is the foundation of all life on the surface. It determines the distribution patterns of plants and animals.

It is important to take note of geology because:
- Parent rock weathers into particular types of soil, and the nature of that soil determines which plants will grow there;
- Many animals feed directly on plants (herbivores) and will only occur where there are enough of the right kind of plants; and
- Animals that feed on other animals (carnivores/predators) will only be in an area if there is enough food for them.

Since the beginning of time, cycles of change have constantly been at work. Almost four billion years ago the Earth was much hotter than it is today and its landmass still formed one huge supercontinent called **Pangaea**.

The entire landmass was covered by **granite,** which originated from fluid volcanic **magma**. Over time, heat and pressure caused the granite to undergo changes in places and caused some of it to transform into **gneiss** – coarse-grained rock with a banded structure.

Gradually, over the next billion years, the landmass cracked in places and boiling lava from the centre of the earth filled these fractures. The lava cooled down as it approached the surface. The rock formed by such intrusions is called **gabbro**.

Parts of the supercontinent broke away until eventually only a central piece called **Gondwanaland** was intact. About 300 million years ago an extremely wet spell caused a huge inland lake. When the lake dried up the sediments left behind were compacted into soft rock that formed the **Ecca shales**. A dry spell followed and sand was blown in over the Ecca shales.

About 200 million years ago, violent, cataclysmic, volcanic eruptions took place, which affected the entire Gondwanaland. Lava poured over thousands of kilometres and resulted in a thick layer of **basalt** covering the landmass.

When Madagascar broke away from Gondwanaland, about 135 million years ago, this caused a massive geological upliftment and a tilting of the African continent in the east towards the Indian Ocean. This is how the Drakensberg was formed. This tilting affected not only the formation of KwaZulu-Natal but also the entire Lowveld, including the Kruger National Park. The tilting exposed the different superimposed layers in cross section. Wet and dry cycles followed. Rocks weathered down over millennia. The properties of rock types differed, as did the rate at which they weathered and the resultant soil types and landscapes into which they transformed.

About 50 million years ago the Lebombo Mountain range was formed by a tectonic upliftment and the resultant **rhyolite** is also a kind of igneous rock related to basalt.

Granite and gneiss are the oldest and hardest rocks and are very resistant to weathering. They are both coarse in texture and, when exposed, take many thousands of years to weather away.

The rhyolite of the Lebombo Mountains is also resistant to weathering, but less so than granite. The gabbro, Ecca shales and basalt are softer and weather into the flat plains.
What all of this means for the park:
- In terms of age, granite and gneiss are the oldest rocks, followed by gabbro, then the Ecca shales. The youngest rocks are basalt and rhyolite.
- The huge granite boulders represent some of the oldest rocks on Earth.
- The rocks formed over aeons have unique compositions and erode to form different soils.
- The soil types, in association with climate, determine the presence or absence of life.

CLIMATE – CONTRIBUTING CONDITIONS

- **Temperature, wind** and **rainfall** are the main climatic factors contributing to conditions in the park. **Altitude** is another determining factor.
- Summers in the park are hot and humid with temperatures rising to 44°C in places.
- The hottest months are October to March, when maximum temperatures average 34°C and night temperatures 18°C. Winters are mild and dry with night temperatures ranging from 5–12°C and day temperatures reaching an average of 26–28°C.
- The park lies within a semi-arid region and rainfall ranges between 200 mm and 750 mm a year. Rainfall is erratic and subject to regional fluctuations of 'wet' and 'dry' cycles of between seven and eleven years.
- In the 'wet' years there can be extensive flooding; in the 'dry' years droughts are equally devastating.
- The highest rainfall occurs around Punda Maria in the north (650–700 mm per annum) and Pretoriuskop in the south (700–750 mm per annum).
- The driest area is north of Pafuri, which receives only 250–300 mm per annum. Rain falls mainly in summer from November to March.
- Kruger has a frost-free subtropical climate.
- Altitude varies from 200–900 m above sea level. The highest areas are in the far south-western parts of the park.

THE SANDVELD
LANDSCAPES/ECOZONES

In the far northern corner of the park there is a pocket of sandveld with an origin not based on geology alone but also on sand blown in from the west. The soils here are sandy and well drained. The landscape is mainly rugged and mountainous with prominent ridges and hills, steep slopes and deep valleys with clearly defined drainage lines.

LANDSCAPES/ECOZONES OVER GABBRO

Gabbro rock was formed by major intrusions of magma into cracks that formed in the granite floor aeons ago. Heat and pressure caused the granite to undergo changes. Gneiss was formed in this way but is still similar to granite. Magma penetrated the cracks and formed intrusive dykes of gabbro rock. This rock is similar to basalt in that it is igneous in origin, but is generally older and harder. The soils derived from gabbro are finer than those from granite, and are thick, black cotton-type soils that become waterlogged and sticky when wet, but which support nutritious grasses with knob-thorn and marula trees. The general features of these landscapes are rolling and undulating plains, with several conspicuous boulder-strewn inselbergs e.g. Ship Mountain in the south.

LANDSCAPES/ECOZONES OVER GRANITE

Landscapes of an undulating nature with pronounced hilly areas and deeply incised drainage systems are typical of the western parts of the park and are most pronounced in the south. The soils here are derived from granites. The vegetation on the hills, mid-slopes and valley bottoms differs. The granite rocks underlying the hills are igneous, acidic, crystalline and slow weathering. The resultant soils are sandy, relatively infertile and rich in silicon. Due to the higher rainfall and their age, the soils are leached (poor in minerals) so the grasses growing there are predominantly unpalatable and attract fewer grazers. However, fine clay soils rich in minerals are produced in the weathering process but are eventually washed down the slopes into the valleys. This makes the slopes and especially the valleys more fertile. Notice the size of the trees in the valleys. The grasses growing there are sweeter and more palatable, thus attracting more grazers.

FLOODPLAINS AND RIVERINE HABITATS
WITHIN LANDSCAPES/ECOZONES

Floodplains traversed by tourist roads are largely confined to the lower reaches of the Shingwedzi and Mphongolo rivers and further north to the area between the Limpopo and Luvuvhu rivers. The soils are alluvial and deep; the floodplains are broad, with gentle slopes, and feature large grass-covered plains. Along the rivers, both perennial and seasonal, the soils are usually deep and fertile with more nutrients and water available than in the surrounding landscapes. Strictly speaking, riverbanks are part of the surrounding landscapes or ecozones and are merely special habitats within them.

LANDSCAPES/ECOZONES OVER BASALT

The fertile flat plains stretch along the entire eastern half of the park. The reason for the flatness of these plains is that they are underlain by basalt. Basalt weathers relatively rapidly, leaving no hills, and generates dark, nutrient-rich, clay soils. The dark colour is because of a high concentration of organic matter, making these soils rich in nitrogen. This in turn causes year-round palatable grasses to grow, attracting high game populations. The tree cover on these plains seems to be sparse, but browsing and regular veld fires control dense tree stands.

LANDSCAPES/ECOZONES OVER RHYOLITE

The Lebombo hills form the eastern boundary of the park. These hills are composed of rhyolite, a type of rock that is also hard and very resistant to weathering. The origin of rhyolite is however vastly different from the other slow-weathering rock type (granite) in that it is a form of lava, and similar in origin to basalt. Rhyolite originated relatively close to the surface of the molten magma and is acidic and rich in silica. The soil erodes from the slopes of the hills nearly as fast as it forms, is stony and poor in nutrients. The result is that grasses growing in these soils are rather unpalatable and are therefore not much grazed.

LANDSCAPES/ECOZONES OVER ECCA SHALES

A strip of clay soils originating from Ecca shales occurs on the fringes of the flat, basaltic eastern plains. It roughly divides the eastern fertile plains from the western granite-based undulating landscapes. Ecca shales are sediments from prehistoric swamplands and these layers contain fossils and coal. They are often mixed with sandstone and erode easily.

ECOZONES OR LANDSCAPES

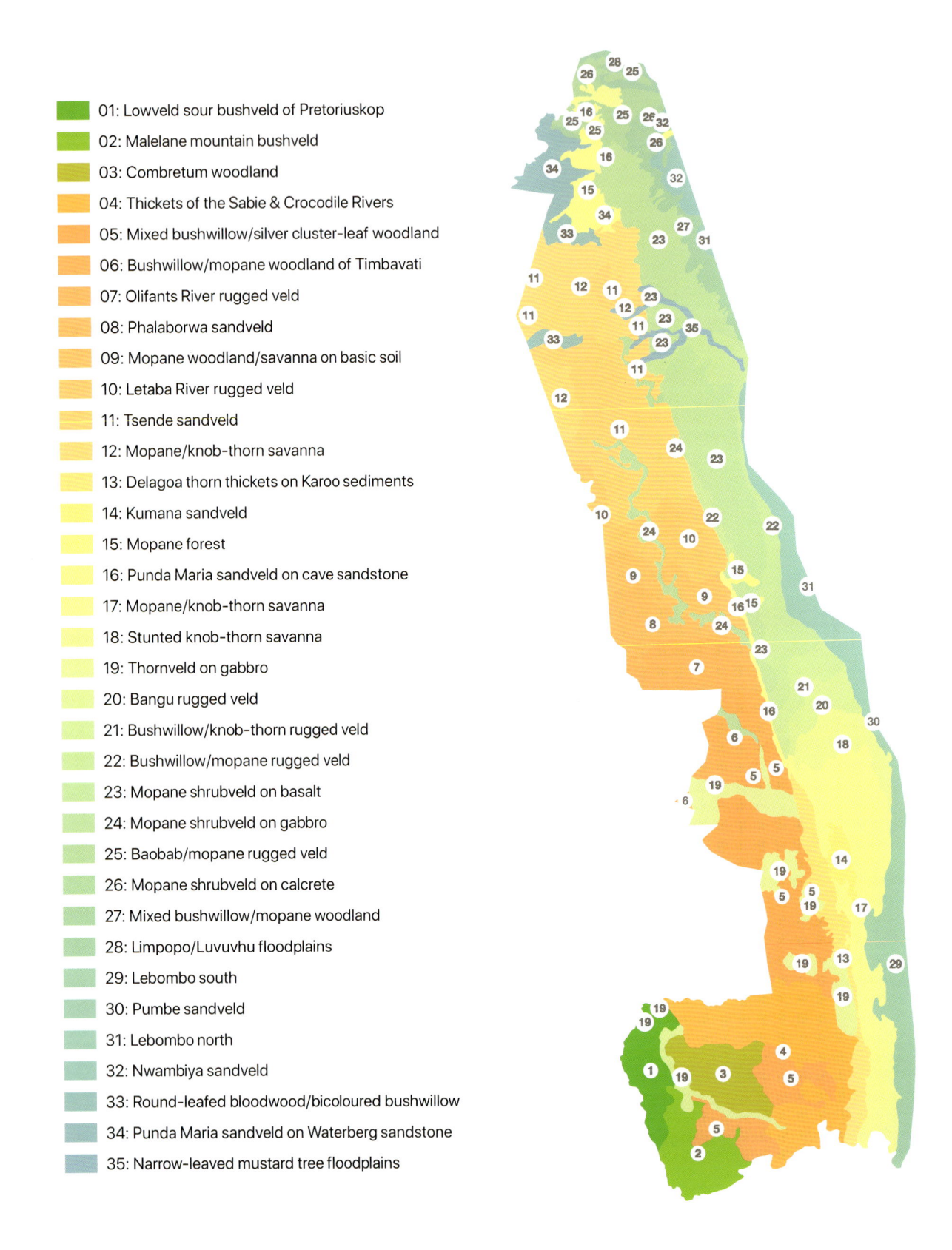

- 01: Lowveld sour bushveld of Pretoriuskop
- 02: Malelane mountain bushveld
- 03: Combretum woodland
- 04: Thickets of the Sabie & Crocodile Rivers
- 05: Mixed bushwillow/silver cluster-leaf woodland
- 06: Bushwillow/mopane woodland of Timbavati
- 07: Olifants River rugged veld
- 08: Phalaborwa sandveld
- 09: Mopane woodland/savanna on basic soil
- 10: Letaba River rugged veld
- 11: Tsende sandveld
- 12: Mopane/knob-thorn savanna
- 13: Delagoa thorn thickets on Karoo sediments
- 14: Kumana sandveld
- 15: Mopane forest
- 16: Punda Maria sandveld on cave sandstone
- 17: Mopane/knob-thorn savanna
- 18: Stunted knob-thorn savanna
- 19: Thornveld on gabbro
- 20: Bangu rugged veld
- 21: Bushwillow/knob-thorn rugged veld
- 22: Bushwillow/mopane rugged veld
- 23: Mopane shrubveld on basalt
- 24: Mopane shrubveld on gabbro
- 25: Baobab/mopane rugged veld
- 26: Mopane shrubveld on calcrete
- 27: Mixed bushwillow/mopane woodland
- 28: Limpopo/Luvuvhu floodplains
- 29: Lebombo south
- 30: Pumbe sandveld
- 31: Lebombo north
- 32: Nwambiya sandveld
- 33: Round-leafed bloodwood/bicoloured bushwillow
- 34: Punda Maria sandveld on Waterberg sandstone
- 35: Narrow-leaved mustard tree floodplains

PAFURI MAKULEKE CONCESSION AREA
Driest place in the park; main winter-feeding ground for elephants from the park and adjoining areas in Zimbabwe and Mozambique; rare bird and animal sightings.

PUNDA MARIA AREA
Sandveld is the flower garden of the park; scarce Sharpe's grysbok and suni; leopard; plenty elephants and buffalo; African grey hornbill and Arnot's chat in the mopane tree forest; lions at Klopperfontein and Dzudzwini.

MPHONGOLO AREA
Large elephant breeding herds; big buffalo herds; rare antelope e.g. tsessebe; Sharpe's grysbok; waterbuck, kudu, giraffe; various mongoose species; leopard and lion; good birding.

MOPANE AREA
Tsendze River and Pioneer Dam attract crocodile, hippo, waterbuck and waterbirds; overnight hide is popular; lion, hyena and leopard; Mooiplaas Picnic Site hotspot for game watching while having a picnic meal; Nshawu marsh good habitat for reedbuck; Tropic of Capricorn Road good for big tuskers, ostrich, and ground-living birds.

PHALABORWA AREA, H14 AND H9
Sable Hide a hotspot for game viewing; wild dog packs frequent the area; leopard, lion and hyena occur; big elephant and buffalo herds; Nandzana Waterhole a hotspot for leopard; Masorini Archaeological Site a hotspot for klipspringer.

ORPEN AREA AND SOUTH ON S36
Broadleaf vegetation attracts browsers including elephant; good game viewing including leopard along Timbavati River; regular lion and wild dog sightings; sable antelope favour high grass cover; Talamati area good for giraffe; cheetah often encountered.

SKUKUZA AREA
Riverine vegetation along the Sabie and Sand rivers is home to the highest concentration of leopards in the world; excellent lion sightings can be expected; buffalo and elephant herds are plentiful; klipspringer on granite koppies; black rhino in thorn-thickets; good birding in the camp and along rivers.

PRETORIUSKOP AREA
Browsers are prolific; home of some rare antelope such as sable, Lichtenstein's hartebeest; and eland; leopard on granite hills.

BERG-EN-DAL AREA
The mountain bushveld attracts mainly leopard, but hyena and lion also occur; wild dog packs frequent the area; Majulu Waterhole is excellent for game viewing; buffalo herds, occasional elephants, baboons, zebra, kudu and impala are to be expected; this is the only place where grey rhebuck may be found; Afsaal area good game viewing.

LUVUVHU AREA
Crook's Corner where Luvuvhu and Limpopo rivers meet; leopard in the riverine forest; plenty crocodile and hippo in the rivers; baboons in the fever tree forest; tropical conditions attract several scarce bird species; picnic site hotspot for birding; look for nyala and bushbuck.

SHINGWEDZI AREA
Confluence of Shingwedzi and Mphongolo rivers; big buffalo and elephant herds; home of many of the big tuskers; baboons, vervet monkeys, nyala and bushbuck along rivers; lion and leopard at red rocks and along rivers; hyena; riverine forest attracts many bird species including raptors and waterbirds; good birding.

LETABA AREA
Large hippo pods in Letaba River; good winter game viewing area due to availability of water in Letaba River all year round; elephants prolific; big tuskers; good predator sightings along the river; good birding along river, S62 and camp; bushbuck often seek refuge in camp; zebra, waterbuck, impala prolific.

OLIFANTS AREA
Olifants River is the divide between mopane veld in the north and mixed bushwillow woodlands in the south; best scenery in park with huge elephant herds, tuskers, waterbuck, impala etc. in and around the Olifants River; high concentration of crocodiles in the Olifants River Gorge.

SATARA AREA
Famous for big grazing herds; highest concentration of predators in the park; big lion prides, leopard along the rivers, hyena, and cheetah on open plains; giraffe, kudu, steenbok, and waterbuck; N'wanetsi area good summer game viewing; Sweni Hide a hotspot for game viewing and birding; Nsemani Dam popular sundown game viewing.

TSHOKWANE AREA
Good predator sightings; diverse habitats attract diversity of animals; plenty of grazing and browsing areas.

LOWER SABIE AREA
Sunset Dam is a hotspot for a diversity of game and offers good birding; the bridge over the Sabie is a popular place to linger and watch waterbirds and hippo; Mlondozi area is excellent for huge herds that come down to drink at the dam; overall excellent sweet grazing; cheetah frequent the H10 area; lion and leopard sightings are regularly reported.

CROCODILE BRIDGE AREA
Grassland savanna excellent for grazers; great diversity of game including predators such as leopard, lion and cheetah; S25 good area for spotting raptors; the south of the park is Big Five territory.

WHY THE PARK IS DEMOLISHING SOME OF THE ARTIFICIAL WATER SOURCES

The matter of water management has always been a concern since **only five perennial rivers** flow through the park and the annual rainfall is not consistent. Wet periods alternate with years of drought, but this cycle was unclear until later in the 20th century. When artificial watering points were first mentioned by the Parks Board in 1927, the **idea was to stabilise water supplies and make the arid central and northern regions more accessible to game.** In those early years the Board believed that this would help to spread

Plains zebra drinking, S28

Congregation of game at Welverdiend drinking place, S126

animals more evenly over the entire Kruger and prevent them emigrating out of the park. At that stage the park was still unfenced and unbeknown to the decision makers, game simply followed their age-old migration routes in and out of the park.

The establishment of the **first artificial watering points started in 1929** and peaked in the late eighties. By this time almost 300 artificial watering points were already established across the Park. These included boreholes, earth dams as well as dams within seasonal and perennial rivers. In the meantime, fencing the Park started and was almost completed by the mid-seventies. The result was that no migrations could happen any longer, and game was completely dependent on local natural resources and artificial watering points.

During the first years after the implementation of the artificial water policy, it seemed as if this contributed to a more even distribution of the game population, but as early as the late sixties, it was gradually noticed that **all was not well**. It became evident that game no longer migrated but rather settled around the artificial watering points. This influenced the spatial distribution and utilisation patterns of almost all the larger animals, both herbivores and predators.

By 1975 the park was almost completely fenced, and the **new picture was beginning to emerge**. Former inaccessible areas of the park which were too dry to support many of the herbivore species, gradually became available to them because of the artificial waterholes. As species such as buffalo and zebra (as well as possibly wildebeest and elephant) prospered, lion and hyena followed. In some places, predator numbers doubled because of the availability of easy prey. This situation became **a disaster for specialist antelope** such as roan, sable and tsessebe, not only because of intensified grazing pressures and the resulting habitat destruction, but also because of their vulnerability to predation.

Ongoing research revealed that the well-meant **'water for game' project of the past was a mistake**. With greater knowledge about short-term and long-term rainfall cycles, animal populations, the removal of part of the western boundary fence and a better understanding of herbivore population dynamics, **the removal of certain artificial water points started**. The main aim was to push zebra and lion off the plains and therefore provide more tall grass refuges for species such as roan.

Artificial dams within natural water courses do help to provide water throughout the drought season, but the negative impact is that the **dams and weirs serve as barriers along fish migration routes**. All rivers in the park serve as biodiversity hotspots for the 48 fish species that occur, of which 22 species are migratory. Therefore, some of the 53 artificial dams are now being demolished as part of the ongoing programme to restore natural water sources and river connectivity.

Some of the artificial watering points and dams have been chosen to remain due to the continued drought stress, but the overall decline in biodiversity goes against the South African National Parks' core biodiversity conservation objectives and therefore measures are being taken to restore the natural landscape.

TREES

Tree spotting is an entertaining activity on game drives. Trees give so many clues about geology, animals and the entire web of life that they simply cannot be ignored. Start with a tree-spotting activity and be surprised how revealing and satisfying it becomes.

South Africa is home to an astounding diversity of tree species – 1 300 are indigenous and 336 of these occur in the Kruger National Park. This means that the park has an indigenous tree diversity that equals 25% of all the species occurring in South Africa and three times more than those indigenous to the whole of Europe. Even more astonishing is that the park covers only about 2.5% of the surface area of South Africa.

The Kruger National Park is about the size of Wales or Israel, yet it has a tremendous botanical diversity. Plant diversity goes hand in hand with geographical diversity since geology, soil types, topography, climate and rainfall are all interlinked. All this helps to define different landscapes and ecozones. This in turn influences the plant-feeders, and the presence of plant-feeders influences the occurrence of predators.

Even though the park's geology is fairly simple, its landscapes are quite varied and diverse. The park's landscapes were mapped and defined as a detailed vegetation map by Rebelo and Low (1996). They described 35 different landscapes.

Baobab flower, H1-3

☐ Red Bushwillow (Rooiboswilg)
Combretum apiculatum

☐ Russet Bushwillow (Kierieklapper)
Combretum hereroense

☐ Large Fruit Bushwillow (Raasblaar)
Combretum zeyheri

☐ Leadwood (Hardekool)
Combretum imberbe

☐ Marula (Maroela)
Sclerocarya birrea

☐ Bushveld Apple-leaf (Appelblaar)
Philenoptera violacea

☐ Knob-thorn (Knoppiesdoring)
Senegalia (formerly Acacia) nigrescens

☐ Delagoa Thorn (Delagoadoring)
Senegalia (formerly Acacia) welwitschii subsp delagoensis

☐ River Thorn (Brakdoring)
Vachellia (formerly Acacia) robusta

☐ Horned Thorn (Horingdoring)
Vachellia (formerly Acacia) grandicornuta

☐ Umbrella Thorn (Haak-en-steek)
Vachellia (formerly Acacia) tortilis

☐ Fever Tree (Koorsboom)
Vachellia (formerly Acacia) xanthophloea

Trees

☐ Greenthorn Torchwood (Groendoring)
Balanites maughamii

☐ Small-leafed Sickle-bush (Sekelbos)
Dichrostachys cinerea subsp. africana

☐ Silver Cluster-leaf (Vaalboom)
Terminalia sericea

☐ Purple-pod Cluster-leaf (Sterkbos)
Terminalia prunioides

☐ Cape Date Palm (Wildedadelpalm)
Phoenix reclinata

☐ Lala Palm (Lalapalm)
Hyphaene coriacea

☐ Bushveld Gardenia (Bosveldkatjiepiering)
Gardenia volkensii

☐ Sycomore Fig (Sycomorusvy)
Ficus sycomorus

☐ Large-leafed Rock Fig (Grootblaarrotsvy)
Ficus abutilifolia

☐ Tamboti (Tambotie)
Spirostachys africana

☐ African Weeping Wattle (Huilboom)
Peltoforum africanum

☐ Many-stemmed Albizia (Meerstamvalsdoring)
Albizia petersiana subsp. evansii

☐ Baobab (Kremetartboom)
Adansonia digitata

☐ Nyala Tree (Njalaboom)
Xanthocercis zambesiaca

☐ Ebony Jackalberry (Jakalsbessie)
Diospyros mespiliformis

☐ Weeping Boer-bean (Huilboerboon)
Schotia brachypetala

☐ Sausage Tee (Worsboom)
Kigelia africana

☐ Pod Mahogany (Peul-mahonie)
Afzelia quanzensis

☐ Bushveld Natal-Mahogany (Rooiessenhout)
Trichilia emetica

☐ Tree Wisteria (Vanwykshout)
Bolusanthus speciosus

☐ Mopane leaves and flowers (Mopanie)
Colophospermum mopane

☐ Long-tail Cassia (Sambokpeul)
Cassia abbreviata

☐ Round-leafed Bloodwood (Dopperkiaat)
Pterocarpus rotundifolius

☐ Impala Lily (Impalalelie)
Adenium multiflorum

INVERTEBRATES

Invertebrates constitute a substantial component of the savanna. Although they usually don't feature as important game-drive sightings, there are a few groups that draw attention and are featured below.

Scorpions can be extremely dangerous, and in South Africa a few people die every year from being stung. There are two scorpion families, namely the *Scorpionidae* (slender tails with a small sting and large pincers – these are less poisonous variants even if the sting hurts) and *Buthidae* (the more dangerous ones with smaller pincers and a large, thick tail and sting).

☐ Less poisonous *Scorpionidae* scorpions

☐ More poisonous *Buthidae* scorpions

☐ More than 3500 spider species

☐ Various ant lion species

☐ Larvae such as the mopane worm

☐ Various moth species like the luna moth

☐ More than 270 butterfly species

☐ Many grasshopper and locust species

☐ Numerous beetles such as dung beetles

BIRDS

Birding is becoming more popular than ever. Start to notice birds and enrich your game-drive experience. It is surprising how much other game you will see while watching for birds.

There are more than 420 bird species regularly seen in the park; some occasional visitors take the number beyond the 500 mark. For a novice birder it may be difficult to identify any of these. If you are interested in getting started, a visual guide may be useful. Once you can identify the most common birds in the park and a few others, you are on your way to discovering a fascinating new world.

This section shows all birds of the park as thumbnail images.

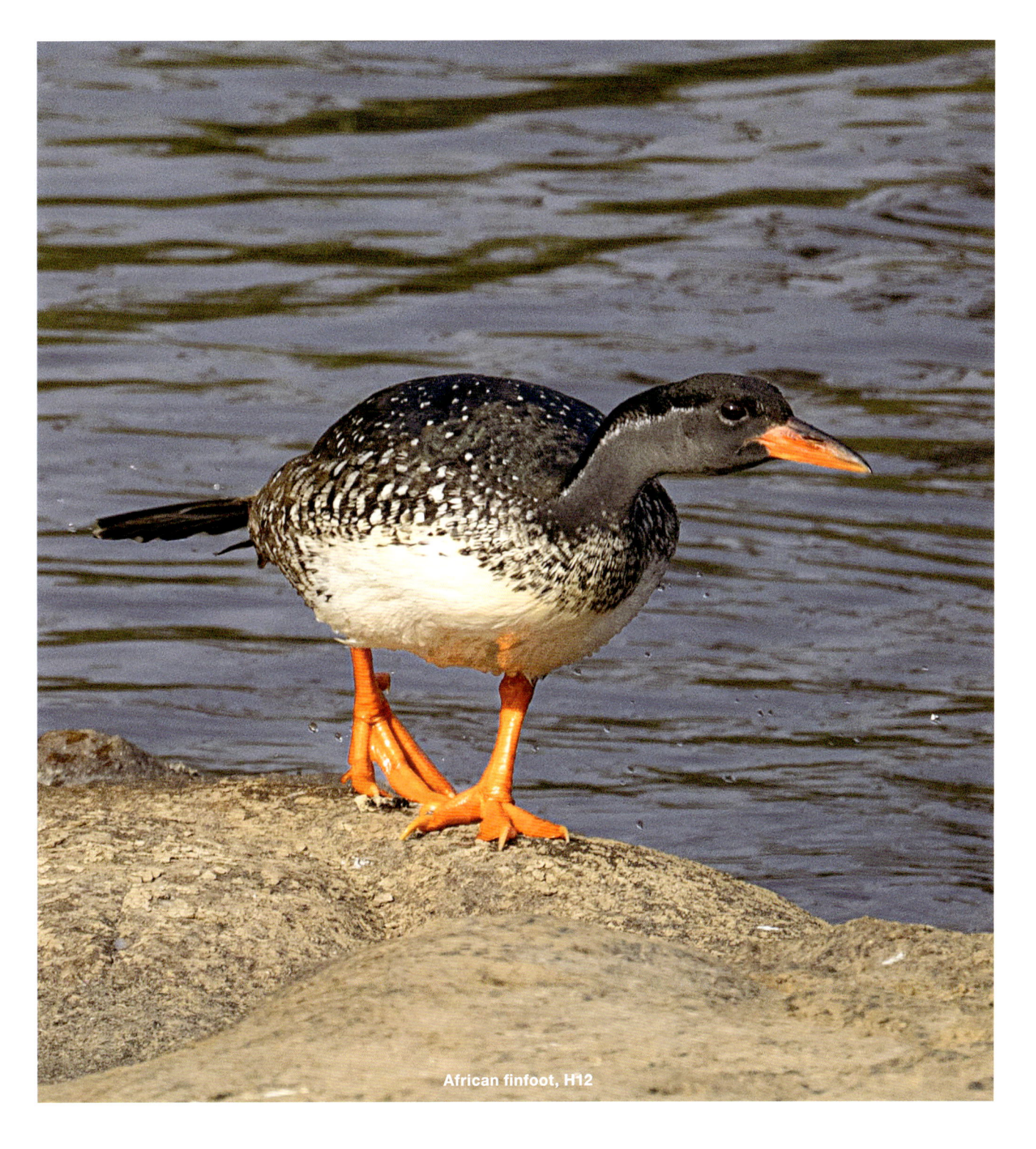

African finfoot, H12

Birds

- Common Ostrich — *Volstruis*
- Crested Guineafowl — *Kuifkoptarentaal*
- Helmeted Guineafowl — *Gewone Tarentaal*
- Harlequin Quail — *Bontkwartel*
- Coqui Francolin — *Swempie*
- Crested Francolin — *Bospatrys*
- Shelley's Francolin — *Laeveldpatrys*
- Greater Flamingo — *Grootflamink*
- Lesser Flamingo — *Kleinflamink*
- Natal Spurfowl — *Natalse Fisant*
- Swainson's Spurfowl — *Bosveldfisant*
- Southern Pochard — *Bruineend*
- African Black Duck — *Swarteend*
- Yellow-billed Duck — *Geelbekeend*
- African Pygmy Goose — *Dwerggans*
- Fulvous Whistling Duck — *Fluiteend*
- Knob-billed (Comb) Duck — *Knobbeleend*
- Egyptian Goose — *Kolgans*
- Spur-winged Goose — *Wildemakou*
- White-backed Duck — *Witrugeend*
- White-faced Whistling Duck — *Nonnetjie-eend*
- Hottentot Teal — *Gevlekte Eend*
- Red-billed Teal — *Rooibekeend*

- [ ] Little Grebe
  Kleindobbertjie
- [ ] Hamerkop
  Hamerkop
- [ ] African Openbill
  Oopbekooievaar
- [ ] Abdim's Stork
  Kleinswartooievaar
- [ ] Reed Cormorant
  Rietduiker
- [ ] White-breasted Cormorant
  Witborsduiker
- [ ] African Darter
  Slanghalsvoël
- [ ] Marabou Stork
  Maraboe
- [ ] Saddle-billed Stork
  Saalbekooievaar
- [ ] Great White Pelican
  Witpelikaan
- [ ] Black Stork
  Grootswartooievaar
- [ ] Yellow-billed Stork
  Nimmersat
- [ ] White Stork
  Witooievaar
- [ ] Woolly-necked Stork
  Wolnekooievaar
- [ ] Black-crowned Night Heron
  Gewone Nagreier
- [ ] Green-backed Heron
  Groenrugreier
- [ ] Squacco Heron
  Ralreier
- [ ] White-backed Night Heron
  Witrugnagreier
- [ ] Purple Heron
  Rooireier
- [ ] Black Heron
  Swartreier
- [ ] Goliath Heron
  Reusereier
- [ ] Black-headed Heron
  Swartkopreier
- [ ] Grey Heron
  Bloureier
- [ ] Great Egret
  Grootwitreier
- [ ] Little Egret
  Kleinwitreier
- [ ] Western Cattle Egret
  Veereier
- [ ] Yellow-billed (Intermediate) Egret
  Geelbekwitreier

Birds

☐ Dwarf Bittern
Dwergrietreier

☐ Little Bittern
Kleinrietreier

☐ Western Osprey
Visvalk

☐ Shikra
Gebande Sperwer

☐ Hadeda Ibis
Hadeda

☐ Glossy Ibis
Glansibis

☐ African Marsh Harrier
Afrikaanse Vleivalk

☐ Montagu's Harrier
Blouvleivalk

☐ African Sacred Ibis
Skoorsteenveer

☐ African Spoonbill
Lepelaar

☐ Secretarybird
Sekretarisvoël

☐ Pallid Harrier
Witborsvleivalk

☐ African Cuckoo Hawk
Koekoekvalk

☐ African Harrier-Hawk
Kaalwangvalk

☐ Dickinson's Kestrel
Dickinsongrysvalk

☐ Bateleur
Berghaan

☐ Bat Hawk
Vlermuisvalk

☐ Black Kite
Swartwou

☐ Common (Steppe) Buzzard
Bruinjakkalsvoël

☐ European Honey Buzzard
Wespedief

☐ Black-shouldered Kite
Blouvalk

☐ Yellow-billed Kite
Geelbekwou

☐ Jackal Buzzard
Rooiborsjakkalsvoël

☐ Lizard Buzzard
Akkedisvalk

☐ African Goshawk *Afrikaanse Sperwer*	☐ Dark Chanting Goshawk *Donkersingvalk*	☐ Black-chested Snake Eagle *Swartborsslangarend*	☐ Booted Eagle *Dwergarend*
☐ Gabar Goshawk *Witkruissperwer/klein singvalk*	☐ African Fish Eagle *Visarend*	☐ Brown Snake Eagle *Bruinslangarend*	☐ Crowned Eagle *Kroonarend*
☐ African Hawk Eagle *Grootjagarend*	☐ Ayres's Hawk Eagle *Kleinjagarend*	☐ Lesser Spotted Eagle *Gevlekte Arend*	☐ Long-crested Eagle *Langkuifarend*
☐ Martial Eagle *Breekoparend*	☐ Steppe Eagle *Steppe - arend*	☐ Little Sparrowhawk *Kleinsperwer*	☐ Ovambo Sparrowhawk *Ovambomsperwer*
☐ Tawny Eagle *Roofarend*	☐ Verreaux's Eagle *Witkruisarend*	☐ Red-crested Korhaan *Boskorhaan*	
☐ Wahlberg's Eagle *Bruinarend*	☐ Black Sparrowhawk *Swartsperwer*	☐ Black-bellied Bustard *Langbeenkorhaan*	☐ Kori Bustard *Gompou*

Birds

Egyptian Vulture *Egiptiese Aasvoël*	Hooded Vulture *Monnikaasvoël*	Palm-nut Vulture *Witaasvoël*	Common Moorhen *Grootwaterhoender*	Lesser Moorhen *Kleinwaterhoender*	African Rail *Grootriethaan*
Cape Vulture *Kransaasvoël*	Lappet-faced Vulture *Swartaasvoël*		Red-knobbed Coot *Bleshoender*	African Crake *Afrikaanse Riethaan*	Black Crake *Swartriethaan*
			Corn Crake *Kwartelkoning*	Striped Crake *Gestreepte Riethaan*	Allen's Gallinule *Kleinkoningriethaan*
White-headed Vulture *Witkopaasvoël*	White-backed Vulture *Witrugaasvoël*		African Swamphen *Grootkoningriethaan*	Red-chested Flufftail *Rooiborsvleikuiken*	African Finfoot *Watertrapper*
Spotted Thick-knee *Gewone Dikkop*	Water Thick-knee *Waterdikkop*	Black-winged Stilt *Rooipootelsie*	Senegal Lapwing *Kleinswartvlerkkiewiet*	White-crowned Lapwing *Witkopkiewiet*	Greater Painted-Snipe *Goudsnip*
Pied Avocet *Bontelsie*	Caspian Plover *Asiatiese Strandkiewiet*	Common Ringed Plover *Ringnekstrandkiewiet*	African Jacana *Grootlangtoon*	Lesser Jacana *Dwerglangtoon*	Ruff *Kemphaan*
Kittlitz's Plover *Geelborsstrandkiewiet*	Three-banded Plover *Driebandstrandkiewiet*	White-fronted Plover *Vaalstrandkiewiet*	Common Sandpiper *Gewone Ruiter*	Curlew Sandpiper *Krombekstrandloper*	Green Sandpiper *Witgatruiter*
African Wattled Lapwing *Lelkiewiet*	Blacksmith Lapwing *Bontkiewiet*	Crowned Lapwing *Kroonkiewiet*	Marsh Sandpiper *Moerasruiter*	Wood Sandpiper *Bosruiter*	Common Greenshank *Groenpootruiter*

☐ Little Stint *Kleinstrandloper*	☐ African Snipe *Afrikaanse Snip*	☐ Kurrichane Buttonquail *Bosveldkwarteltjie*	☐ Eurasian Hobby *Europese Boomvalk*	☐ Lesser Kestrel *Kleinrooivalk*	☐ Rock Kestrel *Kransvalk*
☐ Bronze-winged Courser *Bronsvlerkdrawwertjie*	☐ Temminck's Courser *Trekdrawwertjie*	☐ Three-banded Courser *Driebanddrawwertjie*	☐ Amur Falcon *Oostelike Rooipootvalk*	☐ Lanner Falcon *Edelvalk*	☐ Peregrine Falcon *Swerfvalk*
☐ Collared Pratincole *Rooivlerksprinkaanvoël*	☐ Grey-headed Gull *Gryskopmeeu*	☐ African Skimmer *Waterploeër*	☐ Red-footed Falcon *Westelike Rooipootvalk*	☐ Sooty Falcon *Roetvalk*	☐ Double-banded Sandgrouse *Dubbelbandsandpatrys*
☐ Whiskered Tern *Witbaardsterretjie*	☐ White-winged Tern *Witvlerksterretjie*				
☐ African Green Pigeon *Papegaaiduif*	☐ Speckled Pigeon *Kransduif*	☐ African Mourning Dove *Rooioogtortelduif*	☐ Brown-headed Parrot *Bruinkoppapegaai*	☐ Grey-headed Parrot *Savannepapegaai*	
☐ Cape Turtle-Dove *Gewone Tortelduif*	☐ Emerald-spotted Wood-Dove *Groenvlekduifie*	☐ Laughing Dove *Rooiborsduifie*	☐ Meyer's Parrot *Bosveldpapegaai*		
☐ Namaqua Dove *Namakwaduifie*	☐ Red-eyed Dove *Grootringduif*	☐ Tambourine Dove *Witborsduifie*	☐ Grey Go-away-bird *Kwêvoël*	☐ Purple-crested Turaco *Bloukuifloerie*	

Birds

Black Coucal *Swartvleiloerie*	Burchell's Coucal *Gewone Vleiloerie*	Diederik Cuckoo *Diederikkie*	Great Spotted Cuckoo *Gevlekte Koekoek*	
Senegal Coucal *Senegalvleiloerie*	African Cuckoo *Afrikaanse Koekoek*	Jacobin Cuckoo *Bontnuwejaarsvoël*	Klaas's Cuckoo *Meitjie*	Levaillant's Cuckoo *Gestreepte Nuwejaarsvoël*
Black Cuckoo *Swartkoekoek*	Common Cuckoo *Europese Koekoek*	Red-chested Cuckoo *Piet-My-Vrou*	Thick-billed Cuckoo *Dikbekkoekoek*	
African Grass Owl *Grasuil*	African Scops Owl *Skopsuil / Witwanguil*	Pearl-spotted Owlet *Witkoluil*	African Barred Owlet *Gebande Uil*	
African Wood Owl *Bosuil*	Marsh Owl *Vlei-Uil*	Western Barn Owl *Nonnetjie-Uil*		
Pel's Fishing Owl *Visuil*	Southern White-faced Owl *Witwanguil*	Verreaux's Eagle-Owl *Reuse-Ooruil*	Spotted Eagle-Owl *Gevlekte Ooruil*	

- European Nightjar / *Europese Naguil*
- Fiery-necked Nightjar / *Afrikaanse Naguil*
- African Black Swift / *Swartwindswael*
- African Palm Swift / *Palmwindswael*
- Alpine Swift / *Witpenswindswael*
- Freckled Nightjar / *Donkernaguil*
- Pennant-winged Nightjar / *Wimpelvlerknaguil*
- Rufous-cheeked Nightjar / *Rooiwangnaguil*
- Square-tailed Nightjar / *Laeveldnaguil*
- Common Swift / *Europese Windswael*
- Horus Swift / *Horuswindswael*
- Little Swift / *Kleinwindswael*
- Narina Trogon / *Bosloerie*
- Red-faced Mousebird / *Rooiwangmuisvoël*
- Speckled Mousebird / *Gevlekte muisvoël*
- White-rumped Swift / *Witkruiswindswael*
- Böhm's Spinetail / *Witpensstekelstert*
- Mottled Spinetail / *Gevlekte Stekelstert*
- African Pygmy Kingfisher / *Dwergvisvanger*
- Malachite Kingfisher / *Kuifkopvisvanger*
- Half-collared Kingfisher / *Blouvisvanger*
- Blue-cheeked Bee-eater / *Blouwangbyvreter*
- European Bee-eater / *Europese Byvreter*
- Brown-hooded Kingfisher / *Bruinkopvisvanger*
- Grey-headed Kingfisher / *Gryskopvisvanger*
- Giant Kingfisher / *Reusevisvanger*
- Little Bee-eater / *Kleinbyvreter*
- Southern Carmine Bee-eater / *Rooiborsbyvreter*
- Pied Kingfisher / *Bontvisvanger*
- Striped Kingfisher / *Gestreepte visvanger*
- Woodland Kingfisher / *Bosveldvisvanger*
- Swallow-tailed Bee-eater / *Swaelstertbyvreter*
- White-fronted Bee-eater / *Rooikeelbyvreter*

Birds

Broad-billed Roller — *Geelbektroupant*

European Roller — *Europese Troupant*

Lilac-breasted Roller — *Gewone Troupant*

African Grey Hornbill — *Grysneushoringvoël*

Crowned Hornbill — *Gekroonde Neushoringvoël*

Purple Roller — *Groottroupant*

Racket-tailed Roller — *Knopsterttroupant*

Green Wood-Hoopoe — *Rooibekkakelaar*

Southern Yellow-billed Hornbill — *Geelbekneushoringvoël*

Southern Red-billed Hornbill — *Rooibekneushoringvoël*

African Hoopoe — *Hoephoep*

Common Scimitarbill — *Swartbekkakelaar*

Trumpeter Hornbill — *Gewone Boskraai*

Southern Ground-Hornbill — *Bromvoël*

Bearded Woodpecker — *Baardspeg*

Bennett's Woodpecker — *Bennettspeg*

Chestnut-backed Sparrowlark — *Rooiruglewerik*

Dusky Lark — *Donkerlewerik*

Cardinal Woodpecker — *Kardinaalspeg*

Golden-tailed Woodpecker — *Goudstertspeg*

Fawn-coloured Lark — *Vaalbruinlewerik*

Flappet Lark — *Laeveldklappertjie*

Greater Honeyguide — *Grootheuningwyser*

Grey-backed Sparrowlark — *Grysruglewerik*

Monotonous Lark — *Bosveldlewerik*

Red-capped Lark — *Rooikoplewerik*

Lesser Honeyguide — *Kleinheuningwyser*

Scaly-throated Honeyguide — *Gevlekte Heuningwyser*

Brown-backed Honeybird — *Skerpbekheuningvoël*

Rufous-naped Lark — *Rooineklewerik*

Sabota Lark — *Sabotalewerik*

Bushveld Pipit — *Bosveldkoester*

☐ Black Saw-wing *Swartsaagvlerkswael*	☐ Brown-throated Martin *Afrikaanse Oewerswael*	☐ Common House-Martin *Huisswael*	☐ Wire-tailed Swallow *Draadstertswael*	☐ African Pied Wagtail *Bontkwikkie*	☐ Cape Wagtail *Gewone Kwikkie*
☐ Rock Martin *Kransswael*	☐ Sand Martin *Europese Oewerswael*	☐ Barn Swallow *Europese Swael*	☐ Mountain Wagtail *Bergkwikkie*	☐ Western Yellow Wagtail *Geelkwikkie*	☐ Yellow-throated Longclaw *Geelkeelkalkoentjie*
☐ Grey-rumped Swallow *Gryskruisswael*	☐ Lesser Striped Swallow *Kleinstreepswael*	☐ Mosque Swallow *Moskeeswael*	☐ Plain-backed Pipit *Donkerkoester*	☐ Striped Pipit *Gestreepte Koester*	☐ African Pipit *Gewone Koester*
☐ Pearl-breasted Swallow *Perelborsswael*	☐ Red-breasted Swallow *Rooiborsswael*	☐ White-throated Swallow *Witkeelswael*	☐ Buffy Pipit *Vaalkoester*	☐ Black Cuckooshrike *Swartkatakoeroe*	☐ White-breasted Cuckooshrike *Witborskatakoeroe*
☐ Terrestrial Brownbul *Boskrapper*	☐ Dark-capped Bulbul *Swartoogtiptol*	☐ Sombre Greenbul *Gewone Willie*	☐ Croaking Cisticola *Groot Tinktinkie*	☐ Desert Cisticola *Woestynklopkloppie*	☐ Lazy Cisticola *Luitinktinkie*
☐ Yellow-bellied Greenbul *Geelborswillie*	☐ Willow Warbler *Hofsanger*	☐ Stierling's Wren-Warbler *Stierlingsanger*	☐ Rattling Cisticola *Bosveldtinktinkie*	☐ Red-faced Cisticola *Rooiwangtinktinkie*	☐ Rufous-winged Cisticola *Swartrugtinktinkie*
☐ Burnt-necked Eremomela *Buinkeelbossanger*	☐ Green-capped Eremomela *Donkerwangbossanger*	☐ Yellow-bellied Eremomela *Geelpensbossanger*	☐ Zitting Cisticola *Landeryklopkloppie*	☐ Green-backed Camaroptera *Groenrugkwekwevoël*	☐ Grey-backed Camaroptera *Grysrugkwekwevoël*
☐ Bar-throated Apalis *Bandkeel-kleinjantjie*	☐ Rudd's Apalis *Ruddkleinjantjie*	☐ Yellow-breasted Apalis *Geelborskleinjantjie*	☐ Neddicky *Neddikkie*	☐ Tawny-flanked Prinia *Bruinsylangstertjie*	☐ Long-billed Crombec *Bosveldstompstert*

Birds

☐ African Reed Warbler *Kleinrietsanger*	☐ Broad-tailed Warbler *Breëstertsanger*	☐ Dark-capped Yellow Warbler *Geelsanger*	☐ Southern Hyliota *Mashonahyliota*	☐ Common Whitethroat *Witkeelsanger*	☐ Chestnut-vented Tit-Babbler *Bosveldtjeriktik*
☐ Garden Warbler *Tuinsanger*	☐ Great Reed Warbler *Grootrietsanger*	☐ Icterine Warbler *Spotsanger*	☐ Collared Palm-Thrush *Palmmorelyster*	☐ Groundscraper Thrush *Gevlekte Lyster*	☐ Kurrichane Thrush *Rooibeklyster*
☐ Lesser Swamp Warbler *Kaapse Rietsanger*	☐ Little Rush Warbler *Kaapse vleisanger*	☐ Marsh Warbler *Europese Rietsanger*	☐ Capped Wheatear *Hoëveldskaapwagter*	☐ African Stonechat *Gewone Bontrokkie*	☐ Cape Robin-Chat *Gewone Janfrederik*
☐ Olive-tree Warbler *Olyfboomsanger*	☐ River Warbler *Sprinkaansanger*	☐ Sedge Warbler *Europese Vleisanger*	☐ Red-capped Robin-Chat *Nataljanfrederik*	☐ White-browed Robin-Chat *Heuglinjanfrederik*	☐ White-throated Robin-Chat *Witkeeljanfrederik*
☐ Bearded Scrub Robin *Baardwipstert*	☐ White-browed Scrub Robin *Gestreepte Wipstert*	☐ Thrush Nightingale *Lysternagtegaal*	☐ Southern Black Flycatcher *Swartvlieëvanger*	☐ Spotted Flycatcher *Europese Vlieëvanger*	☐ Cape Batis *Kaapse Bosbontrokkie*
☐ Arnot's Chat *Bontpiek*	☐ Familiar Chat *Gewone Spekvreter*	☐ Mocking Cliff Chat *Dassievoël*	☐ Chinspot Batis *Witliesbosbontrokkie*	☐ Black-throated Wattle-eye *Beloogbosbontrokkie*	☐ African Paradise Flycatcher *Paradysvlieëvanger*
☐ Ashy Flycatcher *Blougrysvlieëvanger*	☐ African Dusky Flycatcher *Donkervlieëvanger*	☐ Fiscal Flycatcher *Fiskaalvlieëvanger*	☐ Blue-mantled Crested-Flycatcher *Bloukuifvlieëvanger*	☐ Arrow-marked Babbler *Pylvlekkatlagter*	☐ Crested Barbet *Kuifkophoutkapper*
☐ Grey Tit-Flycatcher *Waaierstertvlieëvanger*	☐ Marico Flycatcher *Maricovlieëvanger*	☐ Pale Flycatcher *Muiskleurvlieëvanger*	☐ Acacia Pied Barbet *Bonthoutkapper*	☐ Black-collared Barbet *Rooikophoutkapper*	☐ Yellow-fronted Tinkerbird *Geelblestinker*

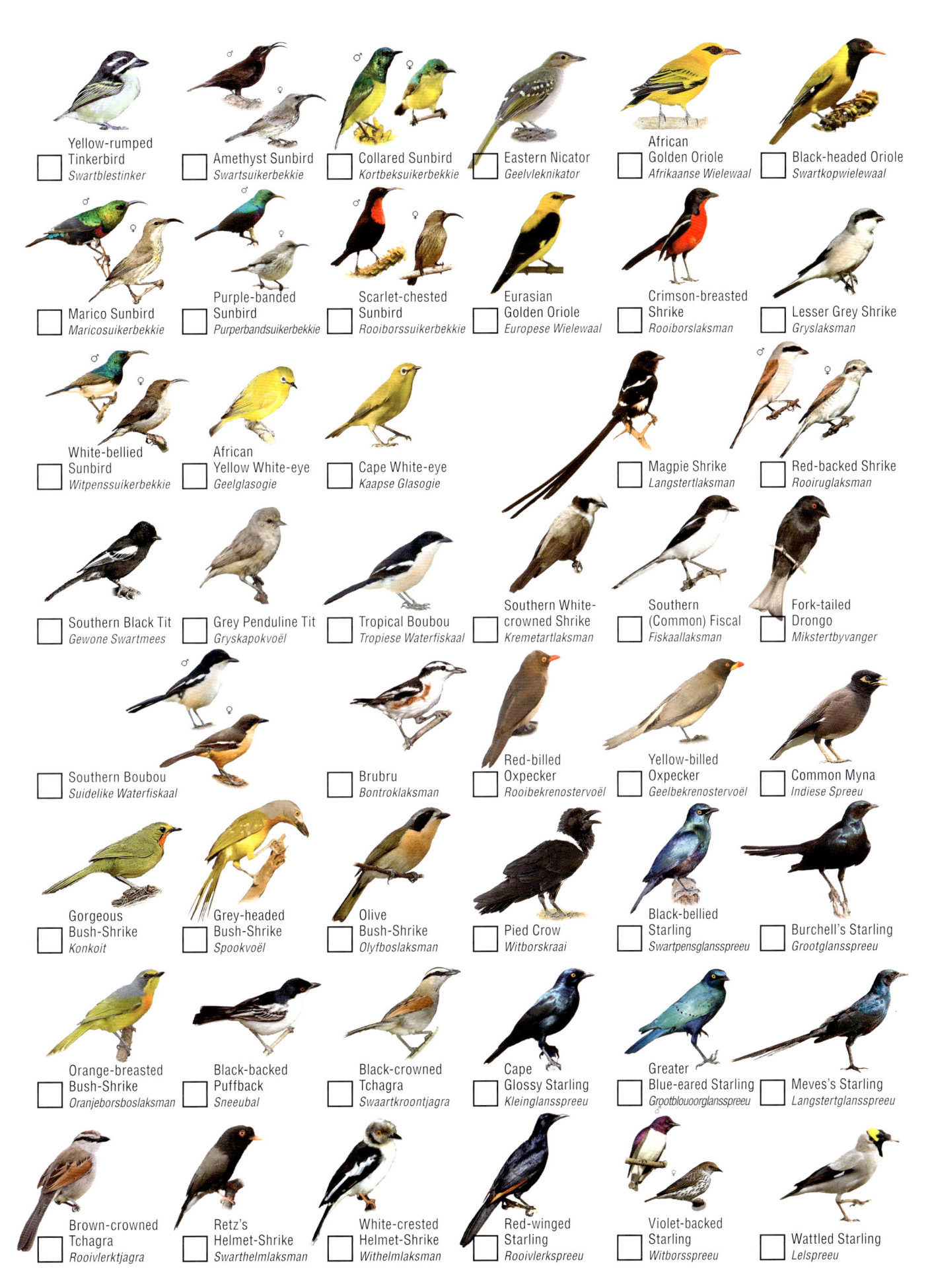

☐ Yellow-rumped Tinkerbird *Swartblestinker*	☐ Amethyst Sunbird *Swartsuikerbekkie*	☐ Collared Sunbird *Kortbeksuikerbekkie*	☐ Eastern Nicator *Geelvleknikator*	☐ African Golden Oriole *Afrikaanse Wielewaal*	☐ Black-headed Oriole *Swartkopwielewaal*
☐ Marico Sunbird *Maricosuikerbekkie*	☐ Purple-banded Sunbird *Purperbandsuikerbekkie*	☐ Scarlet-chested Sunbird *Rooiborssuikerbekkie*	☐ Eurasian Golden Oriole *Europese Wielewaal*	☐ Crimson-breasted Shrike *Rooiborslaksman*	☐ Lesser Grey Shrike *Gryslaksman*
☐ White-bellied Sunbird *Witpenssuikerbekkie*	☐ African Yellow White-eye *Geelglasogie*	☐ Cape White-eye *Kaapse Glasogie*		☐ Magpie Shrike *Langstertlaksman*	☐ Red-backed Shrike *Rooiruglaksman*
☐ Southern Black Tit *Gewone Swartmees*	☐ Grey Penduline Tit *Gryskapokvoël*	☐ Tropical Boubou *Tropiese Waterfiskaal*	☐ Southern White-crowned Shrike *Kremetartlaksman*	☐ Southern (Common) Fiscal *Fiskaallaksman*	☐ Fork-tailed Drongo *Mikstertbyvanger*
☐ Southern Boubou *Suidelike Waterfiskaal*		☐ Brubru *Bontroklaksman*	☐ Red-billed Oxpecker *Rooibekrenostervoël*	☐ Yellow-billed Oxpecker *Geelbekrenostervoël*	☐ Common Myna *Indiese Spreeu*
☐ Gorgeous Bush-Shrike *Konkoit*	☐ Grey-headed Bush-Shrike *Spookvoël*	☐ Olive Bush-Shrike *Olyfboslaksman*	☐ Pied Crow *Witborskraai*	☐ Black-bellied Starling *Swartpensglansspreeu*	☐ Burchell's Starling *Grootglansspreeu*
☐ Orange-breasted Bush-Shrike *Oranjeborsboslaksman*	☐ Black-backed Puffback *Sneeubal*	☐ Black-crowned Tchagra *Swaartkroontjagra*	☐ Cape Glossy Starling *Kleinglansspreeu*	☐ Greater Blue-eared Starling *Grootblouoorglansspreeu*	☐ Meves's Starling *Langstertglansspreeu*
☐ Brown-crowned Tchagra *Rooivlerktjagra*	☐ Retz's Helmet-Shrike *Swarthelmlaksman*	☐ White-crested Helmet-Shrike *Withelmlaksman*	☐ Red-winged Starling *Rooivlerkspreeu*	☐ Violet-backed Starling *Witborsspreeu*	☐ Wattled Starling *Lelspreeu*

Birds

White-browed Sparrow-Weaver — *Koringvoël*

African (Holub's) Golden Weaver — *Goudwewer*

Lesser Masked-Weaver — *Kleingeelvink*

Fan-tailed Widowbird — *Kortstertflap*

Red-collared Widowbird — *Rooikeelflap*

White-winged Widowbird — *Witvlerkflap*

Red-billed Buffalo Weaver — *Buffelwewer*

Red-headed Weaver — *Rooikopwewer*

Southern Brown-throated Weaver — *Bruinkeelwewer*

Red-billed Quelea — *Rooibekkwelea*

Southern Red Bishop — *Rooivink*

Yellow-crowned Bishop — *Goudgeelvink*

Spectacled Weaver — *Brilwewer*

Thick-billed Weaver — *Dikbekwewer*

Cuckoo Finch — *Koekoekvink*

Cut-throat Finch — *Bandkeelvink*

Red-headed Finch — *Rooikopvink*

Southern Masked Weaver — *Swartkeelgeelvink*

Village Weaver — *Bontrugwewer*

Yellow Weaver — *Kaapse wewer / Geelwewer*

African Firefinch — *Kaapse Vuurvinkie*

Jameson's Firefinch — *Jamesonvuurvinkie*

Red-billed Firefinch — *Rooibekvuurvinkie*

Green-winged Pytilia — *Gewone Melba*

Orange-winged Pytilia — *Oranjevlerkmelba*

African Quail-finch — *Gewone Kwartelvinkie*

Bronze Mannikin — *Gewone Fret*

Red-backed Mannikin — *Rooirugfret*

Green Twinspot — *Groenkolpensie*

Long-tailed Paradise-Whydah — *Gewone Paradysvink*

Shaft-tailed Whydah — *Pylstertrooibekkie*

Pin-tailed Whydah — *Koningrooibekkie*

Pink-throated Twinspot — *Rooskeelkolpensie*

Blue Waxbill — *Gewone Blousysie*

Common Waxbill — *Rooibeksysie*

Dusky Indigobird — *Gewone Blouvinkie*

Purple Indigobird — *Witpootblouvinkie*

Village Indigobird — *Staalblouvinkie*

Orange-breasted Waxbill — *Rooiassie*

Violet-eared Waxbill — *Koningblousysie*

Cinnamon-breasted Bunting — *Klipstreepkoppie*

Golden-breasted Bunting — *Rooirugstreepkoppie*

Lark-like Bunting — *Vaalstreepkoppie*

☐ Brimstone Canary
Dikbekkanarie

☐ Lemon-breasted Canary
Geelborskanarie

☐ Yellow-fronted Canary
Geeloogkanarie

☐ Streaky-headed Seedeater
Streepkopkanarie

☐ Yellow-throated Petronia
Geelvlekmossie

☐ Cape Sparrow
Gewone mossie

☐ House Sparrow
Huismossie

☐ Southern Grey-headed Sparrow
Gryskopmossie

Southern yellow-billed hornbill, Skukuza Camp

Southern ground hornbill, S34

REPTILES

Numerous reptile species occur in Kruger, but many are small and seldom seen from a game-drive vehicle.

The reptiles most likely to be spotted may include the Nile crocodile, the largest reptile on earth, marsh terrapins in pools near rivers, leopard tortoises on the road, rock leguaans in the veld and water leguaans near bodies of water. Snakes do well in savanna and a special sighting would be to see a python.

Although several snake species are harmless, there are a few that should be avoided. The black mamba is extremely poisonous, as are cobras and adders. Use a flashlight when walking in the camp at night and look where you are going. Reptiles are fascinating creatures and should be treated with care and respect.

☐ Spotted Bush Snake (Gespikkelde Bosslang)
Philothamnus semivariegatus

☐ Mole Snake (Molslang)
Pseudaspis cana

☐ Boomslang or Tree Snake (Boomslang)
Dispholidus t. typus

☐ Twig Snake (Takslang)
Thelotornis capensis

☐ Snouted Cobra (Egiptiese Kobra)
Naja a. annulifera

☐ Mozambique Spitting Cobra (Mosambiek Kobra)
Naja mossambica

☐ African Python (Gewone Luislang)
Python sebae natalensis

☐ Rhombic Night Adder (Nagadder)
Causus rhombeatus

☐ Puff Adder (Pofadder)
Bitis a. arietans

☐ Black Mamba (Swartmamba)
Dendroaspis polylepis

☐ Brown House Snake (Bruin Huisslang)
Lamprophis fuliginosus

☐ Giant Plated Lizard
(Reuse Pantserakkedis)
Gerrhosaurus validus

☐ Tree Agama (Boomkoggelmander)
Acanthocercus atricollis

☐ Striped skink
(Gestreepte Gladde Akkedis)
Trachylepis striata

☐ Flap-necked Chameleon
(Gewone Verkleurmannetjie)
Chamaeleo d. dilepis

☐ Rock or Tree Leguaan (Veldlikkewaan)
Varanus albigularis albigularis

☐ Water Leguaan (Waterlikkewaan)
Varanus niloticus

☐ Nile Crocodile (Nyl Krokodil)
Crocodylus niloticus

☐ Leopard Tortoise (Bergskilpad)
Geochelone pardalis babcocki

☐ Marsh Terrapin (Platdop Waterskilpad)
Pelomedusa subrufa

MAMMALS

Most people go to the park to see animals. Some think only about sighting the Big Five – lion, leopard, elephant, buffalo and rhino. Most people go there to hunt with their eyes and cameras, to see action and to marvel at the diversity. There is a lot to discover, and many information sources, but the most rewarding insights will be those you reach by yourself as you simply watch what animals do and try to understand why they do it.

When you come across animals, slow down and approach with caution. Be quiet and watch. Let things happen and be there to witness the action.

Animal numbers of the different species fluctuate all the time. For the species where a range of numbers is given e.g. impala, the population estimate for these species is between the two numbers. These species are counted with a sample survey giving these ranges or confidence intervals.

GOOD TO KNOW

• The Kruger National Park is home to about **148 mammal species**.

• Mammals, like all other animals and plants, prefer certain habitats and can tolerate certain environmental conditions. Their preferences are basically determined by the kind of geology and weather of the region, because that in turn will determine the plants that may occur. Plant feeders differ in how specific their preferences are. Some will feed on a broad range of plant species, while others are partial to specific types. Carnivores follow plant feeders and are found wherever there are enough of them to prey on.

• Of all the mammals in the park, **78 species are small and not usually seen** on regular game drives. Of these, 42 are bat species; six shrews; three elephant shrews; two are golden moles; and 25 are rodent species.

• Of the rest there are five primates; 27 carnivores; 23 bovids (including the buffalo and 22 antelopes); three rodents and 11 others.

• Of the **carnivores** six are cats; four belong to the dog group; three are of the hyena group; eight are mongooses; and the others are the civet, genet, badger, otter and polecat.

• Mammals seen on the game drives include the **biggest** (elephant), the **tallest** (giraffe) and the **fastest** (cheetah) land mammals on Earth.

• **Early mornings** are good for **predator and scavenger** sightings, while **mid-mornings** are recommended for game **at drinking points**. During the **hot midday hours** most animals prefer to **rest and shelter** from the sun, and antelope use the time to ruminate. Animals that regularly **wallow** often do so when it is hot and muggy. These include buffalo, rhino, warthog and elephant.

• **Leopards** are basically nocturnal, but sightings are nevertheless reported throughout the day. They often rest on horizontal branches of marula, tamboti or jackalberry trees or in the deep shade of low shrubs where they blend perfectly with the dappled shadow patterns. It is estimated that there are about 1 000 leopards in the park.

• Surprisingly, there are fewer **lion** than leopard in the park, with numbers estimated at 1 750. They are also mainly nocturnal and most active in the early mornings and late afternoons. They spend 20 hours per day sleeping. Most lion kills are reported within two to three kilometres of their prey's drinking places.

• **Cheetah** are diurnal and can be encountered throughout the day. Their hunting technique requires open savanna where they can run down their prey. Since they are independent of water to a larger extent than other predators, they keep to drier areas where they can avoid competition from other predators. Sightings of these speedsters are special since their numbers are estimated at a mere 120 to 150 in the park.

• The extremely successful **spotted hyena** is an opportunist and mainly nocturnal. Their numbers are estimated at 5 340. Although regarded as prime scavengers, they actively hunt for most of their food. In Kruger they cover distances of up to 20 km in search of food but require regular access to water.

• **Wild dogs** are the most endangered of all predators. In the park they number between 120 and 150 and move and hunt in packs. They are most active during early morning or late afternoon and usually rest during the hottest part of the day. These dogs need lots of living space and prefer open savanna. It is difficult to predict where to find them.

Dwarf mongoose, S56

• Both **black-backed and side-striped jackal** are low-key predators in Kruger. Both are nocturnal but while the side-striped jackal is rarely seen, only at dawn or dusk or on heavily overcast days, the black-backed jackal is bolder during the day and often seen at carcasses or skulking around.

• **Caracal** sightings are rare, partly because they are nocturnal, but also because they are much smaller than the other predators and scavengers. Although they are widely distributed, look out for them in dry, rocky areas with adjacent plains.

• **Serval** are rarely seen on self-drives in Kruger since they are mainly active at dawn and dusk. They occur in wetland habitats where they hunt rodents and birds.

• The **African wild cat** is another rare sighting, but in Satara Camp there is often one wandering about scavenging at night. The very rare **black-footed cat** is occasionally seen on night drives in the Klopperfontein Dam area.

• **Smaller predators** such as the diurnal mongooses appear suddenly and are often gone before you can get a proper look. The slender mongoose with its long, black-tipped tail is always solitary; the banded mongooses move around in groups, usually close to rivers and trees; and the tiny dwarf mongooses use termite mounds as their castles and forage in surrounding grassland for insects.

• **Elephants** are distributed all over the park, but 60% occur in the north, 30% in the central parts and 10% in the south. They spend 18 to 19 hours per day feeding and are both nocturnal and diurnal. In most parts of Kruger they drink every day, preferring to do this in the late afternoon. The latest census estimated their numbers at 13 750.

• Look for **white rhino** in short grassland. They feed for at least 12 hours per day, and need shade, shelter and access to water and wallows. In summer they may drink twice a day but usually prefer to drink in the late afternoon or early evening and wallow in the middle of the day. Most white rhino occur in the south of Kruger but their numbers have increased in the centre as they are slowly spreading north.

• **Black rhino** are extremely elusive and shy. Look deep into the bush and undergrowth. As browsers they prefer dense bush with tamboti as their favourite browse. Look for them in the dense Sabie/Crocodile River thorn thickets along the rivers, but also further afield close to watercourses, since they drink regularly in the late evening or at night. The far side of Sunset Dam is a favourite drinking spot just before dusk.

• **Hippo** will be found along the major perennial rivers of the park. In the south they occur in the Crocodile and Sabie Rivers; in the central area they may be found in the big perennial dams and deep pools such as Orpen Dam, Nsemani Dam, the N'wanetsi Dam and the Piet Grobler Dam in the Timbavati. Northwards, the Olifants River, and particularly the Letaba River, are home to big hippo pods. In the north, the Shingwedzi perennial pools and the Grootvlei Dam house a few, as do the deep perennial pools of the Luvuvhu and Limpopo rivers. Their present numbers are estimated at 3 100.

• Central Kruger ranging from the Sabie to the Olifants River is the hub for **giraffe**. Only 10% of the estimated population of 6 800–10 300 occur north of the Letaba River. They favour thorn trees such as umbrella thorn, knob-thorn, Delagoa thorn, horned thorn and others such as bushwillow and cluster-leaf. In the mopane veld, giraffe are mainly found along river courses where thorn trees grow.

- **Buffalo** are considered the most dangerous of all animals to hunt and are therefore included as one of the Big Five. Mixed herds (i.e. including males, females and young) numbering hundreds are often encountered on their way to drink. Being bulk grazers, they have to drink daily and sometimes even twice a day. There are probably in excess of 37 000 of these bovids in the park, of which more than 60% roam the northern parts where the biggest herds occur.

- **Plains zebra** are fussy when it comes to fresh drinking water, of which they require a regular supply. That is the driving force behind zebra migrations. When water supplies become inadequate, they move to find water and good grazing. The zebra migrations in the park are not as pronounced as those in the Serengeti, but north–south mini migrations do take place. The 30 000+ zebra are distributed all over the Park but they always keep within 10 km of water.

- **Blue wildebeest** are often seen in close association with zebra. They do not compete for food as the zebra crop the taller grass and the wildebeest follow in their wake, as they like shorter pastures. About 6 400-13 100 or more of the estimated 15 000 individuals occur south of the Olifants River.

- **Impala** are prolific and occur from south to north in the park, but almost 80% occur south of the Olifants River. Their numbers are estimated at between 132 300 and 176 400.

- **Kudu** numbers in the park are estimated at 11 200–17 300. They are the second-tallest antelope, and have remarkable jumping abilities. They prefer thickets, and browse a wide variety of plant species.

- **Nyala and bushbuck** are almost lookalikes. They occupy the same kind of habitat and feed on similar plant species. Nyala used to be confined to the Pafuri area but are now slowly spreading southwards along perennial rivers. There are only about 300 in the park.

- **Eland** are extremely rare in the park (estimated at 460), are seldom seen and very skittish.

- **Tsessebe** are also rare and skittish but are more often seen despite their low numbers (estimated at 180–220).

- The most beautiful and impressive antelope, the **sable**, is often seen in the Pretoriuskop area and north of N'watindlopfu on the H1-2 and along the S36. Numbers are estimated at 290.

- **Roan** numbers have diminished to such an extent that they are in danger of becoming extinct in the park. These antelope are very seldom seen. Only between 90 individuals have been counted. Most sightings occur along the H1-7 and H1-8. There may still be a small population around Pretoriuskop.

- **Waterbuck** are favourite prey in certain parts of the park. They have increased in numbers over the years and estimations are that there may be 3 100-7 800 in the park.

- **Southern reedbuck** are scarce (about 300) since there are not many suitable habitats for them in Kruger.

- The **rarest antelope** is the **Lichtenstein's Hartebeest**, of which there are only a few left.

- **Steenbok** are prolific and so are **common duiker**. **Oribi** used to occur in the grasslands west of Pretoriuskop but have not been seen lately. **Mountain reedbuck** were re-introduced in the Berg-en-Dal area but probably did not survive. The occasional **suni** is seen around Punda Maria and **Sharpe's grysbok** are often encountered along riverine vegetation in the northern section of the park.

- **Primates** are usually found close to rivers or water points.

- Between 3 100 and 5 700 **warthogs** occur from south to north and are popular predator prey.

- **The best night-drive sightings** include lion, leopard, hyena, jackal, caracal, serval, wild cat, white-tailed mongoose, civet, pangolin, bushbaby (galago), genet, porcupine, spring hare, scrub hare and Cape hare. In regions where termite mounds are abundant, aardvark may be a very special sighting.

Ground pangolin, S41

☐ Lion (Leeu)
Panthera leo

☐ Leopard (Luiperd)
Panthera pardus

☐ Cheetah (Jagluiperd)
Acinonyx jubatus

☐ Black-backed Jackal (Rooijakkals)
Canis mesomelas

☐ Side-striped Jackal (Witkwasjakkals)
Canus adustus

☐ African Wild Dog (Wildehond)
Lycaon pictus

☐ Spotted Hyena (Gevlekte Hiëna)
Crocuta crocuta

☐ Aardwolf (Aardwolf)
Proteles cristatus

☐ Caracal (Rooikat)
Caracal caracal

☐ African Wild Cat (Vaalboskat)
Felis lybica

☐ Serval (Tierboskat)
Leptailurus serval

☐ Honey Badger (Ratel)
Mellivora capensis

Mammals

☐ Small-spotted Genet (Kleinkolmuskejaatkat)
Genetta genetta

☐ Large-spotted Genet (Grootkol muskeljaatkat)
Genetta tigrina

☐ African Civet (Siwetkat)
Civettictis civetta

☐ Dwarf Mongoose (Dwergmuishond)
Helogale parvula

☐ Slender Mongoose (Swartkwasmuishond)
Galerella sanguinea

☐ Banded Mongoose (Gebande Muishond)
Mungos mungo

☐ White-tailed Mongoose (Witstertmuishond)
Ichneumia albicauda

☐ African Savanna Elephant (Olifant)
Loxodonta africana

☐ White Rhinoceros (Witrenoster)
Ceratotherium simum

☐ Black Rhinoceros (Swartrenoster)
Diceros bicornis

☐ Hippopotamus (Seekoei)
Hippopotamus amphibius

☐ African Buffalo (Buffel)
Syncerus caffer

☐ Giraffe (Kameelperd)
Giraffa camelopardalis

☐ Plains Zebra (Bontsebra)
Equus quagga

☐ Eland (Eland)
Tragelaphus oryx

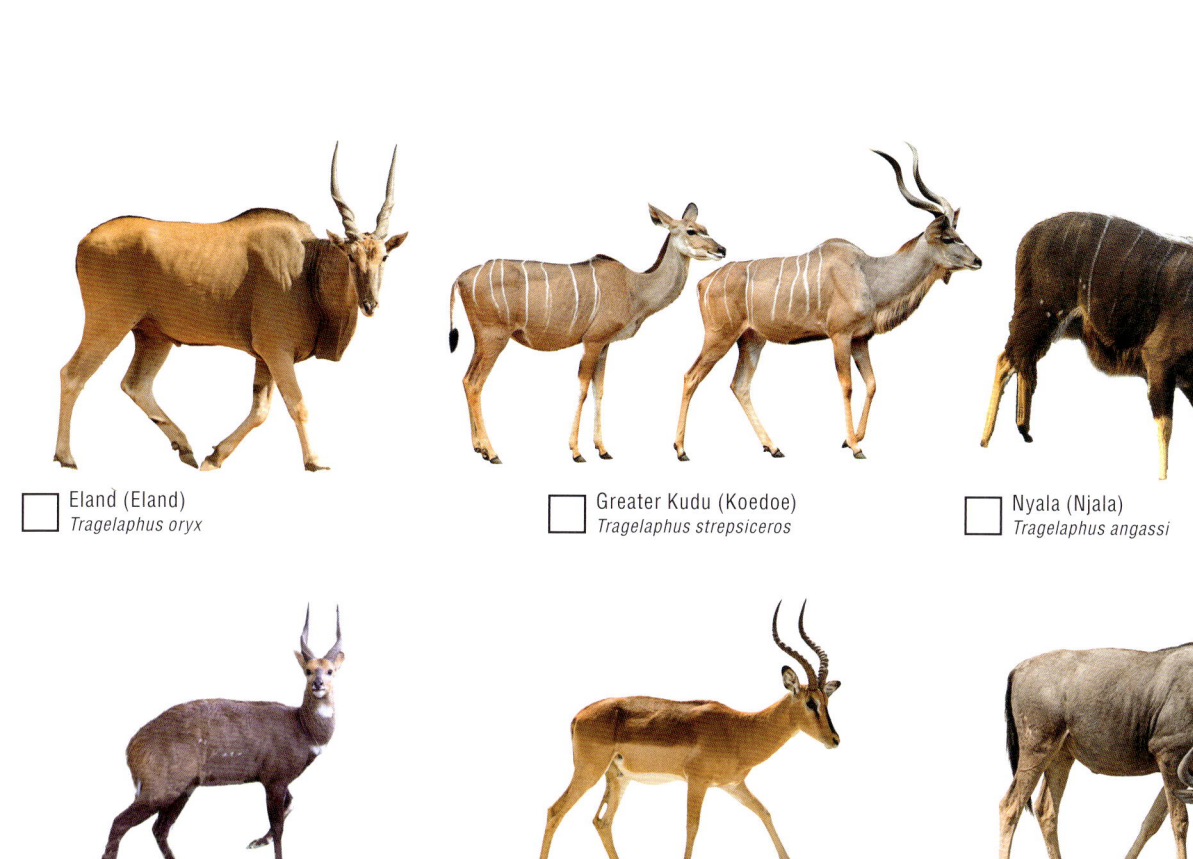

☐ Greater Kudu (Koedoe)
Tragelaphus strepsiceros

☐ Nyala (Njala)
Tragelaphus angassi

☐ Bushbuck (Bosbok)
Tragelaphus scriptus

☐ Impala (Rooibok)
Aepyceros melampus

☐ Blue Wildebeest (Blouwildebees)
Connochaetes taurinus

☐ Waterbuck (Waterbok)
Kobus ellipsiprymnus

☐ Tsessebe (Basterhartbees)
Damaliscus lunatus

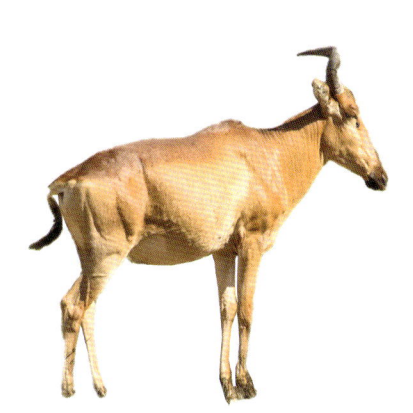

☐ Lichtenstein's hartebeest
(Lichtenstein se hartbees)
Alcelaphus lichtensteinii

☐ Sable Antelope (Swartwitpens)
Hippotragus niger

☐ Roan Antelope (Bastergemsbok)
Hippotragus equinus

☐ Southern Reedbuck (Rietbok)
Redunca arundinum

Mammals

☐ Sharpe's Grysbok (Tropiese Grysbok)
Raphicerus sharpei

☐ Klipspringer (Klipspringer)
Oreotragus oreotragus

☐ Steenbok (Steenbok)
Raphicerus campestris

☐ Common or Grey Duiker (Gewone Duiker)
Sylvicarpa grimmia

☐ Bushpig (Bosvark)
Potamochoerus larvatus

☐ Scrub Hare (Kolhaas)
Lepus saxatilis

☐ Ground Pangolin (Ietermagog)
Manis temminckii

☐ Common Warthog (Vlakvark)
Phacochoerus africanus

☐ Porcupine (Ystervark)
Hystrix africaeaustralis

☐ Rock Hyrax (Dassie)
Procavia capensis

☐ Tree Squirrel (Boomeekhoring)
Paraxerus cepapi

☐ Springhare (Springhaas)
Pedetes capensis

☐ South African Galago or Lesser Bushbaby (Nagapie)
Galago moholi

☐ Vervet Monkey (Blouaap)
Cercopithecus pygerythrus

☐ Chacma Baboon (Bobbejaan)
Papio hamadryas

☐ Greater Galago (Bosnagaap)
Otolemur crassicaudatus

Chacma baboon, H12

SELECTED BIBLIOGRAPHY

Branch, Bill. 1988. *Field guide to the snakes and other reptiles of southern Africa*. Cape Town: Struik.
Carnaby, Trevor. 2006. *Beat About the Bush: Mammals*. Johannesburg: Jacana Media.
Carruthers, Vincent. 2000. *The Wildlife of Southern Africa: A Field Guide to the Animals and Plants of the Region*. Cape Town: Struik.
Chittenden, Hugh. 2012. *Roberts Bird Guide: A Comprehensive Field Guide to Over 950 Bird Species in Southern Africa*. Cape Town: The Trustees of the John Voelcker Bird Book Fund.
Conradie, Riëtte. 2010. *Aardwolf tot Ystervark: Vrae en Antwoorde*. Riëtte Conradie.
Dennis, Nigel J. & Scholes, Bob. 1995. *The Kruger National Park: Wonders of an African Eden*. Cape Town: Struik New Holland.
Emmet, Megan & Pattrick, Sean. 2012. *Game Ranger in Your Backpack: All-in-one Interpretative Guide to the Lowveld*. Pretoria: Briza Publications.
Estes, Richard D. 1993. *The Safari Companion*. Halfway House: Russel Friedman Books.
Grant, Rina, & Thomas, Val. 2006. *Sappi Tree Spotting: Lowveld Including Kruger National Park*. Johannesburg: Jacana Media.
Hall-Martin, Anthony & Carruthers, Jane (Eds). 2003. *South African National Parks: A celebration*. Auckland Park: Horst Klemm.
Hilton-Barber, Brett & Berger, Prof. Lee R. 2007. The *Prime Origins guide to exploring Kruger*. Cape Town: Prime Origins Publishers.
Hockey, PAR, Dean, WRJ & Ryan, PG. 2005. *Roberts Birds of Southern Africa VIIth Edition*. Cape Town: The Trustees of the John Voelcker Bird Book Fund.
Joubert, Salmon. 2007. *The Kruger National Park: A History, Volumes 1, 2 and 3*. Johannesburg: High Branching (Pty) Ltd.
Kloppers, Johan J. 1992. *Plekname in die Nasionale Krugerwildtuin*. Internal Publication, Kruger National Park 1992, revised in 2002 by C van der Merwe.
Mills, Gus & Hes, Lex. 1997. *The Complete Book of Southern African Mammals*. Cape Town: Struik.
Newman, Kenneth. 2003. *What's that Bird? A starter's guide to birds of southern Africa*. Cape Town: Struik Nature.
Pienaar, Uys de Villiers et al. 2007. *Neem uit die Verlede*. Pretoria: Protea Boekhuis.
Skinner, John D & Chimimba, Christian T. 2005. *The Mammals of the Southern African Sub-region*. (Third edition). Cambridge: Cambridge University Press.
Stuart, Chris & Stuart, Tilde. 1997. *Field Guide to the Mammals of Southern Africa*. Cape Town: Struik.

African pygmy-goose male, Leeupan, H1-2

ROUTES AND ROADS INDEX

ROUTES	
SKUKUZA ROUTES	28
BERG-EN-DAL ROUTES	30
PRETORIUSKOP ROUTES	32
CROCODILE BRIDGE ROUTES	34
LOWER SABIE ROUTES	36
ORPEN, TAMBOTI AND MAROELA ROUTES	38
SATARA ROUTES	40
OLIFANTS CAMP ROUTES	42
LETABA ROUTES	44
MOPANI ROUTES	46
SHINGWEDZI ROUTES	48
PUNDA MARIA ROUTES	50

H-ROADS	
H1-1	56
H1-2	58
H1-3	60
H1-4	62
H1-5	66
H1-6	68
H1-6	72
H1-7	74
H1-8	76
H1-9	78
H2-2	80
H3	82
H4-1	84
H4-2	88
H5	90
H6	92
H7	94
H8	96
H9	97
H10	98
H11	102
H12	103
H13-1	104
H13-2	105
H14	106
H15	108

S-ROADS			
S1	110	S82	185
S3	112	S83	186
S4	114	S84	186
S7	114	S85	188
S8	115	S86	188
S10	115	S89	189
S12	116	S90	190
S14	117	S91	192
S21	118	S92	192
S22	120	S93	192
S23	122	S94	194
S25	124	S95	194
S26	126	S96	196
S27	126	S98	196
S28	128	S99	197
S29	129	S100	200
S30	130	S101	204
S32	132	S102	204
S33	133	S103	205
S34	134	S105	206
S35	135	S106	206
S36	136	S107	208
S37	140	S108	208
S39	144	S110	209
S40	146	S112	210
S41	148	S113	210
S42	150	S114	211
S44	152	S118	214
S46	154	S119	214
S47	155	S120	215
S48	156	S121	215
S49	157	S122	216
S50	158	S125	217
S50	159	S126	218
S51	162	S127	220
S52	163	S128	220
S53	166	S129	222
S54	166	S130	222
S55	167	S130	224
S56	168	S131	226
S57	170	S132	227
S58	170	S133	227
S59	172	S134	228
S60	173	S135	228
S61	174	S137	230
S62	176	S140	230
S63	178	S142	231
S64	180	S143	232
S65	182	S144	233
S68	183	S145	233
S76	184	S146	234
S79	185	S147	234

ACKNOWLEDGEMENTS

The Kruger National Park has mesmerised us since our first visit many decades ago. Over the years, changes have taken place, but the special ambience of the park is still intact. Almost a century ago only a few visitors came to the park each year but now the numbers have increased to about 1.5 million. With such an increase in visitor numbers it is inevitable that infrastructure development has to take place. It is however a feather in South African National Parks' cap that it has been done in such a way that the park has retained its wilderness atmosphere in spite of the high visitor numbers. Today, all South Africans can be extremely proud of this wonderful heritage and world-class National Park.

In preparing this book we travelled all the roads in the park many times. The ratings we have given the roads are from our own experience over the many years for which we have been regular visitors, combined with that of others who know the park and its roads well. All photographs were taken along the various roads where they have been placed to illustrate the possibilities each road offers the visitor.

We are indebted to SANParks, our families, friends and many kind people in the preparation of this book and would like to thank them all for their support and encouragement. In particular we would like to mention Jimmy and Lida Pressly; John Deane; Duncan and Linda McKenzie; Dr Sam Ferreira. And a special thanks to Stephen Midzi for supplying the prime water spots in the park.

We also thank the following people who contributed with their photographs: Liz Hart; Elmar Venter; Graeme Mitchley; Mohammed and Sarifa Jinnah; Phil Muller; Hamman Prinsloo; Villiers Steyn; Dustin van Helsdingen; Isak Pretorius; Herman van den Berg; Bruce Crossey; Gerhard Geldenhuys; Hennie Blignaut; Luca Neto; Gerhard Vosloo; Calum Evans; Janus Trotzer; Dorea and Brian Stratton; Rolf Wiesler.

The Van den Bergs

MAPS AND ADDITIONAL INFORMATION

GATE OPENING & CLOSING TIMES

MONTH	ENTRANCE GATES OPEN	CAMP GATES OPEN	ALL GATES CLOSE
January	05:30	04:30	18:30
February	05:30	05:30	18:30
March	05:30	05:30	18:00
April	06:00	06:00	18:00
May	06:00	06:00	17:30
June	06:00	06:00	17:30
July	06:00	06:00	17:30
August	06:00	06:00	18:00
September	06:00	06:00	18:00
October	05:30	05:30	18:00
November	05:30	04:30	18:30
December	05:30	04:30	18:30

HINTS & TIPS

As from the SANParks official website:
www.sanparks.org

- There is a bank at Skukuza (only open Monday to Friday and Saturday morning) and an ATM at Skukuza and Letaba, no cash withdrawal facilities are available elsewhere in the park.
- Vehicle fuel is available in the main rest camps and they accept legitimate petrol/fuel/garage cards, any VISA/MasterCard cards or cash as a form of payment. All accommodation, ablution and kitchen facilities are serviced by cleaning staff daily.
- As outdoor lighting in camps is limited, a torch/headlamp is required when walking outside at night.
- Most rest camps have retail facilities and restaurants. Tariff prices do not include meals.
- Currently, bedding is supplied in all accommodation. Cooking Utensils and Refrigeration are provided in most accommodation units. Exceptions will be indicated while booking. Adult is 12 years or above. Child is 2-11 years, under 2 years – Gratis.
- All rates can be discounted at the discretion of the park or rest camp management.
- Additional Person Supplements are applicable to those units where number of beds exceeds the base occupancy, if these beds are occupied.
- Consult the reservation staff or watch the press for details for out of season discounts and promotions.
- Do not leave any food unattended, as thieving monkeys and baboons are a constant threat.

EMERGENCIES & CONTACT INFORMATION

Kruger National Park Admin Offices: +27 (0)13 735 4000
See each camp's General page for Contact Information on the website **www.sanparks.org**

Tshokwane
Orpen Dam
Massintonto
Shilolweni
Leeupan
Mthombomuni
Nkumbe
Nwatindlopfu
Jones Dam
Rhino Walking Plains Camp
Kruger tablets
Mantimahle Dam
Olifant Drinkgat
Rhino Post Lodge
Mutlumuvi
Mlondozi
Muntshe
Phambana Pans
Hillside
Loskop
Muntshe Loop
Tinga Narina
Sand
Sabie
Tinga – kraal
Salitje Road
Paul Kruger Gate
Paul Kruger Monument
Lake Panic
Skukuza
Nkuhlu Picnic Site
Mafotini
Gabeni
Mlondozi Dam
Mlondozi Dam Picnic Site
Marhambuyanhutlwa
N'waswitshaka
De Laporte
N'watinwambu
N'watimhiri
Old Tshokwane Road
Mlondozi Loop
Granokop
Stevenson-Hamilton grave
Stevenson Hamilton
Napi Road
Transport Dam
Renosterkoppies
Mthomane
Nhlotini
Ntomanene
Sunset Dam
Lower Sabie
Nwari
Albasini's trading post
Trading post
Old Delagoa wagon road
Kwaggaspan
Kemp's cottage
Randspruit Road
Old Randspruit siding
Vurhami
Matjulwungu Road
Mosehla
Nhlowa Road
Mbyamiti
Muhlambamadube
Mpondo Dam
Bume Road
Ntandanyathi
Duke
Nhlanganzwani Dam
Main Jock Lodge
Mitomeni
Malelane Road
Voortrekker
Gomondwane
Sardelli's store
De Cuiper
Francois de Cuiper's attack
Mac's
Biyamiti Weir
Gayisenga
Bume
Afsaal Picnic Site
Blinkwater
Biyamiti
Mpemane
Zambhala
Camp Shawu
Renosterpan
Glen Leary
Rhenosterkoppies Road
Fihlamanzi
Gezantombi
Crocodile River Road
Old Bume siding
Crocodile Bridge
Crocodile Bridge Gate
Camp Shonga
Shishangeni Lodge
Mlambeni
Ampie-se-Boorgat
James
Lwakahle
Lukimbi Lodge
Gardenia
Gardenia Bird Hide
Hippo Pools
Crocodile
Mjejane
Tsengemanti
Van Graan Dam
Malelane Gate
Harold Trollope hut
H1-1
H1-2
H2-2
H3
H4-1
H4-2
H5
H10
H11
H12
S21
S22
S23
S25
S26
S28
S29
S30
S32
S36
S42
S65
S66
S68
S76
S79
S82
S83
S84
S85
S102
S107
S108
S110
S112
S113
S114
S118
S119
S120
S121
S122
S128
S129
S130
S137
S139

SANPARKS REGULATIONS

Visit the SANParks website at **www.sanparks.org**

It is the function of SANParks to protect, conserve and control the Kruger National Park. Kindly adhere to the rules and regulations under the Protected Areas Act. Transgression of the rules and regulations as summarised below may result in prosecution and or penalties.

- Please sign the **INDEMNITY** documents when entering the park.
- Remember to bring all your **IDENTIFICATION** documents along.
- **CONSERVATION FEES** are payable on entry or acquire a Wild Card as an alternative to paying daily conservation fees.
- A 1% **COMMUNITY LEVY** on all reservations is also payable. This is used to fund projects that support surrounding communities in bettering their livelihoods.
- **STAY IN YOUR VEHICLE** – no part of your body may protrude from a window or sunroof and doors should always remain closed since there are dangerous animals out there.
- Adhere to the **MAXIMUM SPEED LIMIT** – tarred roads (50 km/h) and gravel roads (40 km/h).
- The consumption of **ALCOHOL** is prohibited in public areas. Day visitors are prohibited from entering the park with any alcohol in their vehicles.
- **DRIVE SAFELY** – General rules of the road apply within the park.
- **GATE TIMES** must be strictly adhered to. After-hours driving is not allowed and could result in a summons being issued.
- **OVERNIGHT VISITORS** are only allowed to stay at a booked and recognised overnight facilities and must report to the relevant reception before occupying accommodation or camping.
- **CAMPING BASE RATES** include one vehicle per campsite. Additional vehicles are charged at a rate equivalent to the campsite base rate per night.
- For safety reasons some activities conducted in parks have **AGE RESTRICTIONS**. Please take note of these to prevent disappointments.
- **DEPARTURE TIMES** – All accommodation and camping sites may be occupied from 14:00 on the day of arrival and must be vacated by 10:00 on the day of departure.
- **OFF-ROAD DRIVING** or driving on closed or no-entry roads is a serious offence.
- **FEEDING OF WILDLIFE IS PROHIBITED**.
- **NO PLANT, ANIMAL, WILDLIFE OR ANY NATURAL OR CULTURAL ITEMS MAY BE REMOVED** from the park without permission. This includes firewood.
- Take note of **VEHICLE RESTRICTION** as to the type of vehicle that may enter national parks.
- **NO PETS** may be brought into a Park.
- **LITTERING** is prohibited and can result in a fine.
- All **FIREARMS**, dangerous weapons of any sort, any explosive, trap or poison must be declared upon entry, and firearms will be sealed.
- The use of **DRONES** inside and over the park is strictly prohibited.
- **BEWARE MALARIA** – A 24-hour malaria hotline is available on 082 234 1800 or consult your medical practitioner.

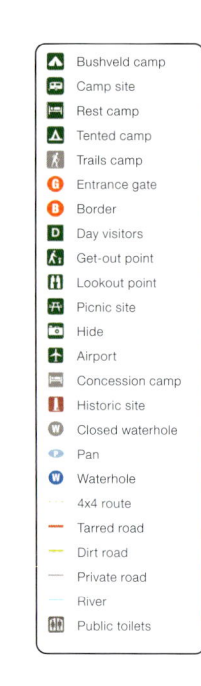

Legend

- Bushveld camp
- Camp site
- Rest camp
- Tented camp
- Trails camp
- Entrance gate
- Border
- Day visitors
- Get-out point
- Lookout point
- Picnic site
- Hide
- Airport
- Concession camp
- Historic site
- Closed waterhole
- Pan
- Waterhole
- 4x4 route
- Tarred road
- Dirt road
- Private road
- River
- Public toilets

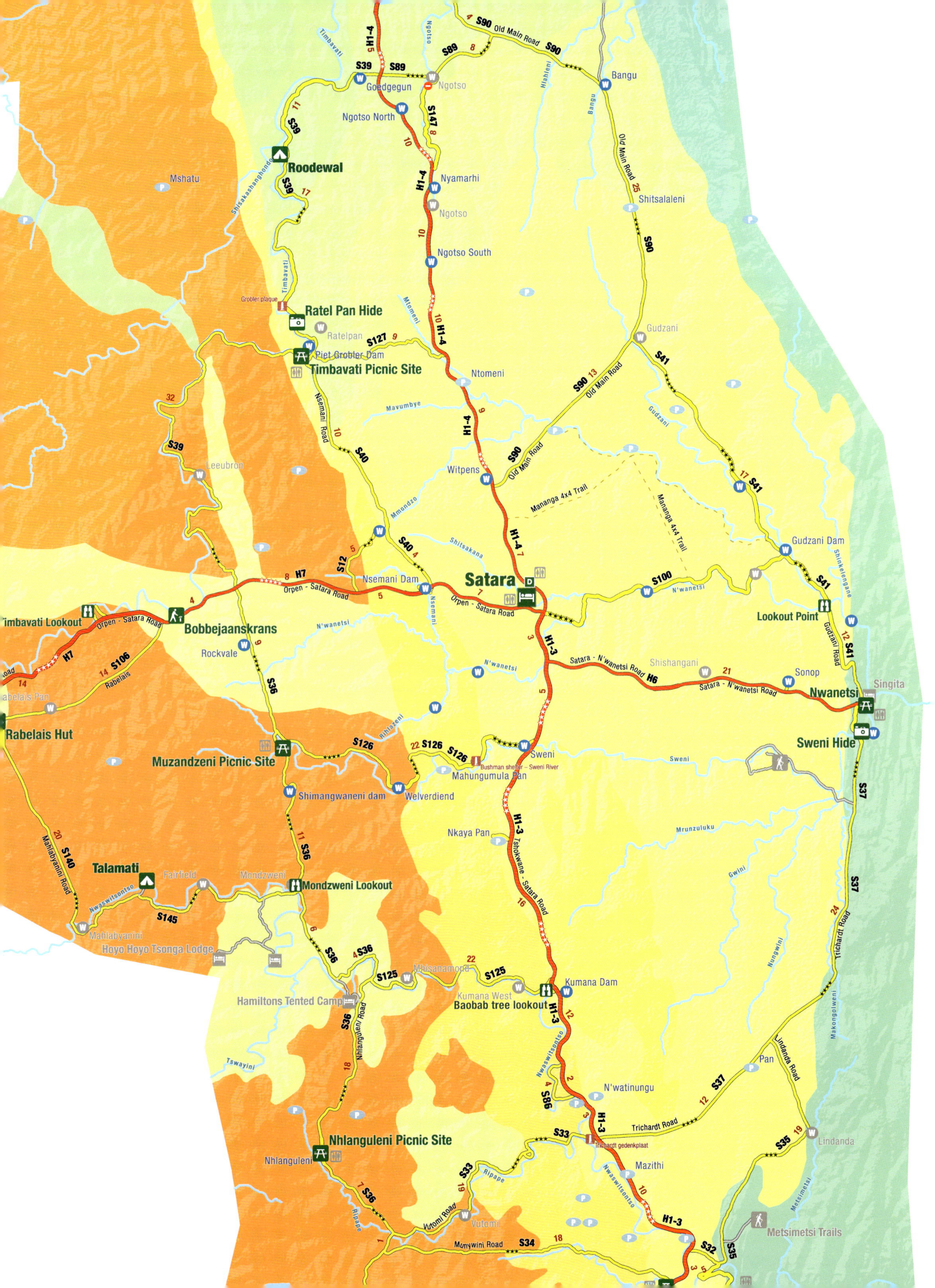

S90 Old Main Road
S89
S39
Goedgegun
Ngotso
Ngotso North
S147
H1-4
Timbavati
Hlahleni
Bangu
Roodewal
Mshatu
Shisakashanghondo
Nyamarhi
Old Main Road
Shitsalaleni
Ngotso South
Grobler plaque
Ratel Pan Hide
Ratelpan
S127
Piet Grobler Dam
Timbavati Picnic Site
Mtomeni
Ntomeni
Gudzani
S41
Mavumbye
Nsemani Road
S40
Witpens
Mananga 4x4 Trail
Leeubron
Mmondzo
Shitsakana
Gudzani Dam
Shinkelengane
S12
H7
Orpen - Satara Road
Nsemani Dam
Satara
S100
N'wanetsi
Lookout Point
Gudzani Road
Timbavati Lookout
Bobbejaanskrans
Rockvale
S106
Rabelais
Rabelais Pan
Rabelais Hut
S36
H1-3
Satara - N'wanetsi Road
H6
Shishangani
Sonop
Nwanetsi
Singita
Sweni Hide
Muzandzeni Picnic Site
S126
Ripape
Bushman shelter – Sweni River
Sweni
Mahungumula Pan
Shimangwaneni dam
Welverdiend
S37
Nkaya Pan
Tshokwane - Satara Road
Mrunzuluku
Gwini
S140
Mahlabyanini Road
Talamati
Fairfield
Mondzweni
Mondzweni Lookout
Nwaswitsontso
S145
Mahlabyanini
Hoyo Hoyo Tsonga Lodge
S125
Mhusanamond
Kumana West
Kumana Dam
Baobab tree lookout
Trichardt Road
Nungwini
Hamiltons Tented Camp
Nhlanguleni Road
Makongolweni
Tswayini
Lindanda Road
Pan
N'watinungu
S86
Nhlanguleni Picnic Site
Nhlanguleni
S33
Trichardt gedenkplaat
S35
Lindanda
Mazithi
Vutomi Road
Vutomi
Metsimetsi
Metsimetsi Trails
Munywini Road
S34
S32

BE BUSHWISE

Be safe and stay in your vehicle unless you are at a place signposted as a 'get-out' point. Hanging out of the windows breaks the familiar outline of the vehicle and frightens animals away. They are comfortable with vehicles, but not with people.

TIME OF DAY

• **Early risers** may encounter predators that spent the night on the warm tarred or sandy roads – especially in winter.

• **Hyena** are often seen returning to their dens and running along the road in the **early mornings**. They often den in culverts along the road.

• Predator activity is **at a minimum during midday periods** and even herbivores seek shade.

• **Cheetah** are diurnal and hunt during **any time of the day**. They prefer open spaces to run down their prey and avoid areas where they have to compete with lions.

• Look up into trees – you may have a pleasant surprise and spot a **leopard resting on a branch**.

KNOWLEDGE OF THE LATEST SIGHTINGS

• Visit the **sightings board** at each camp – it will give you an indication of the latest and best sightings.

• Consult the **visitor's book** at Reception.

• **Talk to people** and share knowledge of sightings.

• Many sightings are **fleeting glimpses** of predators and it is not always worth pursuing these.

• Predators with **young cubs or pups** tend to keep to a specific area for some time. Ask around.

• **Lions at a big kill** often take days to feed. Once they have had their fill, the scavengers arrive.

• **Denning animals** (such as hyena and wild dog) with young tend to stay in a specific area for a long time. Repeated sightings are almost a certainty.

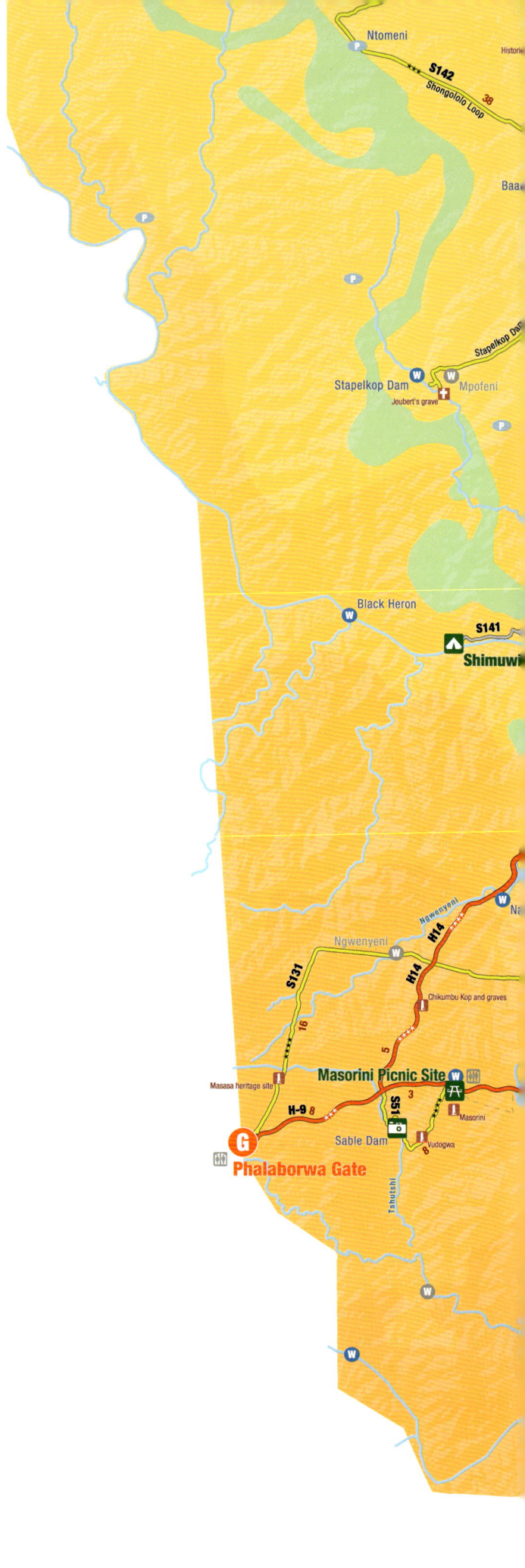

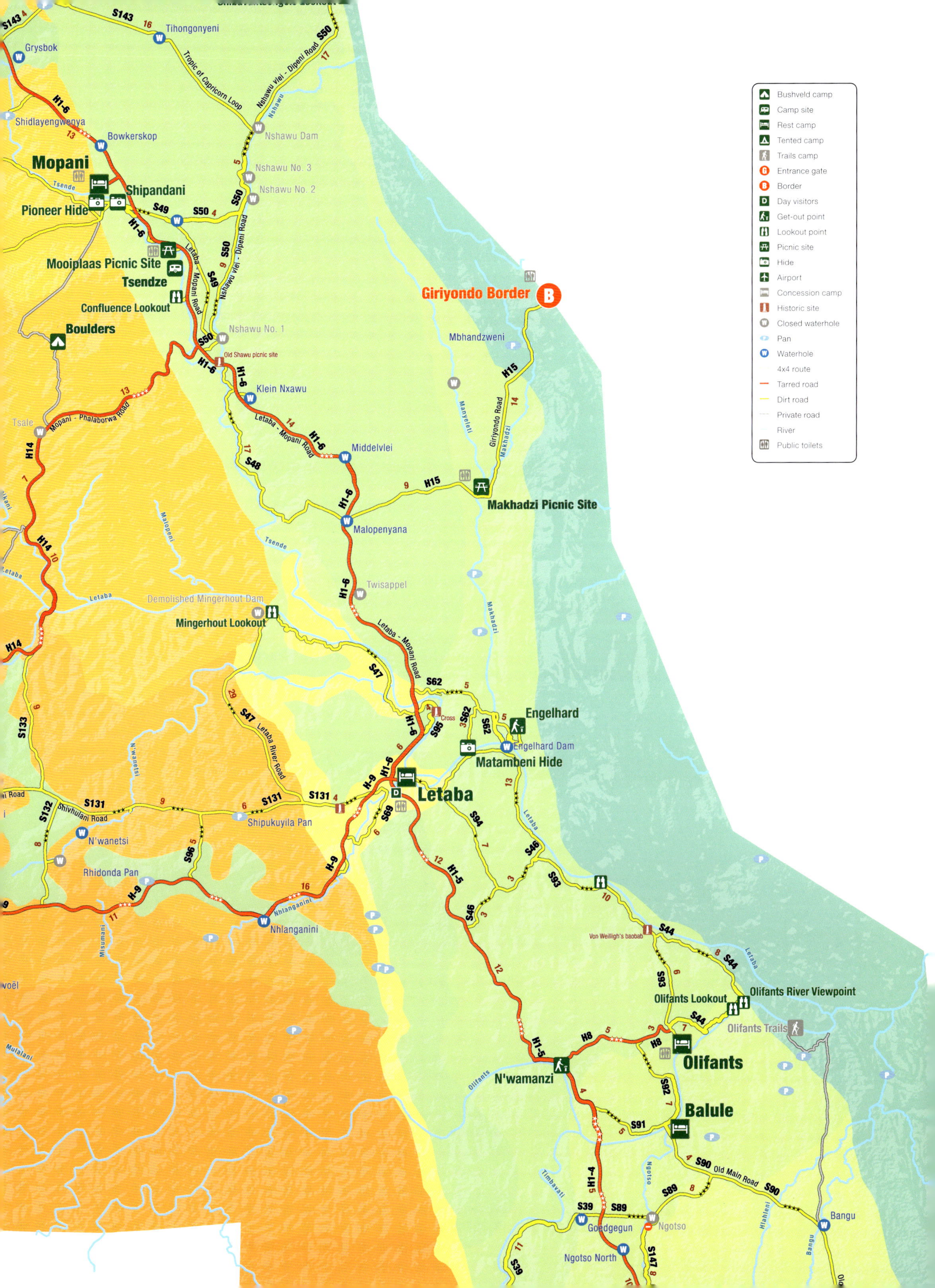
Bushveld camp
Camp site
Rest camp
Tented camp
Trails camp
Entrance gate
Border
Day visitors
Get-out point
Lookout point
Picnic site
Hide
Airport
Concession camp
Historic site
Closed waterhole
Pan
Waterhole
4x4 route
Tarred road
Dirt road
Private road
River
Public toilets
S143
Tihongonyeni
Grysbok
Tropic of Capricorn Loop
Nshawu vlei - Dipeni Road
S50
Nshawu
Shidlayengwenya
Bowkerskop
Nshawu Dam
Mopani
Nshawu No. 3
Tsende
Shipandani
Nshawu No. 2
Pioneer Hide
S49
H1-6
Letaba - Mopani Road
Nshawu vlei - Dipeni Road
Mooiplaas Picnic Site
Tsendze
Giriyondo Border
Confluence Lookout
Boulders
Nshawu No. 1
Mbhandzweni
Old Shawu picnic site
Klein Nxawu
H15
Tsale
Mopani - Phalaborwa Road
Giriyondo Road
Manyeleti
Makhadzi
H14
S48
Middelvlei
Makhadzi Picnic Site
Malopenyana
Malopeni
Tsende
Letaba
Twisappel
Demolished Mingerhout Dam
Mingerhout Lookout
S47
Letaba - Mopani Road
S62
Engelhard
Cross
S95
Engelhard Dam
Matambeni Hide
S133
Letaba River Road
N'wanetsi
H1-9
Letaba
S131
S132
Shivhulani Road
S69
Shipukuyila Pan
S94
N'wanetsi
S96
S46
Rhidonda Pan
H1-5
S93
H-9
Nhlanganini
Von Weilligh's baobab
S44
Misumani
Olifants Lookout
Olifants River Viewpoint
Olifants Trails
H8
Olifants
N'wamanzi
S92
Balule
S91
H1-4
Timbavati
Ngotso
S90
Old Main Road
S89
S39
Goedgegun
Ngotso
Hlahleni
Bangu
Ngotso North
S147

ORIGIN OF PLACE NAMES

Place names in the Kruger National Park reflect the legacy of the diverse ethnic and cultural groups over many centuries that occupied, visited, traded in or crossed the area where the park is today. These groups ranged from Stone Age hunter-gatherers, to tribes such as the Swazi, Sotho, Tsonga and Venda, to Arab and Portuguese traders, European traders, explorers of Dutch, Greek, Hungarian, Irish and British origin, hunters (legal and illegal) and Voortrekkers (emigrants who left the British Cape Colony and moved into the interior during the 1830s and 1840s as part of the Great Trek).

The origins of several place names are included in the text, but the following may also be of interest:

The name of the **Balule** Camp was derived from the Tsonga name for the Olifants River, which they called 'Rimbelule'.

Numbi Gate is named after the fruit of the 'stamvrug' (stem fruit – *Englerophytum magalismontanum*), which grows in rocky places in its vicinity.

Phabeni Gate was named after the Sotho word for a shelter or a cave and the gate and town called **Phalaborwa** means the place that is better (warmer) than the south, from which the Sotho people originally migrated.

Masorini is the name of a hill near the Phalaborwa Gate and was the name of a Sotho person who once lived where the Archaeological Museum is today.

The word **mlondozi** means a strong-flowing stream in Swati. The Mlondozi Dam was built in this stream with the Mlondozi Picnic Site overlooking it. The nearby **Lebombo Mountains** can also be seen from there. The Zulu and Swati call these mountains the 'amabombo', which means the direction one takes when journeying.

The H4-2 runs parallel to the **Vurhami River**, whose name is the Tsonga word for 'cold'. The name given to the **Vutomi River** along the S33 means healthy and alive. When the dam was built in the Vurhami Stream, the Swati called this place **Gezantombi**, which means 'the place where the young maidens bath'.

N'wanetsi is the name given to a seasonal river and also a picnic site after the Tsonga word for water that glitters and shines, is clean and clear. The river called **N'waswitsontso** is so named because of its subterranean nature – it shows itself only here and there. On the other hand, the Swati word for good or clean water is **Mantimahle** and this name is given to a dam, windmill and a seasonal stream.

The name for the **Timbavati River** is derived from the Tsonga term *ku bava*, which means bitter or brackish water. The name given to the **Tsendze River** means to wander around like somebody roaming in the bush.

The **Luvuvhu River** derives its name from *mvuvhu*, the Venda word for the River Bushwillow (*Combretum erythrophyllum*). The Tsonga call the thin reed (*Phragmites* sp.) growing in marshy areas *fayi*. Dense stands of this reed are found along the S14 or **Fayi** loop road.

Nkaya Pan near Satara is named after the Tsonga name for the knob-thorn tree (*Senegalia nigrescence*), while **Nkuhlu** is the name for the Natal mahogany (*Trichilia emetica*) and **Ntoma** the name of the jackalberry (*Diospyros mespiliformis*). **Ntomeni** means the place where this tree grows.

Sweni means to 'wrap up tightly' in Tsonga, while **talamati** means an abundance of water. The Sweni River, the Sweni game-viewing hide and the Sweni Trails Camp are all close to Satara. Talamati Camp is indeed situated in a place where there is an abundance of water.

AT WATERHOLES

- In summer or after rain there may be enough water in **temporary pans further away** from regular waterholes. The best time to watch game at watering points will be in the dry season, which usually peaks in September/October.

- **Big herds** only appear at waterholes around **mid-morning** – buffalo, zebra, wildebeest, waterbuck, kudu, giraffe and impala.

- **Mid-afternoon** is excellent for sightings of elephant drinking and bathing. White rhino may also appear.

- On **hot days,** rhino, buffalo, warthog and elephant may wallow in the mud.

- **Black rhino** usually drink **in early to late evening** and may be seen on night drives or at Sunset Dam just before gate-closing time.

NIGHT DRIVES

- **Self-drive** after gate-closing time is **not allowed** but **guided night drives** in a park vehicle may be booked at Reception.

- You can expect to **see any of the following** on a night drive: civet, genet, porcupine, white-tailed mongoose, honey badger, aardvark, pangolin, African wild cat, black rhino, the Big Five and hyena.

Bushveld camp
Camp site
Rest camp
Tented camp
Trails camp
Entrance gate
Border
Day visitors
Get-out point
Lookout point
Picnic site
Hide
Airport
Concession camp
Historic site
Closed waterhole
Pan
Waterhole
4x4 route
Tarred road
Dirt road
Private road
River
Public toilets
Babalala
Babalala Picnic Site
Boyela
Sirheni
Mphongolo
Ribye
Early borehole
Nkulumbeni
Phugwane
Lamont
Mandzemba
Shingwedzi
Kanniedood Hide
Kanniedood Dam
Bran Key memorial tablet
Shipirivirhi
Bububu
Mashagadzi
Mashakadzi
Joa'o
Juwawa camps
Gubyane
Red Rocks
Silwervis Dam
Bateleur
Tshanga
Rooibosrant Dam
Dipeni
Dipeni dip tank
Dzombo
Nkokodzi
Dzombo West
Dzombo East
Nyawutsi Hide
Nyawutsi
Mopani - Shingwedzi Road
Olifantsbad Pan
Nkokodzi N'wamba Pan Road
Grootvlei Dam
Nshawu vlei - Dipeni Road
Kumba
N'wambu
Tsende
Outspan Pan
Eendrag
N'wambu Pan
Shibavantsengele Lookout
Ntomeni
Historic Tsende tented camp site
Grysbok
Tihongonyeni
Tropic of Capricorn Loop
Shongololo Loop
Frazersrus
Shidlayengwenya
Bowkerskop
Nshawu Dam
Nshawu
Baanbreker
Mopani
Nshawu No. 3
Nshawu No. 2
Shipandani
Pioneer Hide
Stapelkop Dam Road
Mooiplaas Picnic Site
Tsendze
Letaba - Mopani Road
Confluence Lookout
Giriyondo Border
Don
Stapelkop Dam
Mpofeni
Joubert's grave
Boulders
Nshawu No. 1
Mbhandzweni
Old Shawu picnic site
H1-7
H1-6
S56
S57
S53
S55
S135
S101
S52
S134
S50
S144
S103
S143
S142
S49
S146

Distances between camps and gates

	Berg-en-Dal	Crocodile Bridge	Letaba	Lower Sabie	Malelane	Mopani	Numbi Gate	N'wanetsi	Olifants	Orpen	Pafuri Gate	Paul Kruger Gate	Phalaborwa Gate	Phabeni Gate	Pretoriuskop	Punda Maria	Satara	Shingwedzi	Skukuza
Berg-en-Dal	-	149	234	113	12	281	97	180	219	213	453	83	285	110	92	415	165	344	72
Crocodile Bridge	149	-	196	34	141	243	130	142	181	175	415	88	246	115	125	377	127	306	77
Letaba	234	196	-	162	226	47	216	94	32	117	218	173	51	200	211	176	69	109	162
Lower Sabie	133	34	162	-	105	209	95	108	147	141	380	53	213	91	90	342	93	271	43
Malelane	12	141	226	105	-	272	94	170	210	204	444	74	277	102	85	408	156	333	64
Mopani	281	234	47	209	272	-	263	141	86	164	172	220	74	247	258	130	116	63	209
Numbi Gate	97	130	216	95	94	263	-	162	201	195	434	65	267	32	9	396	147	325	54
N'wanetsi	180	142	94	108	170	141	162	-	79	63	312	119	145	146	156	274	25	203	108
Olifants	219	181	32	147	210	86	201	79	-	102	250	158	83	185	195	212	54	141	147
Orpen	213	175	117	141	204	164	195	63	102	-	335	152	167	175	184	297	48	226	137
Pafuri Gate	453	415	218	380	444	172	434	312	250	335	-	392	246	413	438	76	287	109	380
Paul Kruger Gate	83	88	173	53	74	220	65	119	158	152	392	-	224	50	60	354	104	283	12
Phalaborwa Gate	285	246	51	213	277	74	267	145	83	167	246	224	-	251	261	201	119	137	213
Phabeni Gate	110	115	200	91	102	247	32	146	185	175	413	50	251	-	23	380	131	309	38
Pretoriuskop	92	125	21	90	85	258	9	156	195	184	438	60	261	23	-	389	140	318	49
Punda Maria	415	377	176	342	408	130	396	274	212	297	76	354	201	380	389	-	254	71	342
Satara	165	127	69	93	156	116	147	25	54	48	287	104	119	131	140	245	-	178	93
Shingwedzi	344	306	109	27	333	63	325	203	141	226	109	283	137	309	318	71	178	-	271
Skukuza	72	77	162	43	64	209	54	108	147	137	380	12	213	38	49	342	93	271	-

The table shows distances between Kruger National Park rest camps and gates. If you are planning a self-drive safari to the Kruger National Park it is important to take note of the gate opening and closing times. You also need to take into account the distances between camps and gates. This is important as there is a speed limit of 40 km/h on dirt roads and 50 km/h on tar roads within the park.

For more information visit www.sanparks.org

Leopard, H1-2

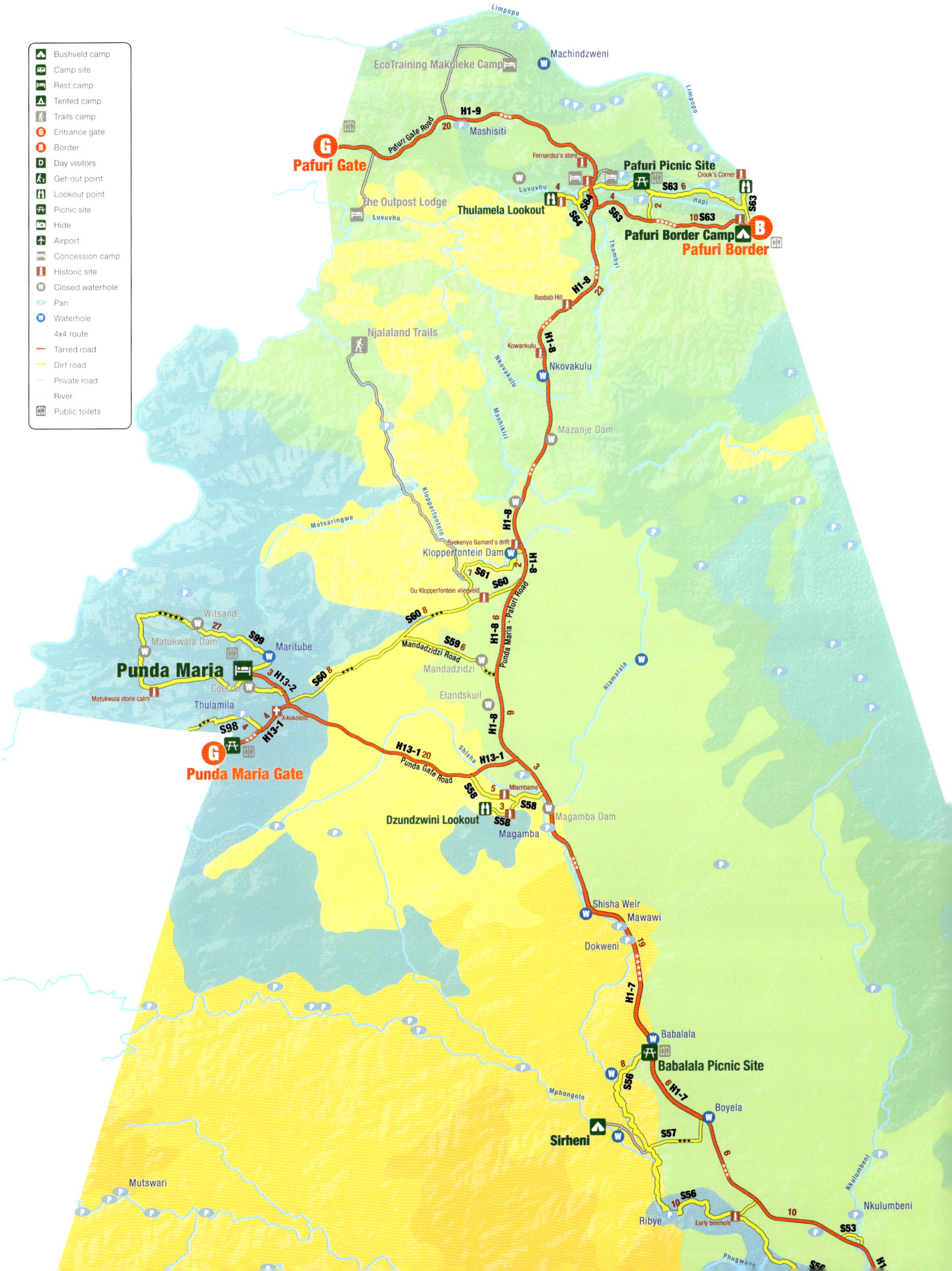
Bushveld camp
Camp site
Rest camp
Tented camp
Trails camp
Entrance gate
Border
Day visitors
Get-out point
Lookout point
Picnic site
Hide
Airport
Concession camp
Historic site
Closed waterhole
Pan
Waterhole
4x4 route
Tarred road
Dirt road
Private road
River
Public toilets
Limpopo
Machindzweni
EcoTraining Makuleke Camp
H1-9
Pafuri Gate Road
Mashisiti
Pafuri Gate
Fernandez's store
Pafuri Picnic Site
Crook's Corner
S63
Luvuvhu
The Outpost Lodge
Thulamela Lookout
S64
Hapi
Pafuri Border Camp
Pafuri Border
Thambyi
H1-8
Baobab Hill
Njalaland Trails
Kowankulu
Nkovakulu
Mashikiri
Mazanje Dam
Klopperfontein
Matsaringwe
Byekenya Barnard's drift
Klopperfontein Dam
S61
S60
Ou Klopperfontein vliegveld
Witsand
Matukwala Dam
S99
Maritube
Punda Maria
H13-2
Coetzer
Matukwala stone cairn
Thulamila
Xikokololo
S98
H13-1
Punda Maria Gate
S59
Mandadzidzi Road
Mandadzidzi
Punda Maria - Pafuri Road
Elandskuil
Hlamalala
Shisha
Punda Gate Road
S58
Mlambame
Dzundzwini Lookout
Magamba Dam
Magamba
Shisha Weir
Mawawi
Dokweni
H1-7
Babalala
Babalala Picnic Site
S56
Boyela
Mphongolo
Sirheni
S57
Mutswari
Nkulumbeni
Ribye
Early borehole
S53
Phugwane

Copyright © 2022 by **HPH Publishing**
Second Edition
ISBN 978-1-77632-322-7
Text by Ingrid van den Berg
Photography by Philip & Ingrid van den Berg,
Heinrich van den Berg
Publisher: Heinrich van den Berg
Edited by John Deane
Proofread by Jane Bowman
Design, typesetting and reproduction by
Heinrich van den Berg, **HPH Publishing** and Nicky Wenhold
Maps by Heinrich van den Berg

All Geographical Information System (GIS) datasets were obtained from Scientific Services, Kruger National Park, South African National Parks, and have been utilised with permission and according to the requirements of the Data User Agreement
Printed in China
All rights reserved. No part of this publication may be reproduced or transmitted in any form or by any means without prior written permission from the publisher.
Second edition, first impression 2022
Published by **HPH Publishing**
50A, Sixth Street, Linden, 2195, South Africa
info@hphpublishing.co.za
www.hphpublishing.co.za